More praise for *The Season*

"Phenomenal. . . . [I]ncludes dozens of captivating interviews with those who've chosen to debut." —*Bitch Reads*

"[Kristen] Richardson's sharp account of how the season evolved . . . is a more absorbing story than any period drama." —Cordelia Jenkins, *Financial Times*

"A detailed examination of modern debutante societies . . . Richardson's engaging study deserves credit for its persistently humane treatment of her subjects." —Robert Leigh-Pemberton, *Sunday Telegraph*

"[A] fascinating social history." —Francesca Carington, *Tatler*

"[A] serious, enlightening look at debutantes throughout history. . . . Richardson reveals a rich and complicated world." —Michael Giltz, *Book and Film Globe*

"Class power has never been about wealth alone. As Kristen Richardson skillfully and colorfully documents, the marriage market—and the courtly ritual of the debutante—lays open a long, troubling, transatlantic history. This engaging book reminds us that 'mock royalty' and the trophy daughter, whether it's Consuelo Vanderbilt in 1894 or Ivanka Trump more recently, are at the center of America's love affair with the rich and beautiful." —Nancy Isenberg, author of *White Trash: The 400–Year Untold History of Class in America*

"Who knew being a debutante was so tough, and so fascinating? Kristen Richardson takes a deep dive into this centuries-old, highly choreographed tribal rite—presentations at court in London, 'Ethiopian Balls' during the American Revolution, Gilded Age Assemblies in New York, the arcane rituals of a secret society in St. Louis, bejeweled dresses more like a suit of armor, and the secret codes embedded in the movement of a fan. And pity the poor Texas girls who had to master the spine-twisting curtsy known as the 'Texas dip.' All this for a husband!"

—Donna M. Lucey, author of *Sargent's Women*

"My grandmother was presented to England's King George V and my mother was Queen of the Veiled Prophet in St. Louis, but it wasn't until I read *The Season* that I understood the enduring fascination and importance of that ritual. Kristen Richardson shows us, with wit and insight, how unmarried girls in long white dresses have publicly embodied the prestige of successful families—across centuries and around the world."

—Carol Wallace, coauthor of *To Marry an English Lord*

"Richardson reminds us in this engaging and thought-provoking history, the use of daughters to cement power and wealth is very hard to give up."

—*BookPage*, starred review

"*The Season* is a must for readers interested in social history, and all will appreciate Richardson's fluid, descriptive prose."   —*Booklist*

"This entertaining, eye-opening portrait captures a tradition that is 'long dead but will never die.' "   —*Publishers Weekly*

The Season

The Season

A SOCIAL HISTORY OF THE DEBUTANTE

Kristen Richardson

W. W. NORTON & COMPANY

Independent Publishers Since 1923

For information about permission to reproduce selections from this book, write to
Permissions, W. W. Norton & Company, Inc., 500 Fifth Avenue, New York, NY 10110

For information about special discounts for bulk purchases, please contact
W. W. Norton Special Sales at specialsales@wwnorton.com or 800-233-4830

Manufacturing by Lake Book Manufacturing
Book design by Chris Welch
Production manager: Lauren Abbate

Library of Congress Cataloging-in-Publication Data

Names: Richardson, Kristen, author.
Title: The season : a social history of the debutante / Kristen Richardson.
Description: First edition. | New York, NY : W.W. Norton & Company, [2020] | Includes
bibliographical references and index.
Identifiers: LCCN 2019027203 | ISBN 9780393608731 (hardcover) | ISBN 9780393608748
(epub)
Subjects: LCSH: Debutantes—History. | Upper class women—Social life and customs. |
Debutante balls—History.
Classification: LCC GT3430 .R53 2020 | DDC 305.48/21—dc23
LC record available at https://lccn.loc.gov/2019027203

ISBN 978-0-393-35853-7 pbk.

W. W. Norton & Company, Inc., 500 Fifth Avenue, New York, N.Y. 10110
www.wwnorton.com

W. W. Norton & Company Ltd., 15 Carlisle Street, London W1D 3BS

1 2 3 4 5 6 7 8 9 0

For Henry

They dream in courtship, but in wedlock wake.

—ALEXANDER POPE

CONTENTS

The Season

Too Many Daughters

The debutante ritual flourished roughly from 1780 to 1914—beginning with the first debutante ball in London and ending with the outbreak of World War I. In this period the debutante season functioned as it was intended to, allowing parents to broker their daughters' marriages in the way that benefited them most. During these years, Great Britain became the dominant power in the West, and its culture spread outward from the fashionable capital of London to provincial cities in Britain and eventually to its far-flung colonies. His Majesty's British subjects, and later Americans, too, waited on coral atolls and in bustling port cities for ships that brought newspapers filled with word of fashionable music, dance, and conversation. Daughters had their seamstresses copy dresses they saw, adapting them to climates with Spanish moss and pink sand or icy winters and salty air. In the outlying areas of England and America alike, one would encounter not only glamorous debutantes, but also their aspirant little sisters. Some were daughters of aristocrats, some were heiresses to bourgeois fortunes, and more still were simply members of families with some money, who had become, at last, respectable people in their small towns. Even the daughters of an innkeeper at a ferry on the Shenandoah walked for seven miles three times a week to attend the lessons with a French dancing master who taught them to trace the same quadrilles danced by aristocrats in distant, foreign courts.[1] These young women who were presented to monarchs, who were betrothed to waning aristocrats, or whose fathers scrounged for money so they could walk across a stage and curtsy to a small-town mayor or rodeo clown, were united by an irresolvable dilemma—the only respectable career for women was marriage, and the best marriages were made by debutantes.

The debutantes we think of today, bowing deeply in frosty dresses, originated and evolved in England and America quite simply because they were needed to solve a problem. The Protestant Reformation in sixteenth-century England and northern Europe ended the extremely convenient practice of cloistering unmarriageable girls in convents. While Catholic aristocracy in Europe continued this practice, the English aristocracy now had a daughter problem. Protestants, you see, don't have convents. When an exasperated Mr. Bennett says of his five daughters in Jane Austen's *Pride and Prejudice*: "What's to be done with all these girls?" he was speaking to a marriage problem that had existed, unresolved, for several hundred years already. The Reformation left wealthy or titled Englishmen with a glut of daughters, whose marriages had to be considered most delicately since, by law, they could not inherit their fathers' estates. The type of marriage the debutante ritual would provide was safe—the girls were presented to vetted company—and prevented a bad marriage from dragging down the status of an entire family, like Lydia's threatened to do in Austen's novel. The Reformation was not the only factor in the development of debutante culture. The Dutch, for example, underwent the Reformation but lacked an active, powerful aristocracy. They had had a strong and integrated middle class of burghers, and did not need to control and arrange marriages in a court setting to perpetuate an aristocratic caste.

To understand how and why the ritual developed specifically in England and its colonies requires considering to what extent the marriage market was indeed a *market*, born, not coincidentally, during England's long, slow industrialization. England experienced commercialization earlier than did other countries due in large part to the social upheaval that followed the Reformation. Free market experimentation was destabilizing and changed the way people thought and behaved, replacing guaranteed income from inherited land with the boundless possibility of new speculative ventures. Freer markets, however, created insecurity and uncertainty where little had previously existed. Men quitted their villages and traveled in search of jobs, leaving the English countryside dotted with upper-middle-class girls with no source of respectable income, like Austen's Bennetts. The Bennett girls couldn't marry the men who stayed in the country—they were small farmers. But neither did they really have access to the elite stratum in London. They were respectable not fashionable, genteel not noble, and were therefore left only to hope that a partner who would meet with approval might find them and would see something in their country freshness. Mrs. Bennett is aware of this and seeks to put them in every good light she can, often looking ridiculous in the process. Given the context of near-impossible marriage prospects, one can suddenly sympathize with Mrs. Bennett's delight when Mr. Bingley arrives in town, and brings his friend Mr. Darcy to the local assembly.

Greater economic mobility and freedom created a social insecurity that played particular havoc with society's most pleasing commodity, young women, who etched their conflicted feelings about their debutante experiences into countless diaries and letters. Some participated, but resented newcomers and competition. Some crouched in corners and hid from the throngs. Sometimes a young woman bloomed and performed well under inspection, convincing herself, perhaps, that she had some choice in a process that might fashion her salvation or downfall, all of which begs the question, if we are indeed trapped, should we try to enjoy it?

What does it feel like to be a debutante? Numerous journals and letters suggest conclusions far less varied than I anticipated, perhaps because the disenchanted are more enthusiastic about writing their recollections. In the early years of debutante presentation, there was less dissent. But as options for women grew, women became more conflicted about what a debutante presentation meant, and more aware of their status as objects or pawns within a larger schematic process. Some women felt as Edith Wharton did, describing her season as a "long, cold agony of shyness." Eleanor Roosevelt hated her debut, which she made at the White House alongside her more glamorous cousin, Alice, daughter of then-president Theodore Roosevelt. Eleanor then came out at a larger Assembly Ball in New York, an event she described similarly as Wharton did, an "utter agony." But in her memoirs she also recalls how deeply important it had been to her beautiful mother, Anna, who died when she was a child, that she also be a debutante. Those who enjoyed the process were happy to have their names peppered throughout gossip columns and in fashion magazines. Some kept journals listing their conquests. Brenda Frazier, the most famous debutante of the twentieth century, whose face sold cars and perfumes, claimed in a 1963 *Life* magazine article that her mother had forced her into the limelight at seventeen and said "I was a fad that year, the way midget golf was once a fad, or flagpole sitting." And there are, too, innumerable nameless girls who went through this process, whose only legacy is their debutante scrapbook, a record of press clippings and photos of fellow debutantes. These scrapbooks are generally found at the tail end of family archives, where one first must riffle through the recorded deeds of great and accomplished tycoons, politicians, and landowners. Even though these daughters played a vital role in the transmission of their fathers' power, their lives remain obscure.

It is ironic then that the season was the only chance a debutante would have to experience even the barest hint of control over her own body and mind. The transitional space between her parents' house and her husband's was the freest she would likely ever be. At a party, this might mean noting the texture of champagne sliding down her throat or the restraint of a corset, or the pain from her beautiful shoes. She would hear the din of an orchestra, the buzz of the lights, whispers in corners, mur-

murs of assent, reluctant demurrals. She would smell the heavy scent of
flower arrangements, the deep, humid smoke of cigars and the dryness
of cigarettes. The terror of everyone focusing on her, the tightness of
her hair, the immobility of her smile, the boredom of civic responsibility.

*W*hen I was seventeen a woman phoned my mother and asked her if I
wanted to be a debutante. I was home from boarding school for the summer and we were standing in the kitchen of our house in Connecticut.
My mother put the phone on the counter and asked me and I laughed
and curtsied and shook my head. My mother told the woman "no thank
you" and we went on with our day. That I was invited by phone and so
casually might seem at odds with what people generally think about the
debutante ritual, with its formality and frothy rigor, but at our house we
received a steady stream of phone calls from strangers bearing invitations. My father rarely answered the phone at all, but particularly not
in the evening, when the social calls would begin—when the women
would begin to call. These women had been, in their younger years,
facsimiles of Ali MacGraw, attending women's colleges, toying with
protest, perhaps even voting for McGovern, but had long since settled
into pastel colors. Bobbed and head-banded, in the evening hours they
spoke on corded phones that stretched around the narrow doorways of
colonial houses, as they worked to organize their lives, which revolved
around their children with their lessons in dance, golf, tennis, sailing,
music, and riding. The world of my childhood was fueled by such calls,
and by a web of invitations between members of the same tribe. Yacht
club people, hunt club people, country club people—we were, at various times, all three.

Would my brother and I be going to dancing school (yes for both of
us), to sailing lessons (yes for him), to riding camp (yes for me)? My
father did all those things and we would, too, at the same places. I didn't
receive an invitation to debut because I was pretty, or smart, or charming. The invitation was an entreaty to contribute to the community as

much as it was a service rendered unto me, the teenager. We would lend our family name to the festivities, and I would emerge from my chrysalis, ready to carry the values I was meant to embody into the wider world, a kind of upper-class mascot. Right before I was set to go to college, to leave the privileged, interconnected world I grew up in, I was being called on to affirm that I would stay.

I couldn't do it. At seventeen, I was shy and had no interest in being on display. To embrace an open show of wealth ran contrary to everything I had been taught, or had passively absorbed, about how to behave. I was not yet aware that the people around me—girls and their families—were attempting to purchase their social legitimacy for the same reasons my ancestors had purchased theirs years before—so their children didn't have to. My friends who did make a debut mostly did so to appease their mothers and grandmothers.

Even if my mother, who is from a middle-class Irish-Catholic background, had been invested in my making my debut, she could not have forced me to come out without the imprimatur of my father's family. They were the ones with the social credentials, though worn reluctantly and awkwardly. Nobody in my father's family had ever taken any interest in my social education, but I was put in the places where I would acquire the desired attitude, and correct education. Once there, I was mostly left alone to learn how to behave on my own via absorption. My paternal grandmother, who traditionally would have taken the leading role in my coming out, loathed anything pretentious. One of her own daughters had been brought out by my grandfather's sister—my great aunt—a former debutante, whose ball in Manhattan had been attended by a chorus of blue bloods, as well as the ornamental minor aristocracy who often turn up to lend the necessary gravitas to American social events. But my grandmother was from a navy family, and any debut she might have made—none is my guess—was squashed by the Second World War, during which she drove a taxi in Newport. It seemed to me she continued to operate her life in this same directional way for as long as I knew her. She loved art and had beautiful taste but was suspicious of all fanfare. She eschewed logos and told us that "we are not anyone's advertisement." When I was left in her care, she would entertain me by handing me a wooden pail of sailing knots to untie with my tiny fingers. When, at six, I wove myself between warp and weft of her large loom that had its own room on the fourth floor of their house, I was relieved to be found and unraveled by my grandparents' housekeeper, who laughed and warned me to never, ever do that again. The notion of the two of us lovingly perusing scrapbooks filled with old social news or bonding over the tulle explosion that would be my debutante's dress makes me laugh to think of it.

But many women in my family have been debutantes. I have this information because my great-grandfather, a North Carolina industrialist who had married a Virginian belle from an old family, paid several genealogists to construct a lineage for us. The book they produced is four hundred pages long and traces his family back to thirteenth-century England and France and seventeenth-century British America, and places us among the colonial elite, spending much more time on our ancestor who owned much of Williamsburg and the other who was an explorer than on the many more who were pig farmers in Virginia and the Carolinas. From this book, I learn that a debutante ancestor captivated a young George Washington, who sent her several short letters of admiration (mimeographed into the book, of course). A second book, also written by genealogists, traces my great-grandmother's ancestry. Her history was more direct than his. Her family was old and connected, and there was nothing to invent. Her ancestors weren't indentured servants sent to Jamestown, but King James's men, who arrived on the second boat, the money boat. Having been granted thousands of acres land by the king instead of the money they'd put into the Virginia Company (a failure), her ancestors arrived to colonize what is now Colonial Williamsburg. They intermarried with other similar families and began an unbroken chain of daughters who acted as vessels for their fathers' property, allowing the family to make key alliances that have sustained us, through ups and downs, for the four centuries we have been in America.

When I was a senior at boarding school, remembering these books in our library, I cannily chose "family history" to be my independent study project, written over a semester, which I could use to get out of playing on the tennis team. It took me only a matter of days to rewrite what the Jazz Age genealogists had turned up. I used my newly free time to lie flat in the tall grass behind the soccer fields reading and sending thin reeds of smoke into the air. At the end of the semester my teachers were astonished at the depth of the history I had unearthed.

These illustrious, and often tenuous, connections to seemingly refined historical predecessors serve to set my family into history, to validate our contemporary place, and to let me, an entitled teenager, sit back and coast, as I did with my family history project. This is the function the debutante ritual serves and has served for the families who decide to pursue it. It's like a good cleanse—whatever grime covered the climb to the top, a white dress and a good party will hide a multitude of sins.

After deciding not to make a debut myself, I didn't give my decision much thought. I went to college in North Carolina, a nod to my family's southern roots. Over the Christmas holidays, I attended some of my prep-school friends' coming-out parties in New York. A few of the friends I had made in college flew home to make furtive debuts, but there was no fanfare at school. There remained an unarticulated sense that this was something to be endured but not discussed, a favor to one's family, a duty.

At the beginning of the George W. Bush presidency, with its resurgent conservatism, lavish parties came back into style. I started to understand what my father had felt during the evening—don't answer the phone, go to bed early, read books, walk dogs. I stopped going to these parties quickly but many of my friends stayed in that scene, using their social lives to advance their own careers in fashion, magazines, publicity, and business. I was particularly interested to see that the debutante scene, nearly rendered extinct by nineties grunge, was booming once again in the new millennium. My more distant, younger southern cousins began to come out, one by one, at various debutante presentations in the Carolinas.

As the debutante ritual gained traction once again, I wondered how it would align with the changing values of a twentieth-century upper class, a group led less by WASPs and minor aristocrats and more by tech billionaires, Wall Street money men, and entertainment industry superstars whose wealth and reach eclipsed anything since the Gilded Age. What had felt arcane to me was clearly relevant to my young cousins, who lived in the banking centers of the new South, their status still a trump card and parameter of exclusion. But I didn't see their young male counterparts embarking on revived eighteenth-century style grand tours. I wanted to know why the social advancement of families seemed only to happen through young women.

Since it became institutionalized in the late eighteenth century, the debutante ritual has been unkillable. Though there is a moment at every debutante party when an elderly relative sounds a dirge for the passing of the age of debutantes, it is not a ritual in mellow decline but one that is completely bulletproof. Its very outmodedness is part of its value—its built-in nostalgia is fundamentally necessary to its continuation. With each successive generation, this nostalgia further fogs the ritual's mercenary origins in a mist of glamour, so much so that when I asked debutantes at a recent ball in Manhattan where and how it began not a single one could answer my question, and none was interested in trying, either. We learn early that it is better not to look too closely when money and status are at stake, a message I received as well.

When I began to mention this book to members of my father's family, it quickly became clear to me that seeing this project through wouldn't be breezy conversations at the club, or drinks on the terrace. Some of my relatives pushed back against my work with social warnings like "now, make sure you don't say anything mean" and "don't say anything arch, now." The more people tried to corral me into a soothing and uncomplicated worldview, the more I wondered if they knew in their hearts, too, that this isn't something we should do to girls. At the same time, their defensiveness spoke to something that bothered me. Criticisms of the debutante ritual are most commonly aimed at the young women themselves, who bear a certain burden for being standard bearers of upper-class values when they are barely adults themselves.

But my research revealed that the debutante ritual is far more complex and interesting than I could have anticipated. It took time for the barter of daughters to acquire an agreeable sheen, for the debutante ritual to become so beautiful and exclusive that girls themselves began to crave participation. The debutante ritual was so effective a social-climbing tool that parents jockeyed over presentation venues; it was so costly that it created new industries for its supporting staff. It launched the careers of fashionable dressmakers, hairdressers, makeup artists, designers, florists, and dancing masters. It created markets for women's magazines and gazettes that were the prototypes of today's fashion magazines. It provided steady work for painters, photographers, and musicians, and for the social secretaries who were the forerunners of publicists, the gatekeepers of today's social scene. The debutante ritual created a soft economy wherein people with knowledge and family history, but no money, could earn a living as guardians of ancient social rules. Crucially, there were roles for mothers, widows, and maiden aunts as chaperones. Wealthy gay men, the "committed bachelors," became walkers and arbiters. The more indispensable they were to women, the safer they were in a hostile patriarchal social environment. All of these people worked in service of a system they could participate in only as long as their social knowledge remained both current and vibrant. It was competitive, stressful, and unstable, requiring both ongoing vigilance and a precise balance between conformity and innovation.

Today's social life still follows the rhythm of the debutante season and its focus remains money—fathers didn't only advance through their daughters, they figured out how to make them beg for the right to curtsy. Because of its primal link to coming of age rituals and its success at advancing the social status of its participants, the debutante ritual has been adopted by numerous and varied cultures, who have alternately democratized it or ruined it, depending on whom you ask.

The ritual was a main driver of upper-class marriage in Britain and the United States for several hundred years, but it has never been taken seriously by scholars. When I began to look into the ritual's origins, I was surprised they were so difficult to pinpoint. Historians have been content to describe when it began, but have been uninterested in dealing with why. Elitist rituals are easy to dismiss, and when they shape young women's lives it's easier still. But if we do so, we miss a key part of women's history, and of the history of marriage as well.

The Girl Standard

UNDERSTANDING THE CURRENCY OF DAUGHTERS

Young women have always been for sale. In the 5th century
BCE, Herodotus describes the practice of selling Babylonian
daughters at a yearly auction in his *Histories*. He wrote:

They used to collect all the young women who were old enough to
be married and take the whole lot of them all at once to a certain
place. A crowd of men would form a circle around them there. An
auctioneer would get each of the women to stand up one by one,
and he would put her up for sale. He used to start with the most
attractive girl there, and then, once she had fetched a good price
and been bought, he would go on to auction the next most attractive
one. They were being sold to be wives, not slaves. All the well-off
Babylonian men who wanted wives would outbid one another to
buy the good-looking young women, while the commoners who
wanted wives and were not interested in good looks used to end up
with some money as well as the less attractive women.[1]

The Babylonian men paid a bride price but some of their money would
come back to them because the young women were given dowries,
which their husbands would administer even if they could not raid it.
This exchange seems odd but was not so unusual in the classical world,
where women served to cement together two male-controlled families.

If a married daughter died without children her money would go back to her family, which removed any incentive to harm her.

At the time, virginity was not always necessary to a girl's successful marriage—the Lydians prostituted their daughters to raise money for their dowries. Because of the dangers of childbirth and high rate of early mortality in ancient Greece, it was common for wealthy relatives to provide not just their daughters, but also their poor relations, with dowries. Athenian law even required that the State dower poor women of just passable attractiveness; teeth were all that were required. Because Athens was under constant threat from its rivals, it depended on its young women to provide it with a constant stream of new soldiers.

Classical literature is filled with accounts of creative daughter disposal. In some memorable verses of *The Odyssey*, the father of Penelope, Odysseus's wife, then thought to be a widow, urges her to marry the suitor with the most gifts. Greek fathers took care not to raise more daughters than they could dower. Outright infanticide was abhorrent to ancient Greeks, but they did practice "exposure," wherein parents intentionally left unwanted infants exposed to the elements. They believed that the gods could choose to save the abandoned children, thereby eliminating their agency while achieving their aims. Husbands were not permitted to run through their wives' dowries but neither could the wife. A Greek woman's dowry yielded about 18 percent per year and if the couple got divorced, either party could request the dowry. It was returned to a woman's guardian or, in certain cases, kept by the husband who paid 18 percent interest to his former wife's guardian for her support. The wealthier the family, the more likely it was that a marriage would take place between two young first cousins. Such marriages keep money in one family and tended to correlate with periods of cultural instability, when power was held by a few important families. Cousin marriage was particularly popular among the higher echelons in Elizabethan England, the Antebellum South, and in late eighteenth- and early nineteenth-century Britain.

Greek girls who died in childhood were mourned specifically because they did not fulfill their destiny as wives and mothers. Their epitaphs make reference to their failure to marry, and the girls were quickly writ into myth. Like Persephone before them, they were considered married to Hades and dwelled, as wraiths, in the underworld. All Greeks were buried with a *loutrophoros*, long, slender water vessels that were used exclusively to transport water to a woman's wedding-day bath, but the ghostly funerary rites for ancient Greek women who died young were carved into their *loutrophoroi*, as if to remind them of a life unlived, or fate escaped. Young unmarried women were buried with such *loutrophoroi* from around the sixth to the fourth century BCE. In contrast, vase paintings of women seated on chests allude to dowries brides possessed.

In the Roman period, women did not fare better. Catullus sums up the Roman attitude toward marriage, writing, "If, when [a young woman] is ripe for marriage, she enters into wedlock, she is ever dearer to her husband and less hateful to her parents."

The middle class continued to sell their daughters at regional markets throughout most European countries during the Middle Ages. For the upper middle classes, the social stasis of the period made marrying an heiress one of the only means to improve one's social status, and it was nearly impossible to do without deception. The middle classes began to consult marriage brokers—a growing cottage industry in Europe— who would help them plot their rise, reconstruct their family histories, then help them relocate in order to achieve success in another part of the country. If a woman did marry up, she would find that she had much less control over both her body and her daily life—where she walked and even what she ate, than she had in a middle-class environment. In the upper classes, the legitimacy of heirs continued to be of primary importance, and as such women's movements were intensely regulated. These women were confined to the home, left to pursue needlework with the other gentlewomen of the house. If they were lucky and their new house had a library, they might be able to read.

Women were progressively more visible during the Renaissance. Increased trade created a new culture of conspicuous consumption, propped up by merchants and explorers who transported new goods through Genoa and Venice, Zanzibar and Constantinople, outward to European capitals and the known world. Newly available luxury goods made life easier and more enjoyable—tobacco, tea, coffee, silks, and spices facilitated a culture of male comfort in which wives and daughters played an important though entirely passive role. In ancient Greece and Rome women were kept mostly in the home, but during the Renaissance men put their velvet-swaddled wives and daughters on display, trotting them out in public, where they would often sit separately, saying little if anything, but fulfilling a necessary decorative function. A woman's beauty, or wealth, was most of all a statement about the social status of her presiding male, be he husband, father, or brother.

For much of the Middle Ages and into the Renaissance, sumptuary laws on food and goods defined and limited social space. By legislating who could obtain specific fabrics, foods, drink, and other luxuries, governments prevented servants and the middle classes from masquerading as aristocrats by denying them access to the materials necessary to appear richer than they were. Pre-Reformation Europeans were just beginning to let go of feudal social organization. Though more people now lived in cities, family patriarchs had long made decisions for their large clans and were not interested in giving up a privilege that had served them so well. Daughters were married to create important and lasting connections between families. Those who could not be married off in a way that would benefit the clan were often forced into nunneries. For a noble family, sending a daughter to a convent or forcing her into spinsterhood was far preferable to tainting a family line by permitting her to marry beneath her station.

This system of dispensing with daughters worked peaceably for hundreds of years, until Henry VIII came to need a son and heir. When his attempts to have his first marriage, which had produced no sons, annulled by the pope failed, Henry charged ecclesiastical and secular legal scholars in England with finding a way to divorce his consort Catherine and marry his mistress Anne Boleyn. Their solution was divorce and breaking away from the Catholic Church. Henry began the violent dissolution of Catholic monasteries in 1536. It lasted for four years, during which the crown plundered church lands, sold them off to rich allies, and used the surplus cash to wage dubious wars in France. For wealthy young women, newly Anglican, there was an additional change, perhaps the single most significant social change women would see until suffrage. Their safe haven—the convent—was now gone.

The absence of nunneries sent numerous marriageable aristocratic young women into circulation. When once they would have been in the country, awaiting the marriages arranged for them, or preparing to enter a convent, these young girls were now brought to court, which is where they were most likely to find husbands. By the time Henry's daughter Elizabeth I began her reign in 1558, the atmosphere surrounding marriage had a new urgency. Elizabeth's rule began in religious chaos after her predecessor, her half-sister Mary, violently restored Roman Catholicism to England. Elizabeth spent the better part of her first years on the throne fighting for her father's Protestantism in an effort to fend off those who wished to depose her. Her legitimacy was questioned with every decision she made, and she understood that her courtiers were her key to maintaining the throne. She tightened her control over the aristocracy by reducing its size to a new low. She stripped disloyal aristocrats of their titles or made it known they were not welcome at court.

It was against this tumultuous backdrop that Elizabeth, in an effort to form beneficial social and political alliances, began having young ladies ceremonially presented to her at Court. These presentations were small affairs and limited to the daughters of Elizabeth's most important courtiers. They took place in the queen's "withdrawing room," a private room, but located next to larger public rooms where she could go with a smaller party. The girls were led from a public stateroom into the smaller adjoining room at Hampton Court palace, so that other courtiers would know who was being favored. At the more private ceremony of presentation, the young girls curtsied to the queen. The young girls had a vivid experience of being watched and assessed, enhanced by the fact that of the roughly 1,500 people in regular attendance at court, only fifty were women. These presentations came to be referred to as "drawing rooms" and they engendered a curious experience that blended ostentatious display with the familial and private, a mix that would continue to characterize the debutante ritual for its duration.

Many of the presented young women served her as attendants and became intermediaries between Elizabeth and the wider circle of her court. They helped Elizabeth to exert control over the nobility by creating an elegant buffer between the monarch and her courtiers. In order to present a petition to the queen, one first gave it to a lady-in-waiting, along with a fee that the lady in question would determine based on her closeness with the queen. Elizabeth encouraged her ladies to charge exorbitantly for this service—not so much because they'd have some independence, but so they would have enough money to be able to gamble with her. She also regularly rejected petitions based on their lack of generosity toward her ladies.[2] The queen could also be capricious— Elizabeth's ladies-in-waiting could not marry of their own volition. Elizabeth Vernon spent a week in prison (with her new husband the Earl of Southampton) for marrying without the queen's permission. Lettice Knollys was banished permanently for marrying Elizabeth's favorite courtier, Robert Dudley, Earl of Leicester. When Elizabeth discovered that another lady-in-waiting, Mary Shelton, was secretly married, she attacked her and broke her finger.

Still, proximity to monarchy held many advantages that proved a balm for wounded pride and broken appendages. Elizabeth's favorites received not only riches, but also direct access to power. When her attendants did marry, they became wives to important courtiers and continued to curry favor. When their husbands were on extended overseas diplomatic missions for the queen, it was left to wives to oversee their ongoing status at court.

Elizabeth's social standards and rituals persisted after her death, with queens taking over control of drawing rooms and social presentations even when there was a king on the throne. Elizabethan presentations-at-court served a very clear political purpose. Though they bore little resemblance to the feverish social theater that characterized the fully developed debutante ritual of the nineteenth century, these court presentations provided the foundation for modern debutante culture and served, too, as its myth of origin. They show the important link between society and politics, a symbiotic relationship that only deepened as the ritual became institutionalized and spread outward to all corners of the British Empire. Elizabeth's backroom maneuvers—quick conferences with her ladies or political advisers—provided the precedent for the many political meetings that took place at debutante parties in later centuries, and emphasized the soft power of social settings, which were controlled by women who understood that the way to power was not always hard work or even fortunate birth, but judicious conversation next to a sloshing punchbowl or quivering trifle.

The Stuart monarchs who followed Elizabeth continued the tradition of the drawing room ("with" was dropped from "withdrawing room" in the late seventeenth century), which retained its function as a match-making tool. Elizabeth's successor, James I, arranged the marriage of his favorite courtier, the charming spendthrift James Hay, to Honoria Denny, by granting Honoria's reluctant father a title and royal patent.[3] While these high-level marriages took strategy, marriage law remained chaotic. There was no legislation that defined marriage, and there were no protections for women after they were married. Rather, the absence of law meant that women might be forced into marriage by their fathers, married by capture, tricked into marriage. The age of consent to marriage was twelve for women and fourteen for men, and contracts were often made during the "unripe years." It was a particularly dangerous time to be an heiress. During these years women could inherit property. Inheritance law was not clear on whether her property would become her husband's upon marriage. Without knowing if they could control their property, many women resisted marriage. Restrictive regulations for daughters intensified after they were wives, especially if they were considered to have broken proper codes of behavior. If a wife were to be convicted of adultery, she would lose her dowry or marriage portion and her husband could make a good case that she could punitively lose her property as well. There was no comparable financial forfeiture for adulterous men, and courts habitually disbelieved women who tried to defend themselves against claims of adultery. It is not difficult to explain widespread female acquiescence.

Though the Stuart monarchs' social machinations were truncated by the religious English Civil War, the Puritan leader Oliver Cromwell was hardly progressive when it came to women's property rights. Born into the gentry, he had the intense social aspirations of the upper middle rung, a group that was close enough to view power but had no real experience of it. Cromwell sought out an heiress not only for the benefit of his son, but also so that he could use the bride's money to provide dowries for his two daughters. He haggled until he obtained a £2,000 cash payout from the girl's father. This common practice illustrates how the fortunes of an entire family were intertwined and could hinge upon marriage to a wealthy young woman.

The restoration of monarchy upended the stringent puritanism of Cromwellian rule but left women in the same subordinate social position. The aristocratic classes still controlled the land, which remained the primary source of wealth. More important still, they controlled most of Parliament. Unlike European countries, England had a small, stable aristocracy. In Spain, for example, almost half a million people could claim some manner of nobility. By the turn of the eighteenth century, there were around two hundred noble families in England and one hundred more families that were not titled but who held over 10,000 acres of land. English younger sons and daughters did not inherit titles and, even if they did have a courtesy title, they were commoners by law. This meant that England's small, concentrated, and powerful upper class intermarried strategically. It also meant that it had a large middle class with untapped economic power and roiling social ambition.

The small size of the English aristocracy was a significant factor in the development of the debutante ritual. The oldest son would inherit the family title and most of the land. Unless the family was exceptionally rich, younger sons needed professions. This led to a kind of downward leveling of society. While any daughter could marry a member of the aristocracy, younger sons were eventually reabsorbed, albeit with ideals and manner intact, into the upper middle and middle classes. Some made up part of what was known as the gentry, a group of well-born landowners who did not have titles but who did administer their own land. Others went into respectable professions like the law or military. The upward and downward mobility in English society meant that the manners and customs of the middle class and gentry bore a large resemblance to those of the aristocracy and peerage, and that the upper rungs absorbed middle-class manners, too, through intermarriage. The gentry, as landowners, were seen as socially fit to mix with the aristocracy and peerage but not as their true financial or social equals. The panoply of country squires, military officers, and the clergyman who might help make twelve at dinner had significant roles in small villages. Their daughters would lead the dances, tend to local food or flower festivals, and take food to poor but respectable relations, like Emma Woodhouse did with her aunts in Jane Austen's *Emma*. However, these young women would only have a London season as a companion to a more aristocratic friend, or because of the kindness of a rich relation. Country squires modeled their behavior on members of the nobility, who owned many thousands of acres of land and employed numerous farm managers to oversee many tenants. The country squires and their families replicated this pattern on a much smaller scale and with much more personal involvement. Yet there was one group of wealthy people who were excluded from this system: city merchants. Trade was still considered vulgar because proprietors worked for a living. Many urban merchants made efforts to buy country estates so they could begin to cross this most significant barrier in English society.

$\mathcal{B}$ecause the upper and upper middle classes were interacting already, the development of a more structured debutante ritual to support this intermingling was one way to make it more palatable and to try to control it at least to some extent. Downward mobility also created an interesting phenomenon—aristocratic financial climbing, wherein economically stretched noble families would seek a rich spouse for their child of either gender to bolster flagging bank accounts. Younger sons, too, needed to seek financially attractive marriages, and they made up another part of the marriage market, trading access to their family's status for money from a lower-status woman who could help dower their sisters. But the threat of loss of status did not always ignite the fires of entrepreneurship in a younger son. The forces of entitlement and denial were no weaker in the eighteenth century than they are today. Younger sons from aristocratic families could marry women with lower status but more money. If he didn't make that marriage, he would have to go into a respectable profession, like law or the military, or embark upon his own speculative business venture, perhaps in the colonies, where the hot shame of his trade would be hidden among the palms.

Not-as-wealthy aristocratic husbands of rich brides didn't always preserve their newly gained money. Usurious loans, expensive mistresses, and not uncommon gaming debts meant that many an heir squandered his new wife's fortune before addressing the creeping damp that was overrunning his house or his sisters' need to marry. Squandered wealth was not just humiliating, but ruinous, and would mean diminished wealth and prestige for an entire family. Most aristocratic families would do anything to avoid losing their money, including aligning themselves with a newly rich family through marriage. Although aristocratic sons had sought money through their brides for many years, as many as one-third of all British brides were marrying down during the eighteenth century, which indicates, too, that increasing numbers of merchant sons were marrying aristocratic daughters. When a daughter married out of the aristocracy, her dowry went to her new family, diluting her family's resources. This intensified the competition between girls to make a good match within the aristocracy. As fortunes were diluted over genera-tions, and more young women entered the marriage market, aristocratic power waned. Loss of status among the aristocracy came at the same time as the merchant classes were making major gains in theirs. It took a minimum of £25,000 (£5,450,000 today) to "hook a peer." According to historian Roy Porter, every class of people watched marriages with rabid interest, and their cost was reported feverishly by newspapers.

Marriages
25 March 1735, John Parry, Esq. of Carmarthenshire, to a daughter of Walter Lloyd, Esq. member for that county, a fortune of £8000. The Lord Bishop of St Astaph to Miss Orell, with £30,000. Mar-ried, the Rev Mr Roger Waind of York, about twenty six years of age, to a Lincolnshire lady, upwards of eighty, with whom he is to have £8000 in money, £300 per annum and a coach-and-four during life only.[4]

Upward mobility is ever a thorny issue, the drama of which has been a major preoccupation of English literature since at least the early eigh-teenth century. In *Clarissa* (1748), Samuel Richardson tells the story of Clarissa Howe, a virtuous daughter of a striving nouveau riche family attempting to buy their way into the aristocracy. When they try to force

Clarissa to marry a rich but horrible man, she runs off with a duplicitous rake. Clarissa, reputation damaged beyond repair, succumbs first to madness, then illness, and finally death and the redemption of heaven. Richardson shows a world closing in on young women as a dissipated aristocracy sought to bolster its fortunes by entering into alliances with a vulgar but rich middle class that hoped to gain position and connections. The possibility of losing one's standing, and the need to constantly maintain it once established, fed a class anxiety in England that was absent in the more static European cultures of France, Spain, and Italy, with their infinite supply of redundant princelings.

The more fluid class structure that developed in early modern England led to an increased emphasis on behavior as a means for people to locate themselves, and others, in society. Education was more common. What constituted a gentleman was widely understood. As Sir Richard Steele wrote in the magazine *Tatler* in 1711, "the Appellation of Gentleman is never to be affixed to a Man's Circumstances, but to his Behaviour in them."[5] The "English gentleman" soon became a categorization that members of all levels of society employed to describe the male ideal of the time. Ubiquitous in period literature, this mighty oak was a kindly, paternalistic character, surrounded by hounds and wide acreage. In eighteenth-century art, he is often depicted surveying his wild and rangy land, itself liberated from the geometric incarceration of French gardens. Paintings by Thomas Gainsborough and George Romney show the English gentleman standing in a landscape that stretches back unencumbered by fences or boundaries, so that his domain appears infinite; his wives and children sit behind him, displayed in the same way as land or property.

The domain of the English gentleman, the countryside, had become a refuge during the English Civil War and the center of social life as well, and this led to a more relaxed social rhythm, more informal values, and a new emphasis on house parties, out of which an itinerant social season began to grow. Daughters became accustomed to greater freedom of

movement. They visited cousins in other counties, and families traveled
to be with family friends and to forge connections outside of their immediate neighborhoods. With improvements in infrastructure allowing for
better mobility, the aristocratic class could control rural estates and get
to London more easily. Economic power became increasingly decentral-
ized, a departure from the previous century's more central control of
resources and finances in the capital.

Decentralization was due in part to a growing market environment
that was creating a relationship between earner and buyer where once
there had been only patronage. A debutante buying dresses might now
have more than one dressmaker from which to choose even in her small
market town. Most of all, as she began to see herself as part of this consumer system, she might develop preferences and even a bit of her own
taste. Samuel Johnson noted in his diary the nature of this new market when he observed "the shoe-black at the entry of my court does
not depend on me."[6] With more workers flooding into the cities to participate in new industries, even those in trade had more choices about
whom they would serve. The eighteenth century also saw the first mass
printings of conduct literature, a genre that was widely read and instru-
mental in helping many in the middle classes form opinions about what
constituted proper behavior. These etiquette manuals soon helped the
bourgeoisie to copy aristocratic behavior, and eventually to satirize it
as well. Freer thinking was a threat to traditional ways of social organization, and numerous private clubs and societies were founded in this
period in an effort to keep a horde of social climbers, now equipped not
just with money, but convincing manners, at bay. Some of these clubs
were organized for alumni of prestigious schools, those with musical
interests, or around dancing. Some were gaming clubs for men only.

At the same time as aristocrats were taking advantage of more relaxed
market conditions, liberal ideas were bleeding into other sectors of society, penetrating art and literature, music and politics. Historian Margaret Jacob had written that these ideas had some disadvantages for

the powerful, as they encouraged a long-quiet political opposition to reinvent itself. Assorted societies of freethinkers made their way back toward London, filling the spaces vacated by the defunct heresies and radical political groups that had been active during the Civil War. Jacob writes that these groups created "a new zone of social experience separate from court intrigue and clerical influence. Salons, coffeehouses, theaters and literary, scientific, and philosophical associations flourished over the course of the eighteenth century, and their meetings became places where men (only men) theorized about the rules of constitutions and individual rights."[7] The active political underground and burgeoning demimonde demonstrated the need for more defined social spaces, particularly for young women who were reading novels by Daniel Defoe, Henry Fielding, and Samuel Richardson, whose stories featured realistic characters who were making at least some of their own decisions. The idea that it might be acceptable to marry someone you loved grew, and was so seductive and delightful that it threatened the traditional marriage practices of the aristocracy. Young women also had to be protected from the dangers posed by bad men with new ideas.

Protestant English women, though they had more freedom than their Catholic counterparts before marriage, still had few property rights, and this also intensified the importance of marriage, which remained both the only means of advancement and the most secure way to live. In this new environment, defined as it was by market pressures, it was nearly impossible for a woman to make an advantageous marriage if she did not have some combination of competitive dowry, exceptional beauty, and perfect lineage. Contemporary observers like essayist Sir William Temple were startled by the spread of rank commercialism into middle- and upper-middle-class marriages. He wrote that "the custom of making marriages just like other common bargains and sales, by the mere consideration of interest of gain, without any love or esteem" was "of not ancient date."[8] What Temple is getting at is akin to what Johnson recorded in his diary about his shoe-black no longer being dependent on his patronage. The introduction of market-based choices created greater freedom but also new prisons of social confusion and the stress of not knowing one's place. More people had acceptable manners; more people had money. Travel was quicker, easier, and cheaper, and afforded middle-class people with money the ability to see the world and return with information and experiences that were previously available only to the richest people. Even by 1710, the Earl of Shaftsbury complained about the vogue for reading about distant cultures, complaining about authors who give us "monstrous brutes." People hungrily sought out information about other societies. This made it easier to adopt an air of mystery and chic, to hide one's familial origins and, ultimately, to change one's station, like the incomparable social climber Becky Sharp did in Thackeray's *Vanity Fair*.

Men's relationship to marriage was also affected by the market environment. They tended to marry late in the hopes they would attract a young wife of better status if they themselves were more established. Fathers who wanted to marry off their daughters found there were fewer young men looking, leaving them with fewer choices. As in previous periods, according to contemporary literary critic Ian Watt, "young girls were driving into flagrantly unsuitable marriages on grounds of economic advantage." The artist Mary Delany, for instance, was married in 1718, at the age of seventeen, to a man nearly sixty years old because her uncle, Lord Lansdowne, hoped her marriage to a member of Parliament would bring the family political power. Her bleak marriage led her to ask: "Why must women be driven to the necessity of marrying? A state that should always be a matter of choice! And if a young woman has not fortune sufficient to maintain her in the situation she has been bred to, what can she do, but marry?"[9] Still, the fact that Delaney envisioned choosing her husband at all had not existed in the preceding century. Mary Wortely Montagu so hated her father's choice for her that she eloped, putting it in the racist terms of her era: "People in my way are sold like slaves, and I cannot tell what price my masters will put on me," she lamented. Her chosen husband was hardly better.[10]

The urgent need for women to marry, and the absence of partners of a similar age and standing, or agreeable alternatives to marriage, led many to cry that English society needed to return to the convent system, the former safe haven of nonbeauties, nonheiresses, younger sisters, and even the sincerely religious. In *A Serious Proposal to Ladies* (1694), English feminist Mary Astell had urged the establishment of "a monastery or religious retirement." Defoe had put forward a similar idea in his *Essay upon Projects* (1697), while in 1739, the *Gentlemen's Magazine* was very explicit in proposing "a New Method of making women as useful and capable of maintaining themselves as men are, and consequently preventing their becoming old maids or taking ill courses." Similarly, Richardson had the idea in mind: his heroine Clarissa laments the fact that she cannot take shelter in a nunnery, while the eponymous protagonist of another Richardson novel, Sir Charles Grandison, strongly advocates "Protestant Nunneries" where "numbers of young women, joining their small fortunes, might maintain themselves genteelly on their own income, though each singly in the world would be distressed."[11] English writers and thinkers were discussing the problem of marriage openly and widely but without a solution. The institution was slipping into crisis.

The fight between the aristocracy and the middle classes over marriage finally came to a head politically in the 1750s, in the frenzied debate over Hardwicke's Marriage Act. This legislation, sponsored by aristocratic members of the House of Lords and opposed by the urban bourgeoisie who populated the House of Commons, sought to bring marriage under church control and prevent people under the age of twenty-one from marrying without parental consent. The law purported to solve an ongoing problem for the aristocracy, preventing the clandestine marriages of nouveau riche men with the heiress daughters they targeted. Fear of secret marriages was widespread in the eighteenth century. Anglican priests disgraced by personal debt, who couldn't make their livings otherwise, congregated around East London's Fleet prison and performed ceremonies without posting the banns (public notice). Prisons were outside the jurisdiction of the church, so the marriages remained secret but were still valid. These "fleet marriages" were most sought after by the middle rungs of society, but members of Parliament seized them as an excuse to take definitive control of their children's marriages.

A proponent of the bill, Sir Dudley Ryder, described it, saying: "Sir, the Bill is designed for putting an end to an evil which has been long and grievously complained of, an evil by which many of our best families have often suffered, and which our laws have often endeavoured to prevent. . . ." According to Ryder, the bill would "guard against the many artful contrivances set on foot to seduce young gentlemen and ladies of fortune" into marriages unsanctioned by both families. It was unlikely that a male heir would truly make an "infamous" marriage, which meant a marriage to an actress, courtesan, or prostitute. Sir Dudley's real concern was to solve the problem of a marriage a rich father couldn't control, between his son and a respectable but impoverished housemaid, or a daughter and a too-attractive man with too few means, or ill intentions. Of this, the solicitor general, William Murray said, "I cannot suppose that any gentlemen who has ever known what it is to be a father, will be against it."[12]

Both the framers and the opponents of this legislation cloaked their mercenary aims in virtue. The opposition invoked romantic love, self-determination, and the rights of children to argue against it. But in truth their fierce advocacy was a smokescreen designed to hide their own economic self-interest, which showed the rich fathers as being in the right; most of the bill's detractors came from the urban bourgeoisie and many had married heiresses as an essential step on their path to the House of Commons. If parental consent were obligatory, they would have a harder time seducing the young heiresses and making their own way up the social ladder. Robert Nugent, a member of Parliament who opposed the bill, explained it plainly: "Therefore I may prophesy, that if this Bill passes into a law, no commoner will ever marry a rich heiress, unless his father be minister of state, nor will a peer's eldest son marry the daughter of a commoner, unless she be a rich heiress."[13]

In 1753, Parliament passed the law, which made a father's power to veto a marriage absolute and binding. As a result, mothers and children lost their rights to appeal decisions in ecclesiastical courts, which were often less discriminatory to women. Young women impregnated by sons of the aristocracy also lost their rights. Young men were now legally allowed to treat young women of lesser background as they wished without fear of diminished reputation or financial drain. This made a significant impact on marriage—young men who were allowed to sow their wild oats were more likely to comply with an earlier marriage planned by their parents.

Harwicke's Act had wealthy fathers breathing more freely; they could cease worrying about their fortunes. Young heiresses could now attend parties (still chaperoned) with the sons of rich London merchants without inciting fears that they'd fall in love and run off together because the marriage markets of London were now firmly, legally, controlled by their fathers. Harwicke's law was a vital contributor to the development of the debutante ritual because it legally connected the welfare of daughters to political and socioeconomic power. Young women were now official channels of power as a result of an act of Parliament.[14]

With the marriage act passed, and control of marriage firmly in the hands of fathers, young women could be launched into a wider society earlier, ready to take their places as flagship vessels in the family fleet. The London social scene exploded in the latter half of the eighteenth century, not least because it slowly became the place where marriages could be negotiated. A stream of rich young girls poured into the capital and began to coalesce into the first debutante scene, where there were multiple parties designed to make marriages taking place over a period of months. In this period, an official "coming out" could happen any-

where and referred simply to the first appearance a young girl made, with
her parents, as a marriageable adult at an important social event. When
people described a girl as "out" it meant that she was unmarried and in
social circulation looking for a husband. How a family chose to present
its daughters reflected its status. The most eligible debutante of the eighteenth century, Lady Georgiana Spencer, later the Duchess of Devonshire, began her debutante year in Spa, a fashionable hot springs resort
in the Ardennes Forest, in what is now Belgium, where she learned how
to behave in a more socially sophisticated and flexible atmosphere while
her father "took the cure." If he had been well, the family might have
taken Georgiana to London. After the time in Spa, the family decamped
to France, where Georgiana, then fifteen, learned to successfully negotiate the complexities of the court of Louis XVI and Marie Antoinette
and became close friends with the young queen.[15] Georgiana is a good
illustration of what happens when a girl's family is at the apex of society.
There was so little time between her being "out" and her marriage to the
Duke of Devonshire that she was not presented at the British court until
after she was married.

Presentation at court and what we now call "the season" or "the debutante ritual" are related to each other but they are not the same thing.
In this period, as it had been since Elizabeth's proto-debutantes were
presented to her, court presentation was restricted to the top echelon
of young women. It was not a requirement that anyone be presented to
the queen before being considered respectably "out" or a good candidate for marriage. A girl could have any number of seasons before being
presented to the queen. Some were never presented. Even for an eligible family, a court presentation was sometimes prohibitively expensive.
The exquisite and costly gowns required could be worn only once and if
one's parents were not presented, sponsorship could be difficult to come
by. This is why you see kindly aunts and cousins acting as sponsors to
young women in English literature, where a combustible mix of resent-
ment and gratitude often drives the plot forward.

Still, court presentations influenced how the debutante ritual developed, along with influencing its aesthetics. The curtsy developed in this period, and is still practiced in many debutante presentations. The white debutante dress, now associated primarily with virginity, was initially an indicator of exclusivity. Before advancements in textile production that occurred in the late eighteenth century, making luxurious dresses in any color was labor intensive, and even the richest women had relatively few. The drawing rooms where court presentations took place were packed with people, and court dress requirements called for wide dresses with panniers and long trains that were made of many yards of fabric. White dirtied easily and was more vulnerable to the damage sustained when people collided and trod on each other's trains in the crowded rooms. While a few of the wealthiest debutantes did wear white to their presentations before textile production improved, if it had been an obligation, it would have limited the number of debutantes introduced, creating problems for the monarch, for whom court was not just social, but political. At the end of the eighteenth century, improved production techniques allowed dressmakers to produce dresses more rapidly, which lowered their price, after which white dresses grew in popularity. The color white's association with purity and wealth was longstanding. Aristocratic Greek and Roman women wore simple white dresses that set them apart from other women in society. White was a natural match for debutantes, who needed to radiate wealth and appear as ethereal, rarefied beings.

For the girls who were to be presented to the monarch, the required preparation was daunting. When her daughter was about the right age, usually seventeen or eighteen, a mother would send a notification to the head of the monarch's household, the Lord Chamberlain, to let him know she wished to present her daughter at the next drawing room. The chamberlain responded with a date and a list of dress requirements, including number of ostrich feathers, symbolizing grandeur and ascension, the girl was required to wear in her hair. By this time, the girls had been instructed by their mothers or aunts in practicing the necessary protocol again and again. In the country-bound months of the off-season, eager and unenthusiastic daughters alike had been subjected to all manner of social training—lessons in music, dance, French—with the hope that they might pass muster at court and/or with assembly patronesses, to be discussed below, and make a successful marriage. The girls had only twelve weeks in London to secure their future. It's difficult to convey just how sheltered prospective debutantes were. They knew little of the outside world and did not attend many parties, or at least the parties they attended were not significant in their lives, until they were informed by their mother that the time had come to have "a new occupation," as one Regency debutante put it: "My mother told me that my childhood had passed away; I was now seventeen, and must for the future be dressed suitably to the Class of young lady into which I had passed . . . I was so extremely pleased . . . I retained none of my old attire but my bonnets, cloaks and my habits."[16]

Though they might be familiar with country-house etiquette, the court was another thing altogether, and functioned with intrigue, competition, and its own jargon. "A chit-chat, a small talk, which turns upon trifles . . . it is the proper language of levees, drawing rooms and antechambers, it is necessary to know it," wrote Lord Chesterfield in his *Letters* to his son. "Flattery, though a base coin, is the necessary pocket money at court," he advised. And what does a child know of flattery? But all was in the hands of the queen, who kissed the daughters of the peers and often spoke to them as well. If the queen seemed particularly charmed, it would be reported in the Court Circular, and then in the gossip columns. If a girl performed poorly, that too would be reported.

Daughters might have had some general understanding of rank, but at court one had to observe strict rules of precedence. Girls were presented in the order of their father's standing, and people took to the floor to dance in order of their rank as well. The stress could be overwhelming, and most girls, understanding their predicament—they needed to get married—were frankly afraid. The novelist Fanny Burney, who served as a lady-in-waiting to Queen Charlotte, wrote in 1785 that it was preferable to "choke rather than cough, hold one's breath or break a blood vessel rather than sneeze. If a hairpin should prove painful it was not to be removed and if the agony became unbearable it was permitted to bite the inside of the cheek, providing that should a piece of flesh detach itself in the process it was swallowed, as spitting was certainly not allowed at court."[17] Debutantes were required to hold their heavy trains up as a sign of respect, even as they dropped into a curtsy. That fainting was chic was the only possible relief from error.

Over the course of the eighteenth century, as the moneyed sector of society grew larger and more diverse, marriage machinations moved outside of the court. Whitehall Palace, which had previously served to house the royal family and accommodate its social and political functions, was destroyed by fire in 1698, forcing a separation between the private and public lives of the royal family. They made Kensington Palace their home, and political and public ceremonies moved to St. James's Palace. Court presentations took place at the latter and were no longer held in actual drawing rooms near the monarchs' apartments. They retained their name as drawing rooms.

Though the first two Georgian kings, who reigned from 1714–1760, were less social (and barely spoke English, as they were German), King George III and Queen Charlotte expanded and nurtured a newly codified social season. It began in earnest following Parliament's Easter session break with an annual exhibition at the Royal Academy in early May. This was followed by Queen Charlotte's Ball, given first in 1780 by George III to celebrate his wife's birthday. The ball benefited the queen's favorite charity, a maternity hospital, and most debutante presentations today are similarly associated with a charity. Court balls and concerts, private balls and dances, parties, and sporting events took place throughout the summer. When Parliament adjourned on August 12, for the opening of the grouse season, the fashionable and aristocratic deserted London for points north, and the season would end.

The formalization of the season's schedule and its relationship to Parliament's session created ample opportunity for resourceful and ambitious people who wanted to rise in society. It's not that parvenus did not exist in the early eighteenth century; you just saw far fewer of them. In 1720, Daniel Defoe was already ridiculing the gentry for designs beyond their station, scoffing that their daughters "carry themselves to market" at the newly established assemblies. The assemblies that Defoe mocks were a social innovation. While private balls persisted, they remained both infrequent and prohibitively expensive for all but the wealthiest people to hold. Simply defined, assemblies were a gathering of people with some shared social purpose, like a musical or dancing society. They were held frequently enough to allow young people to meet and dance and form romantic attachments under the watchful supervision of a group of chaperones. Assemblies were simpler balls and were held weekly or bimonthly in all corners of Britain. Assembly rooms were built by enterprising proprietors who may have once chosen to open taverns or cafés and were then leased by a group of managers who sold subscriptions for admittance, chose the music, the dances, and who would attend. Between 1720 and 1820, seventy purpose-built assembly rooms were operating in England and Wales.[18]

Assemblies were centered around music and dancing and ranged from quite humble, usually in the countryside, to glamorous in the cities. Assemblies were funded by the price of the ticket for admission, and theoretically anyone who could pay it would be able to attend, particularly in small towns where the price remained low, like the Meryton in *Pride and Prejudice*. After her brother takes the lease at Netherfield, Caroline Bingley expresses her embarrassment at having to attend the local assembly, where she might be forced to mingle with the daughters of successful shopkeepers. At the Bingley's own Netherfield ball, by contrast, she controls the guest list, decoration, menu, and dances. This ball causes great excitement and stress and holds the potential for the greatest embarrassment for Elizabeth and Jane Bennett, whose mother and younger sisters regularly make them cringe. And indeed they are embarrassed—their pious younger sister Mary belabors her time at the piano playing religious tunes off-key. Their other two sisters race around chasing soldiers.

Like all institutions trusted implicitly by the English aristocracy, assemblies originated in the countryside and were tied, symbolically (yet not insignificantly) to the hunt. There were always balls that closed and opened the hunts. Because the hunts drew together acquaintances from all over the country, hunt balls were often places where future husbands and wives met. Balls during the hunting season were scheduled around full moons so that carriages could find their way through darkness along winding country roads. Hunt balls were initially held in the nicest rooms of someone's country house, but as aspirations grew, people wanted balls more often. They began to collectively lease spaces beginning in the 1720s. These evenings did function as marriage markets but they were also designed to be instructive. Like the junior cotillions or dancing school lessons of the twentieth century, young women learned how to behave at these informal balls that took place within a large and safe group of family and vouched-for acquaintances in attendance. This was a place where you could fail a little bit and still recover. These dances were a preparation for the more complex London season, where society was more urbane and its members more judgmental. Immersion among peers was the only guaranteed way to learn this behavior. Assemblies were a major feature of the growing social season, and parents relied increasingly on them as venues for presenting their daughters. They developed rapidly because they filled a social void, providing a predictable, approved space from which the newly established English gentleman could choose his wife or display his daughter, thus securing familial continuity.

Country assemblies would not suffice for the more fashionable aristocrats in London. They wanted to be able to launch their daughters in environments that had fewer members from the middle ranks. And indeed, by the mid-eighteenth century, there were several assembly rooms in London where a young girl might make her début. The most prestigious of these was Almack's, in St. James, where patronesses hosted a weekly Wednesday night ball and supper attended by the higher echelons of London society. From the moment it opened, Almack's set a standard that all other assembly rooms attempted to reach. A hundred years after its founding, social aspirants across the Atlantic in New York would look to Almack's model for guidance. "Almack's" became a by-word for the ultimate fashionable place. And its main function was to get girls married.

The Wednesday night dances at Almack's were the first debutante events to bear a passing resemblance to today's debutante parties. Their role in making marriages was clear even at the time. Writing in 1866 about the society of his younger years, Grantley Berkeley, son of the Earl of Berkeley, described Almack's as:

> One of the matrimonial marts of my time . . . an institution that seemed expressly designed as the slave market at Aleppo for the appreciation and transfer of female attraction. . . . With the title of Lady Patronesses, they issued tickets for a series of balls for the gratification of the crème de la crème of society, with a jealous watchfulness to prevent the intrusion of plebian rich or untitled vulgar; and they drew up a code of laws for the elect who received invitations, which were as unalterable as those of the Medes and Persians.[19]

Almack's was not the only assembly room in London but it was, by far, the most fashionable and exclusive. It was built in 1764–5 by William Macall, a Scotsman who had been valet to the Duke of Hamilton. Macall had saved the duke's life and was rewarded with a rise in salary. He remained in the duke's service, and when he retired he was able to open the club with his proceeds and the duke's social connections. Almack's was, at first, a club comparable to any of any other men's clubs that opened in St. James, the newly fashionable sector of London. A few years after it opened, it underwent a significant change and became a club for both sexes, the first of its kind. In 1770, Horace Walpole would record that the club had promise, writing, "There is a new institution that begins to make, and if it proceeds, will make a considerable noise."[20]

From the outside, Almack's was not overly ornamental for this period. It had a grand facade and entrance with a neoclassical door-case and six large arched windows that followed the ballroom along King Street, St. James. Inside, were three rooms, each dedicated to its own activity—a ballroom with a musicians' gallery for dancing, a card room for gambling, and a room where people were served drinks, usually punch. The interior was dominated by the cavernous ballroom, one hundred feet long and forty feet wide, decorated with gilt columns, classic medallions, and enormous mirrors. The interior architecture of the club would provide the model for all future assembly room design, and it was designed for intimidation. There was no doubt that a young woman was on stage when she danced in front of the spectators who hung over the rafters.[21] An evening there could be so hot and stressful that there is almost a sub-genre within eighteenth century letters of older people begging off of an evening at Almack's.

The biggest innovation of Almack's was, however, that women controlled the marriage market. A group of aristocratic women, the wives of the cabinet ministers and London's wealthiest peers, had come to the conclusion that private balls were unreliable—not everyone knew how to throw one and, even if they did, they could not be depended upon to produce enough perfect bachelors. Additionally, a private ball afforded its host little ability to increase her social influence. Hosting a ball at home was essentially an outgrowth of her already-existing duties as the lady of the house, and was so involved to produce that it could only happen once in a season. In controlling the Almack's, patronesses could exert influence they would not normally have, and much of that came from their working in unison. It's clear that their efforts to increase their power were successful because their husbands complained about it; a contemporary attendee wrote that they despaired at never knowing where their horses were, or when their carriages would be at their own disposal. Still, they must have benefited from their wives' ministrations because they did not stop them, which they could have done at any time.

The group of "lady patronesses," as they were commonly called, joined together and leased the assembly space from Mr. Almack for a weekly ball. The patronesses reconfigured the subscription dance formula that was common in the countryside wherein people would pay up front to buy a kind of season ticket that would fund the expenses of the party. They took that model but made the parties smaller and more exclusive. They chose Wednesday night because Parliament did not have an evening session then, guaranteeing the attendance of the rich, socially connected men the patronesses wanted for their daughters and nieces. The patronesses also made up the admissions committee. They managed the subscriptions fees, paid Mr. Almack, and, most importantly, they controlled the list of who would be sent invitations. Although the women did not make money from the parties, they put their energies into them, gaining social and political power from arranging the dances where matchmaking took place. Some contemporary authors referred to the patronesses as "bawds" and "mothers," the terms used for "madams" in off-color guidebooks to London's increasingly seamy nightlife. Almack's was known throughout all social classes—and even inspired a parody tavern called Allmax in East London where prostitutes pantomimed minuets and contredanse.[22]

Each Monday from April onward the seven Almack patronesses sat at a long table with three baskets: one for applications from friends, relatives, and near connections; another for acceptances; and a third for rejections. Compiled from the third basket were two lists: a list of those who would never be admitted and another made up of those who could try their luck again. After they made their decisions, the patronesses would distribute vouchers of admission. There were never more than 2,000 subscribers at a time, and birth and money did not guarantee admittance. Money was not the point. If you could not dance and behave properly, the women would not let you in. The patronesses took care not to admit men who were not serious about getting married. A contemporary explained the strict criteria:

> So anxious are the committee of Almack's to promote matrimonial matches, that they often refuse to admit a young gentleman whom they think in marriageable circumstances, to a third season, because he has "done no good" in the two first. They reason in this way: The young gentleman who is in circumstances to justify his marrying, and who has withstood the female attractions of two seasons, will, in all probability, become a confirmed bachelor—the sort of animal who has no business at Willis's rooms [another name for Almack's].[23]

By all accounts, the patronesses of Almack's were as stringent about acceptable clothing. This was not a club where aristocrats gathered in confident shabbiness. Even the Duke of Wellington, fresh from victory in the Napoleonic Wars, was refused admittance for wearing the wrong trousers. According to Captain Gronow, who wrote in his 1860 *Reminiscences*, "the Duke, who had a great respect for orders and regulations, quietly walked away." Wellington, added Gronow, was not the only one to suffer such ignominy. "Very often persons whose rank and fortunes entitled them to entrée anywhere else were excluded by the cliqueism of the lady patronesses, for the female government of Almack's was a pure despotism and subject to all the caprices of despotic rule. It is needless to add that, like every other despotism, it was not innocent of abuses."[24] Snubs were common and brutal. In an 1822 letter,

Maria Edgeworth recounts the blackballing of the Duchess of Rutland, who had offended the patronesses by not bothering to pay a special visit to court them, assuming that her rank would make her welcome. They retaliated by removing her from the list. They pleaded that "they really did not know her Grace."[25] Lady Caroline Lamb, best known for being Byron's tragic lover, was barred from Almack's after she satirized patroness Lady Jersey in her novel *Glenarvon*. The duchess was never removed from the black list, and Caroline Lamb was only reinstated because her sister-in-law was a patroness.

Society was transforming into an institution that people recognized, with contours that sheltered or expelled them. It was reliable, and as it expanded it became easier to participate in, as well as to deride. By the time Jane Austen was writing her novels, there were hundreds of parties during each season and mini-seasons had developed in resort towns like Bath and Tunbridge Wells, and in provincial cities like York, complete with their own assembly rooms and authoritarian patronesses. The increase in social requirements changed the lives of young girls in Regency England, who were exposed to the marriage market much earlier than in years past. If a gentry family was sufficiently wealthy and wished to improve their social standing, making their daughter a debutante was often part of their long-range plan to catapult themselves into the aristocracy. With assemblies increasingly accessible to a broader range of people, how soon a young girl was out in society was largely up to her parents. Some families limited their daughters to school and private balls until they were sixteen, but some young girls were launched as early as thirteen.

Marriage mania was fueled in part by national euphoria. The Napoleonic Wars (1803–15), which had drained national resources and forced young men overseas, were drawing to a close, and with their conclusion England emerged as the most powerful nation in the world. Some soldiers returned with new fortunes, and many were granted baronetcies. Young women's obsession with soldiers, so memorable when portrayed by the younger Bennett sisters in *Pride and Prejudice*, was widespread. Society was increasingly fluid and mobile, in part because assemblies had made it so—the assemblies made good behavior their primary focus, and in so doing the patronesses' authorized code of manners and the people who complied with them could blur the lines between the classes.

By developing a glamorous but grueling debutante ritual to entice a younger generation, the English aristocracy attempted to control the social chaos around them. The growing debutante system limited the diminution of aristocratic fortunes and social status by controlling the young men to whom their daughters were exposed and the daughters who could participate. Making a young girl's introduction to society ritualistic and communal built class identity. Making it beautiful cleansed debutante presentations and marriage markets of their blatantly commercial nature, while keeping them for the rich and making them appealing to daughters, for whom glamour was a new and welcome seduction.

CHAPTER 2

Revolution and Republic

THE ANTEBELLUM NORTH

The practice of formally presenting young women to society was exported from England in some form to most of its colonies during the consumer revolution of the mid-eighteenth century. Along with tea and silks came the attitudes that spurred their consumption—ideas arriving slowly on ships. In England, landed aristocracy had always provided an unassailable and grounding standard against which all social interaction could be measured. Even as the bourgeoisie and gentry gained power, the aristocracy remained a social ideal, its power begat by generations, shored up by property and a web of longstanding social connections. In England, the debutante ritual had emerged as a marriage strategy that helped maintain a hereditary upper class by creating opportunities for this class to intermarry with acceptable newcomers. Still, in England, a duke was a duke and his daughter was the daughter of a duke, and no ungainly curtsy or rude behavior could change that. Americans, however, had no titles, and would enthusiastically embrace debutante presentations as a means of delineating social class, barring the masses with an impenetrable wall of complex etiquette and ritual. In America, the debutante ritual and the marriages it facilitated created an upper class with the identifiable characteristics of a group of newly rich merchants and professionals. The ritual gained in importance after the tether to England was cut by the Revolution. Paradoxically, it flourished in a democratic environment, where some were still seen as more equal than others. Here, the debutante ritual reached its most dramatic heights and became the defining ritual not of kings, but of a striving merchant class.

Even in the lean years of early settlement, Americans aspired to proper manners. John Winthrop, the Puritan governor of the Massachusetts Bay Colony, arrived on the *Arbella* with only a few personal items, among them a copy of Baldessario Castiglione's *Book of the Courtier*, and a fork. The old forms of reputation—land and family name—had not been transportable to the colonies, and no matter—few colonists had names they would want transported. The social environment in the Atlantic port cities, where early settlement was concentrated, was dynamic and erratic. Ships came into harbor carrying everything anyone would ever want to buy. This splendor had to have seemed grander still, set against a backdrop wherein enslaved men and women stood for auction, indentured people served their masters, people flung the contents of chamber pots from windows, "bawdy texts" were discarded in the street and picked up by passersby, and where many drank watered-down beer all day because it was safer to drink than the water. From almost the instant Americans arrived, they began to accumulate goods; probate inventories show that the acquisition of objects accelerated quickly and people died with more and more belongings with each successive generation. The upper class that began to coalesce toward the end of the seventeenth century was soon defined by its rapidly increasing wealth, the proliferation of services and products that catered to its members, and its increasing self-consciousness. Wealthy colonists closely followed court rituals. It did not take long for a kind of colonial upper class to develop, and soon after they accumulated the money, behavior, and good manners that helped to separate them from those with less, they formed the basis of a new kind of hierarchy. By 1680, most upper-class colonial families were inheriting, not earning, their wealth. By 1700, the wealthiest 10 percent of Americans controlled 50 percent of all taxable property in the colonies. Fifty years later, they controlled 65 percent of this property.

The change in status can be seen in portraiture. If you compare seventeenth-century portraits of Puritan women to portraits of merchants' wives and daughters that were painted a hundred years later, the difference is dramatic. In the few portraits that remain of Puritan women, they look directly ahead, their gaze plain, "abridged of their superfluities," as John Winthrop put it. In their virtue, there are no secrets. Though artists did paint canvasses with a sense of movement and perspective in the seventeenth century, these paintings are flat, and most of them have matte black backgrounds. In eighteenth-century portraits, women wear rich clothing. A portrait by Ralph Earl of Alexander Hamilton's wife, born Elizabeth Schuyler, shows Mrs. Hamilton sitting on a giltwood bergère covered in blue velvet in front of undulating velvet curtains. She wears a diaphanous white dress with a delicate lace collar and pink sash. She has a black velvet ribbon tied around her neck and a netted veil in her hair. Each item she is wearing conveys her husband's wealth and power as well as her knowledge of the latest fashions. In other eighteenth-century paintings, there are objects on dressing boxes, including fans and the hand mirrors, which demonstrated the time one spent looking and assessing one's looks. At colonial assemblies, debutantes were both coy and inviting, holding fans close to their faces. They lowered them to show off a slender, beautifully angled wrist, one that knew how to make elegant movements that conveyed whether they were romantically available, interested, or bored. Wrist movement was part of a new language of leisure.

The shape of consumer goods began to shift with this new leisured behavior. Furniture changed. It became softer, allowing people to sink into it and lounge. It was up to the sitter to find the elegance in a swollen chair, or one with a back too delicate to lean on. Punchbowls grew larger; their new fluted shape permitting liquids to slosh around appealingly without spilling over the edges of the bowl, as people went back for more and more drinks during parties that ran well into the early morning hours. When John Adams visited Philadelphia, he was embarrassed by the sensuality of all the jellied food he was forced to eat there. He wrote to his wife, Abigail, about trembling aspics and trifles with too much rum to convey that the food of Philadelphia was overly rich and sinful. The size of serving implements grew, too, as tables grew wider. People, too, grew softer and richer and wanted to display their largesse. British Americans received catalogues from London and Paris and viewed the new objects and styles as ciphers to be cracked and learned. Name-dropping was a new frontier. Gentility was a language as much as English was, ever-shifting, with new vocabulary. To not know this language had social consequences.

The most important possessions of a rich teenage girl in a seaboard city would be those concerning dressing. She would have a chamber table, dressing boxes, and any other "accessories to the serious work of self-beautification." Dressing boxes were divided into tiny compartments for cosmetics, powders, and unguents. For a Puritan woman, a pockmark was God's will, meant to be endured. For an eighteenth-century debutante, filling that crevasse was "work akin to prayer."[1] A girl would have had a chest of drawers in which she would keep her lighter clothing, arranged by season, as well as the sort of filmy evening layers worn to an assembly. Though these were not the sack clothes of the cook or ladies' maid, they too were a uniform worn for the serious work of finding a husband.

At around the same time as dancing lessons became popular, English glass manufacturers figured out "how to elongate a squaring face glass into a three-quarter-length living portrait of face and figure fashionably united." Never before in human history had people seen themselves from "top to toe," as one delighted Englishwoman described her first experience of seeing her entire body reflected.[2] In tandem with their ability to view their bodies, and their experience of being viewed by others, young women became aware of their need to perform and measure up to a standard, and understood they were their family's representatives. In 1771, Anna Green Winslow's parents sent her to Boston to live with her prominent family there, so she would learn to be a proper lady. Only twelve, and already sensing her society's preoccupations, she complained about her lack of the right clothes in a letter to her mother back in Halifax, "you don't know the fation [*sic*] here, I beg to look like other folk," even though this would "cost an amasing sight of money." Noah Webster, the lexicographer and educator who gave his name to *Webster's Dictionary*, fretted that "the present ambition of Americans is to, as fast as possible, introduce as fast as possible the fashionable amusements of the European courts."[3]

Complex etiquette and rituals like debutante presentations functioned as codes—Were you in the right circle or were you not? Your movements, gracious or ungainly, would immediately communicate your place to a group of people who waited, watched, and judged. A new word entered the American vernacular—"genteel," from the French word *gentil*, originally meaning "well-born." Used in Europe to describe received good behavior, but not plausibly applied in the colonies in their first century, the word's widespread use in the eighteenth century conveyed that there was now an accepted standard of behavior to which colonists should aspire. Gentility, with its basis in proper behavior, soon transformed all manner of people into critics, because it made every activity into a performance.[4] In an atmosphere where a successful show of one's gentility was the primary means of social advancement, knowing how to dance was the fastest way for a colonist to move upward socially. Early forms of country dancing, or contredanse, originated in fifteenth-century England, and accelerated in popularity at the court of Elizabeth I. In the dance, two lines of people face each other (*contre* is French for "against" or "across"), women on one side, men on the other. These simple dances, and their later derivatives, the quadrille and the cotillion, were performed by groups of men and women and were first danced only in lines, but later in more complicated rounds and squares. These dances were deliberately and self-consciously social and evolved not only to allow men and women to interact within a safely contained space, but also to teach them how to do so elegantly. John Playford's *The English Dancing Master*, which explained a number of different dances using simple terms, was published in 1651, and made its way, with dancing masters, to the colonies. There were eighteen editions, as well as new volumes, by 1728.

Playford's book was among the first in a new genre of etiquette literature that preached that one could actually improve oneself and one's station through successful behaviors, like skill at dance. By the eighteenth century, Europe had produced a large number of itinerant dancing masters who modeled themselves after Playford, some of whom emigrated to the colonies in the early part of the century and began to advise the merchant captains and landowners who made up the colonial elite. By the early eighteenth century, there were enough traveling dancing masters to worry religious figures, who saw them as sly frauds whose instruction would lead to the disruption of the social order. Prominent church leaders inveighed against them and against dance itself, as did Cotton Mather when he wrote in 1700 "the case before us, is not, whether people of quality may not employ a *dancing-master* . . . but, whether the *dancing* humour, as it now prevails . . . be not a vanity forbidden by the values of Christianity."

Mather's speeches could not stop the craze for dancing. In Boston, dancing instruction was offered to young ladies and gentlemen by 1716. Its popularity created such controversy that a group of angry Puritans fell upon and destroyed Boston's main dancing school in 1723. In Philadelphia and Charleston, there was a greater demand for dancing teachers—and in those non-Puritan cities the elite vied for the best dancing masters. In an ad posted in a Philadelphia newspaper in 1780, a dancing school advertised that it had opened "for the ensuing season, for the reception of Pupils to learn that polite and necessary art. And for the convenience of grown Gentlemen, an EVENING SCHOOL will be continued the whole season."[5]

In 1740s Charleston, the two major dancing masters copied each other's advertisements and accused each other of being imposters. Both were eventually driven out of town by a third, Thomas Pike, who arrived from England in 1764, pronounced them both frauds, and rendered them obsolete with his skills that went beyond mere dancing—he also taught fencing, swordplay, and deportment. He was wise to offer private classes at his students' houses after their work hours, sheltering the tradesmen from public humiliation. Pike constructed long rooms that were specific to contredanse and held weekly dance nights and one large scholars' ball each year. Pike remained the preeminent master in Charleston for years. Because of the timidity and conformism of his colonial clientele, he was forced to introduce all innovations on spec—people hesitated to pay for something new until they were sure it was the current fashion. Once convinced, they needed to learn it immediately. Pike eventually went bankrupt after other dancing masters opened new venues there, diluting his clientele. He left Charleston and moved to Philadelphia, where he began again.[6]

Dancing masters traded in information and status. They were masters, too, of gossip and judges of minute mistakes. A dancing master could ruin a young woman's marriage prospects by excluding her from the dance or raise them by naming a dance after her, letting her lead the dance, or choosing the best partner for her. The colonial dancing master was just one in a long line of intimidating experts a potential debutante would rely on as rules for the burgeoning upper classes developed and hardened.

Dancing masters were not the only people in colonial America who organized balls and assemblies. Much like the British gentry, colonial Americans found that their houses were not large enough to accommodate the kind of dancing they wanted to do. Groups first began to sponsor larger gatherings in taverns and, soon, in purpose-built spaces modeled on Almack's and other assembly rooms in England. Philadelphia, New York, Boston, and Charleston all had dancing assemblies in place by the mid-1740s. Smaller cities like Cambridge, Massachusetts, and

Alexandria, Virginia, had theirs by the 1760s. Unlike in England, where assemblies were organized and administered by women, in colonial America, men ran these events and determined who was invited. While in London, merchants were barred from court presentation, in the colonies, they were the social leaders, setting trends and defining the parameters of fashionable society. And it was their daughters who were the most desirable brides.

Because it was the commercial and political center, Philadelphia had the most important dancing assembly in the colonies, which was run by a group who were referred to as "managers." Like the Almack's patronesses, they arranged the rooms so that people could sit and eat or play cards as well as dance. These Assemblies were designed to be exclusive. Initially, cost alone served to keep out most of the people deemed undesirable. In the first season of the Philadelphia Assembly, in 1748–9, a ticket was 40 shillings ($20 today); the next year it went up to £3 ($350 today). The cost increase did its intended job of excluding many—one of the organizers recorded that some "mechanics" complained to him about being unable to attend. Though he did not complain, Benjamin Franklin, easily the most famous man in North America, was a printer who worked with his hands, and thus technically a mechanic, and was not permitted to join the assembly, though he did attend on a few occasions as a guest. Though the assembly kept out the working classes, it did not exclude members of Philadelphia's two most prominent Jewish families. Both David Franks and Samson Levy, wealthy Sephardic merchants, were members of the assembly, and their children married into Protestant families. This religious mixing predated anything similar in England by at least one hundred years, and demonstrates how a society could fashion the debutante ritual to fit the needs of its own culture.

Despite the entry fee, the assembly soon attracted so many subscribers that guests were required to attend in shifts. A group of eighty dancers gathered on one evening and another group of that size two weeks later. In the first season of the Philadelphia Assembly, nine parties were given, and there were fifty-four subscribers. That number is somewhat deceptive because only men were permitted to subscribe, but their wives and grown children and out-of-town guests nearly always attended. The total population of Philadelphia was around 15,000, which means about 1 percent of the population attended the assembly. The parties were held on Thursday nights from the first of January to the first of May. Each party began at six and ended at midnight. Because only men could subscribe, they were told to give tickets to the ladies they wished to invite, suggesting that the first hurdle for young ladies was to impress older men so they could gain entrance to an event where they would once again need to impress men. Invitations were printed on the back of playing cards, as it was impossible to obtain other paper. The ledger that accounted for purchases at the dances shows that rum was consistently the largest order, and the greatest expense.

Because the evening at an assembly was formulaic and the contours of proper behavior were easy to understand, attending was seemingly unthreatening. The parties took a recognizable form each week, the attendees were largely the same, with just enough variation (visiting dignitaries, someone's rich New York relative) for anticipation. The assembly had to be predictable so it could set a standard for behavior against which people, especially young women, could be judged. Unlike in a café or tavern, the conversation tended to follow a well-trodden path. There were the usual introductions, toasts, and promenades, and the order of the dances changed little. Because the ceremony was always the same, it was a natural fit for ritual presentation of daughters.

Against the backdrop of this predictability a frisson could occur when a young woman made her debut. In the early years of the assembly, all a daughter had to do to become a debutante was put her hair up and appear with her parents at the event wearing a dress that exposed more décolletage than usual. She was then "out" and considered marriageable. When, exactly, a young woman came out depended on her age and her family's circumstances. If she had an older sister who had come out and was still

unmarried, her parents might wait a year to present her. If the family fortunes were in need of help, a beautiful girl would debut earlier.

Daughters of wealthy merchants and the kings' representatives in
Atlantic coastal cities were America's first debutantes. Teenage girls
in need of husbands were the first people in the colonies who didn't
have to work in a conventional sense. Spoiled by their father's wealth and
living in cities, on mornings after late dinner parties and assemblies they
slept until noon, their nights spent dancing until 3 a.m. Merchant heiress
Nancy Shippen wrote in her journal in 1780: "Must I acknowledge that
the greatest part of this day was spent in preparing for the assembly?"[7]

Regular attendance at the assembly served, in a dynamic socioeconomic environment where status was not pegged to hereditary titles,
to maintain appearances. As one writer put it, one needed "to be richly
dressed despite rumors or reversals of fortune, to show that the rav-
ages of disease had not disfigured one. When one failed to appear, or
one could not disguise the decline in one's status, beauty, health or ability, these occasions registered the failure that gave contrast to the sheen
of success."[8] Even the clothing worked to control the proceedings, by
influencing movement, and ordering a young woman's experience. The
garments that debutantes wore were designed to enhance the music and
dance steps. A fully boned eighteenth-century corset allowed a woman to
lean backward or from side to side, but she could not bend forward from
the waist without the heavily boned point of her corset reminding her of
her correct bearing. The armholes of her dress were high and tight, making it comfortable to keep shoulders back and her arms ever so slightly
raised, decreasing the tendency to droop. Eighteenth-century shoes had
no right or left. Their pointed toes, rounded soles, and high curved heels
forced the foot forward so a woman was on her tiptoes standing over the
instep. Balancing in such shoes required skill and a great deal of practice.
Executing the intricate footwork of eighteenth-century dances would
quickly separate the agile and graceful dancer from others. The manner
in which a girl moved was also affected by the fabric of her dress. Heavy

damasks or crisp silk taffetas restricted movement and forced elegance and deliberation onto a girl who might have collected eggs from hens earlier in the day. The dances themselves were not about the individual girl; the totality of movement the dancers created was meant to be a reflection of the social order. The dancers worked together to make pleasing figures. The challenge of asserting oneself in this context was difficult. Too much, and you were vulgar. Too little and you were a wallflower. Finding the right balance was a major part of the young women's work.

By 1755, demand for entertainments led the managers of the assembly to extend its season by hosting parties beginning in October, though the truly fashionable people did not attend before Christmas. By 1757, the *Philadelphia Gazette* was printing a list of the "belles and dames of Philadelphia." Just a list, no annotation needed. Membership in the assembly was enough to indicate everything one might want to know about a woman. There never seemed to be enough women, though. Organizers complained about a drought of women, writing "the subscribers may send a ticket to any young lady for the evening; notwithstanding which privilege J Willing tells me that he is almost tired of it because the girls are so little."[9]

On a regular evening, a dancing master or manager would organize and run the event, like a master of ceremony. Ladies would draw for their places in the dance, but to add a competitive element, the most favorable place was reserved for the evening's organizer to choose. The minuet, which always opened a ball, imitated the stylized courtship rituals of the highly controlled court environments. This provided a connection with European grandeur and made a ceremony of the proceedings. In the colonies, the minuet was always led by the most important man at a ball, generally a political leader or the richest man in town, and his chosen partner. In George Washington's papers, he referred to dance as "the gentler conflict" and regularly opened minuets at balls. Contemporaries described Washington and his dancing with admiration. He was known for his endurance. The Revolutionary War general Nathanael Greene described Washington's dancing in a letter to a friend: "His Excellency and Mrs. Greene [Greene's wife] danced upwards of three hours without once sitting down."[10] Another admirer wrote, "the General danced every set, that all the ladies might have the pleasure of dancing with him, or as it has since been handsomely expressed, *get a touch of him*."[11] Washington had an effect on women of all ages and often singled out the most beautiful women at balls, as witnessed by the young jurist Francis Brooke, who recounted in his journal that the general "opened it [the ball] by dancing a minuet with some lady, and then danced cotillions and country dances; was very gallant, and always attached himself, by his attentions, to some one or more of the most beautiful and attractive ladies at the balls."[12] Young women also recollected Washington's strong effect on them. In a letter to her mother, Charlotte Chambers wrote, "We were not long seated when General Washington entered, and bowed to the ladies as he passed round the room. 'He comes, he comes, the hero comes!' I involuntarily but softly exclaimed. When he bowed to me, I could scarcely resist the impulse of my heart that almost burst through my bosom, to meet him."[13]

That colonial leaders included assessments of their own dancing and that of others in their private journals and letters speaks to its importance as an indicator of refinement and as evidence for their participation in the highest reaches of society. Writing about dance skills was not limited to letters and private papers. A vibrant post-ball literary culture had developed by the late eighteenth century. Men concealed by arch pseudonyms wrote about the proceedings on the next day and circulated them among friends, or published leaflets. These writings memorialized the evening and led to further correspondence, and created a culture around the events that served to insert them into history, making them more important and consequential. The pseudonymous "Loquacious Scribble" wrote up his wry commentary on a ball in 1745, decrying the smooth ministrations of "The Reverend Mr Sly" who " tho the gravity of his Cloth would not permit him to dance" did manage to make "much the Smartest figure in Squiring the Ladies, and comparing them, as they stood in a row, to the [stars of the] milky way."[14] The anonymous writer references the flirting reverend in a way that shows that the entire party would understand this as a trope—this married man could ogle young girls more openly than could a single man with marriage prospects. The women are to be observed and are treated as a collective.

For women, success at a ball could take on several forms: she could receive accolades from the organizers, gather to her side an army of suitors, triumph over a particular rival, or win the heart of a desired gentleman.[15] She could also capture the interest of the larger company by being declared a favorite by the colonial press. For those women who had made a success at a ball, there existed a desire to "certify the verdict and fix it in public memory."[16] Young men flattered women by memorializing in verse their presence at a particular evening. A genre, "the survey of beauties," grew up around behavior at balls and assemblies, which resulted in poems that are embarrassing to read. A superior example is an early effort of by Philadelphia grandee Joseph Shippen, whose "Lines written in an Assembly room" is a breathless catalogue of women's virtues:

In lovely White's most pleasing form,
What various graces meet!
How blest with every striking charm!
How languishingly sweet!
With just such elegance and ease
Fair, Charming Swift appears;
Thus Willing, while she lives, can please,
Thus Polly Franks endears . . .

'Tis far beyond the painter's skill
To set their charms to view;
As far beyond the poet's quill,
To give the praise that's due.[17]

That the women are called out individually by name is significant. White, Swift, Willing, and Franks were major names in Philadelphia society at the time, and this sort of poetry added to a woman's prospects by making her seem more desirable while raising the stakes for the women who were not included.

The culture of writing that flourished after assemblies was not limited to florid poetry or wry pseudonymous clippings. Social performances— successful and, quite often, not—were chronicled in numerous letters and journals. Historian Richard Bushman has shown the pervasiveness of criticism, and how it created and delineated the contours of genteel society. First Lady Abigail Adams, who was known as a sober, intellectual woman, made it a practice of writing up assessments of other women after large parties and other social occasions. Adams recounted that the daughters of Captain Middleton, a major planter, were "aukward in their behavior, and dull, and rather saturnine in appearance." Of two Philadelphia socialites, she said, "Miss S. Shippen is pretty in the face but badly Made, and appears to have a fund of good humour. Miss Molly Shippen is very ugly and very formal in her manners, but good natur'd." In London, when her husband was ambassador there, she wrote that the Duchess of Devonshire, Georgiana, generally acknowledged to have been ravishing, was "masculine in appearance" and that Almack's patroness Lady Salisbury, whom nobody liked, had "a bad complexion." Moreover, she wrote to her husband when she was in Boston and he in Philadelphia to beg for his evaluation of a young woman about whom she was curious, saying she longed to read "her character drawn by your pen . . . I know you are a critical observer, and your judgment of people generally plases me."[18] Judgment, itself, proved a pleasure and a sign of one's gentility.

People did not hesitate to critique bad dancing. Eighteen-year-old Lucinda Lee Orr, a Virginia debutante who kept a journal of her social life and rounds of visits, confided in a letter to a friend in 1782 that "I don't think I ever laugh't so much in my life as I did last night at Captain

Grigg's minuet. I wish you could see him. It is really the most ludicrous thing I ever saw; and what makes it more so is, he thinks he dances a most delightful one . . ."[19] It appears that Captain Grigg danced badly in many places and did not improve, as he had already made an appearance in the plantation journal of tutor Phillip Fithian several years earlier: "Miss Prissy told us . . . that Captain Grigg (Captain of an English Ship) danced a Minuet with her; that he hobled [sic] most dolefully, & that the whole Assembly laughed!"[20] It is worth noting that what made Captain Grigg ridiculous was not so much his bad dancing as his firm belief in his abilities.

With even the most serious-minded people in the country regularly turning out the most casual eviscerations, the pressure placed upon young women was intense, and they turned increasingly to imported etiquette manuals for instruction and guidance. A French courtesy book that went through numerous American reprintings likely did not relieve their anxiety. It advised young women that "wherever you are, imagine that you are observed, and that your Behaviour is attentively scanned by the rest of the Company all the while and this will oblige you to observe yourself and to be constantly on your Guard."[21]

Debutantes would need to remain watchful even after the Revolution, as presentations continued to thrive in the years following. When the capital moved to Washington, they centered around the White House, where the president and first lady would receive people at the conspicuously named President's Levée, which bore such a resemblance to European debuts that they drew criticism from republican sectors of government and the public. That said, they were popular with Washington society. A contemporary attendee described these receptions as "numerously attended by all that was fashionable, elegant, and refined in society; but there were no places for the intrusion of the rabble in crowds, or for the mere coarse and boisterous partisan or impudent place-hunter—with boots, and frock-coats, or roundabouts, or with patched knees, and holes at both elbows."[22] The relieved observer continued, "democratic rudeness had not then so far gained the ascendency as to banish good manners." Young debutantes from powerful political families were presented to the president and first lady each New Year's Day, in a ceremony that would have been familiar in formula, if not refinement, to any who had attended one at St. James palace.

In 1827, sixteen-year-old Catharine Wirt, back in her native Baltimore after attending winter parties in Washington, wrote to her father, William, then the US attorney general, to describe the debut of her sister Lizzy, a year her senior, at one of these presidential levées. "This has been a great day with us in as much as it was Lizzy's debut," she wrote. "The rooms were crowded . . . But there was not in the whole room a dress which could at all vie with either of our group . . . After being introduced to Mr. and Mrs. Adams—she took her station at Mrs. A's right hand—where she has the best chance of seeing tout le monde— she says I must tell you that she was very well pleased and gratified." Catherine followed Lizzy and made her own debut there the following year. In the days leading up to the event she had coached herself in her diary "to take it all calmly." Her coming out was a success. She wrote a long entry in her journal the following day, describing her dress, the admiration she received, the crowd's reception of the Wirt family. It was her first late night. She returned home at dawn "in great good humour."[23]

Washington did not last long as a social center, though. Just after Catharine Wirt made her debut in 1828, Andrew Jackson took office, and the installation of this populist everyman and his pipe-smoking wife halted any fledgling efforts to create a national social life in the new capital. New York, already a significant social and commercial center, began to absorb some of the overflow from Washington. Harriet and Maria Trumbull arrived there from Connecticut in the winter of 1801 for their debutante season. The girls' father, governor of Connecticut, understanding that rural Connecticut was no place for young ladies of taste, had paid a family friend, Lady Kitty Duer, to chaperone them. Lady Kitty was an impoverished Anglo-American aristocrat whose husband William, a stock speculator and banker had, in 1792, caused the first true credit crisis and financial panic in United States history. Despite her connection to this scandal, she had survived because she was related to every old family in New York.

Left without money, Lady Kitty began a lucrative career as a social fixer, taking in the daughters of wealthy and connected provincials and shepherding them through a city season. Through her taste and relationships, she found the right dancing master for her charges, and arranged music lessons. She connected them with the dressmaker who would make the "white gowns" for their presentations at the City Assemblies for what Harriet described as "a pritty good price." She introduced the young daughters of Connecticut's governor into a not uncomplicated postwar society in the middle of a national election cycle, wherein many of the families they would meet opposed their father's political party. The fact that the girls navigated their season without detrimental notice was a testament to the skill set of women like Lady Kitty, who smoothed the rough contours of society.

Harriet (seventeen) and Maria (fifteen) wrote letters home to their parents that contain all the excitement and anxiety such privileged provincial girls would experience when plunked down in the middle of sophistication. They wrote of their awe at the shops on William Street, filled with stylish clothing. "You are very good my dear Papa, to be so indulgent to us in letting us have new dresses and encouraging us to appear in a style suited to your station in life," Harriet wrote to her father. New York at the turn of the nineteenth century had a population of 60,000, and those people lived almost entirely in the downtown area now known as the financial district. In 1776, a fire had destroyed 1,000 houses, and the sudden absence of housing stock, at a time when the population was growing dramatically, created a building boom that continued unabated until well into the nineteenth century. A British traveler who visited New York at the same time as Harriet and Maria wrote that the rebuilt New York "differed little from London's West End, except for being constructed entirely of red brick." The comparison to London by a Londoner speaks to the growing sophistication of the city that New Yorkers built, self-consciously, with refinement in mind.

Still, the city's boundaries contained only what now comprises the southernmost tip of Manhattan. The Battery was a fashionable promenade, where the upper classes walked to see and be seen, as they did in London's Hyde Park. But as late as 1808, people were petitioning the city to remove the pigs and chickens from the Battery and implored officials to stop people from beating out their carpets and hanging out their clothes to dry on the seawall. Lady Kitty Duer could no longer afford to live in a genteel neighborhood, so she lived in a respectable, if unfashionable, part of the city near the almshouse and the jail, close to what is now City Hall. The end of her street drifted into meadow. The house was far from the stylish shopping on William Street (which was good for Lady Kitty, who was in considerable debt) and most of the Trumbull girls' friends. Harriet and Maria wrote to their parents that they walked five miles a day on a circuitous round of visits, making social calls and drinking tea with John Jay, who was then serving as New York's governor, after having recently finished his term as first Chief Justice of the United States Supreme Court. Going farther afield required tougher clothing, a horse and a guide, and was, definitively, the country. There was no gradual demarcation; once the paved road stopped, so did society.

For young girls from sleepy Lebanon, Connecticut, New York was also loud. Construction noise was constant, and cart men moved goods from the wharves to the shops beginning before dawn. Observers complained that workers "steered their plodding oxen as much with loud yelling as with their reins."[24] Outside of drawing rooms and assemblies, the girls would have heard drunken men and entreaties from the windows of brothels on Murray and George Streets. The noise of the city was so intense that only the snow could quiet it. Then the sleighs replaced wheeled carts, and the world slowed. Still, despite streets interlarded with farm animals and filled with refuse from open sewers, New York was society's center.

Sending daughters into this environment reminds one that the process of refinement through a debutante experience was not exactly an effort to seal them off in an ivory tower. The kind of refinement Governor Trumbull sought for his daughters was not so much a sequestered innocence, but the ability to be graceful in moments of social complexity, which would have a real bearing on their future. Manners could function as a kind of armor that the girls could don when they needed to create a strong but polite barrier between themselves and a larger world filled with people of uncertain stature, farm animals in the street, and any other challenges to gentility.

While in the city, Harriet and Maria received instruction in painting, lessons in music, and regularly attended classes at Monsieur Laillet's Dancing Academy on Broad Street. There were seven dancing schools operating in New York at the turn of the nineteenth century—many of which were opened by aristocratic refugees from the French and Haitian Revolutions, both unfolding in the last years of the eighteenth century. The preponderance of dancing schools indicates how important social dance was in a city of 60,000, not many of whom could afford dance lessons. Even with rigorous training under M. Laillet, the girls were not totally confident in their new milieu. But a man Maria danced with at an elegant ball proved unnerving in more private surroundings the next day. When one dance partner called on her the following morning, she flailed. "I am sure he takes me for a great fool," she wrote to her mother. "I am so unused to fine things that the only reply I know how to make is either to hang down my head in silence and feel as ashamed as a dog—or else to look all around the room and begin to talk of something else as fast as I can." Her self-consciousness about being courted by someone older and more sophisticated was acute. "He seems a very good natured and clever man, but he don't know how to treat little girls, that is certain." Still, when the girls returned to Connecticut at the end of their debutante season they were considered "well turned-out young ladies."[25]

Only a few decades later, the city's population had increased to 250,000. The fashionable neighborhoods had shifted a bit north. One could rent a two-story house on newly chic Bleecker Street for $300 a year [$5,000/year in today's dollar]. For a hundred dollars more you could plant yourself right on "aristocratic Park Place, among the crème de la crème of New York society." If you weren't yet sure where you wanted to live when you arrived in 1830s New York, you could take a room and four meals at the brand-new Astor House hotel—where the food was putting the famed Delmonico restaurant to shame, according to socialite mayor and prolific diarist Philip Hone—for $1.50 per day. At the Astor, you would receive "all the delicacies of the season . . . served in a most ample manner." It cost less than $3,000 a year to support "a comfortable house, servants, a good table, wine, a horse, hospitality" while an additional $1,000 would allow you to live "like a truly rich man."[26] There were no state or federal income taxes to distress the rich, and there was ample freedom and few expenses. The press had yet to become a watchful nuisance. Part of the reason social life exploded in New York in this period was because it was (relatively) inexpensive and convenient to entertain. But having money wasn't enough to belong.

Society was now complex enough to require a more ambitious fixer than Lady Kitty. The first stop for mothers with debutante daughters in mid-nineteenth-century New York was a visit to Isaac Brown. He was a giant bear of a man, "beadle faced" and weighing in at almost four hundred pounds, whose official job was sexton of Grace Church in Greenwich Village, the Episcopal congregation attended by the families that made up elite New York. In his official capacity Brown was a handyman within the church—indeed he got the job as sexton because he had previously been a successful carpenter during the long real-estate boom of the early nineteenth century. While the priests might have tended to the spiritual lives of parishioners, Brown was the man who kept the physical part of the parish running. But where Brown really flourished was as a keeper of information. From his responsibility collecting all church bills (parishioners rented their pews, and their location within the church had its own hierarchy), he began to glean an understanding of the tiers of New York society. He used that understanding to serve society so well that he became indispensable. Brown knew where all of society's bodies were buried.[27] He sought out servants to get to know a family's taste and habits. He discovered new wines and cuts of meat, recommended furniture and linen rentals for parties. He knew gardeners who crossbred roses so he could supply a hostess with blooms heretofore unseen. He took on a role that was previously unknown in New York society, where servants had not been taught sophisticated manners because their employers were not yet in need of them. Brown slowly became a kind of higher-order handler—part butler, part arbiter, part authoritarian grandmother. When he observed that New Yorkers couldn't be bothered to take their own carriages home from parties—so crowded were the streets—he went into the carriage-hire business, arranging for carriages to line the streets outside of parties so that the fashionable need not worry about having their own coaches return to a party to pick them up. Even after he became rich from his carriage business, he did not leave his position as sexton, suggesting that he understood the hierarchies of society, and that his role therein would evaporate were he to abandon his information-rich post.

Brown was indispensable because he was effective. The upper reaches of New York society, whose members descended from the solidly middle-class Dutch and Englishmen who had made fortunes in city real estate and in shipping, were conservative. While the women went to Paris to buy dresses from Worth, they left them in the closet for a year to cure, so they would not appear too new and therefore considered vulgar. Fearful people depend on perfect etiquette. It was considered a breach to invite a sick person to your party—to have not learned they were ill revealed you were not really in the know. If you did so, you would force them to decline, making them acknowledge their weakness, a faux pas. Sexton Brown would know who was unwell, newly pregnant, low on money, as well as what couple was quarreling because the man of the house saw too many young opera singers. He knew whose humor was too coarse for a debutante party and how it could be managed if they were from a family that made their attendance obligatory. He knew who drank too heavily and stood too close to young women, or held their hands for just seconds too long. It was for these reasons that mothers looking to create a list of people to have to their daughters' debutante presentation always went to see Brown first. And he knew where young women should not go. One nineteenth-century socialite remembered Brown warning her away from a party at a "new" house. Her friend had asked "Many people here, Brown?" "Too many," was the answer in a sepulchral tone tinged with melancholy. "If you ladies will take my advice, you'll go on to Mrs. _____. This is mixed, *very*."[28]

Through his contacts at hotels, Brown told them which visiting dignitaries would be in town for their parties. Hostesses hungered for traveling aristocrats to provide an aura of authenticity to their evenings, and the aristocrats were themselves eager to see moneyed New York's upper echelons, to understand the city where men had made such enormous fortunes that there was a new word on everyone's lips—millionaire. Brown's encyclopedic knowledge of society led naturally to entrepreneurship. Sexton Brown kept a list of men he knew who danced with ease, and he would provide it to the mothers of debutantes, perhaps for a small fee. Over time, he created a coterie of men he called "Brown's boys." They were the "extra men" of their day, and were excellent dance partners for society women who were left alone by husbands who, unlike their aristocratic counterparts in Europe, worked hard for their money. Brown's boys helped to round out a party, adding their elegant manners to the occasion, but they knew better than to cross the line and call on the young debutantes the next day. Just because you met someone at a ball did not mean you had any right to see them in private. Like Brown, his boys made society run smoothly and look beautiful, but didn't threaten its hierarchies. Though Brown had a fierce suspicion of the parvenus who flocked to New York in the years preceding the Civil War and then came in multitudes after it, he also saw it as his role to single out those striving families he felt might slide into society, even if their names weren't Roosevelt or Van Rensselaer. He watched, and recommended young people who had more polish than their parents. Because he was himself a social climber, he knew society had to be at least somewhat organic, and that it functioned best when there were a few people on the verge of exclusion. There also needed to be some places at a table for people who were beautiful or talented if not moneyed, as long as they had the right manners. New York was too big and competitive, too obsessed with money, for society to consist of just the old families. During his thirty-five years at Grace Church, Isaac Brown would witness and help transform New York society from a cabal of families who ran a city ranging from the Battery to Greenwich Village, where cows still wandered the streets along with debutantes, into a huge metropolis that no gatekeeper could control.

CHAPTER 3

Frozen in Time

THE ANTEBELLUM SOUTH

While the New York of Isaac Brown was the prime location for the nation's most socially ambitious, another debutante culture developed in the southern states, informed by planter culture. The bustling port cities of Charleston and Savannah had dancing assemblies that functioned similarly to those that developed in Philadelphia and New York. Daughters of city merchants were presented at evening assemblies in these cities from the mid-eighteenth century on. The coastal cities were cosmopolitan and diverse, and in the early years of colonization shared more characteristics with northern port cities than they did with the smaller, regional towns of the interior. Like their merchant counterparts in the north, the planter elite opened their most elegant balls with the minuet. These balls tended to occur when the rich occasionally gathered, around holidays or other occasions. As in the north, minuets were danced one couple at a time in descending social order. William Byrd, slaveholder, planter, and diarist, wrote about an occasion at a ball in Williamsburg in 1711 at which the colonial governor had chosen Byrd's wife as a dance partner for the minuet. In so doing, he communicated that Byrd ranked above all men but himself. Men with political aspirations and their wives were thus wise to practice their dance steps often, as indeed Byrd did. The note "danced my dance" appears almost daily in his diary.[1]

But the driving force in the development of a distinctly southern debutante culture was not the coastal merchant elite but the social structure of the colonial plantation, where marriages and the rituals that facilitated them were organized with one purpose in mind—to bolster the power of the *paterfamilias*. Southern plantations were unlike anything in the north—even the Dutch patroonships along the Hudson could not rival the size of the largest southern tracts. One French traveler recounted his arrival at a Virginia plantation in 1686: "I thought I was entering a rather large village, but later on was told that all of it belonged to the planter."[2] Planters lived like feudal lords on remote properties that were entirely self-contained, supported by the forced labor due to the work of the enslaved people kept living there. The largest landowner in colonial Virginia, Robert "King" Carter, a tobacco farmer and colonial governor, acquired farmland by seeking out foreclosures, and died with at least 295,000 acres of land.[3] He was a prolific diarist who wrote about everything from his health to his dynastic strategy. When his daughters were to wed, it was not the new couple, nor even the bridegroom-to-be, who wrote to the county clerk for marriage licenses, but Carter himself.[4] The Virginia gentry maintained their power through intermarriage, and this strategy would provide the philosophical underpinnings of the debutante ritual.[5]

Carter ruled his land from his plantation house "Corotoman" on the shores of the Rappahannock River. Everything he needed floated up the river from Williamsburg with his overseers. Even the dancing master, Charles Stagg, drifted over from town, riding with the tobacco hogsheads, to teach the Carter children to dance.[6] Along the riverbank, dancing masters cut particularly glamorous figures, bringing with them tales of Europe, its changing fashions and gossip, and information about the belles of the moment in town. Dance was a vital link to civilization and basic good manners, and the dancing masters' direction and instruction were crucial for young girls in particular, who would be assessed by prospective husbands based on how well they internalized the graces taught them. These teachers would generally hold forth on the small changes in manners and etiquette that were their stock and trade, and whether their information was true or invented did not much matter. If a dancing master started at Carter's plantation when a large trunk of new silk arrived for the Carter daughters, when he reached the Page family up the river, he could tell the Page daughters what color they had ordered, and they could compare it to their own choices. Dancing masters were a vital source of information for colonists stuck on remote plantations, especially the planters' daughters, whose marriages depended on their sophistication, even while they were restricted to their immediate environs.

Some southerners felt their isolation intensely. George Washington used to post an enslaved man at the crossroads near his plantation to invite any passerby to dinner. Washington's granddaughter, Eleanor Park Custis, wrote to a school friend in 1796, "I stay constantly at home . . . I have been out but twice since I came here (which is three weeks.)" A visitor to the region recounted, "Strangers are sought after with Greediness." A circuit judge in North Carolina in the Revolutionary War era stopped at the home of some well-to-do newlyweds who were living on the husband's farm, eighteen miles from the nearest neighbor. He wrote that when a male visitor told the young bride he would bring his own wife to visit her, she wept with gratitude.[7] Young people rarely met except for at the occasional ball, and these events held by planters were not bound by the smooth manners of the city. One man, writing to a friend in London, recounted his experiences of a plantation ball. Everyone gathered and:

> Dined under a large shady Tree or an arbour made of green bushes under which we have benches and seats to sit on when we dine sumptuously all this an old field, where we have a mile Race Ground and every horse on the Field runs, two and two together, by that means we have a deal of diversion and in the evening we retire to some Gentle's house and dance awhile after supper and

then retire to bed, all stay at the House all night (it's not like in your country) for every Gentleman here has ten or fifteen beds, which is aplenty for the Ladies and the Mens Ruffs it, in this manner we spend our time once a fortnight and had other times we have regular Balls as you have in England.[8]

In the rural areas, sometimes a motley arrangement of dancers was the only way to get the numbers necessary for the line dances colonists favored. Locals might be asked to appear at a plantation to dance. They usually attended, whether enthusiastically or grudgingly it's hard to say. These contredanses, with their polite, simple-to-learn steps, were designed to teach people how to interact, and the changing of partners was as important as the dance steps. Good manners during transitions from partner to partner were vital, and mirrored the need for avoiding awkwardness in conversation. Still, plantation hospitality did not always run as smoothly as events in the city did. Meals were often served several hours after the appointed time as people waited for enslaved women to cook and serve food. The process of carrying the dishes from the cookhouse—always located away from the house—left much of the food overcooked and underheated.

A ball on a plantation usually ended with a jig danced later in the night. One visiting Englishmen was alarmed by the sensuality of a plantation ball in Virginia, which he witnessed in 1774: It was "more like a bacchanalian dance than one in a polite assembly. Old women, young wives with children in the lap, widows, maids and girls come promiscuously to these assemblies, which generally continue until morning."[9] After this, at times, enslaved men would play music late into the night. Only in the context of a planter's absolute authority could gender, class, and race mixing like this take place. There was no threat of transgression; the planter's power was absolute and his potential violence hung threateningly in the air, protecting his daughters.

Because of the distance between plantations, southerners invited guests for long periods so that they might attend a ball. Planter daughters rarely encountered people who were not preapproved by their parents. If they did go to town, they were chaperoned, and could not meet someone who did not meet their parents' standards. These parties could be slightly wilder than city assemblies and foreshadowed what would be essential components of old-line southern debutante presentations in places like New Orleans and Charleston—secrecy and control.

After the Revolutionary War, the American South, dependent on slave labor and geographically isolated from the new capital and growing commercial centers of the North, drifted further away from the rest of the country in both temperament and custom. Sectional differences became pronounced, and southerners became more defensive about their slave-based economy as the Revolution, with its moral idealism, ushered in a small, but growing, abolitionist movement in the North. The great planter families like the Carters continued to wield significant power, but a middle class composed of smaller merchants and farmers grew larger.[10] By the end of the eighteenth century, the southern social elite felt a greater need to differentiate themselves from the striving crowds.[11] Robert Carter's grandson would employ a dancing master at his house Nomini Hall to teach cotillion, a complex French dance that was introduced to the colonies during the Revolution. The dancing master was equal in importance to another of his employees, the Princeton-educated academic tutor, Philip Fithian, who despaired in his journal about his inability to dance, writing, "I was strongly solicited by the young Gentlemen to go in and dance. I declined it, however, and went to my Room not without Wishes that it had been a part of my Education to learn what I think is an innocent and an ornamental, and most certainly, in this province is a necessary qualification for a person to appear even decent in Company!"[12] Less well-to-do, Fithian would not have been taught the dance steps, and Carter likely would not have wanted him on the dance floor. This change toward greater exclusion even within white society took place over only fifty years.

In the wake of the war, most US states undertook a series of democratic reforms, and some of the first, significantly, had to do with reforming the way inheritance favored the very rich, at the expense of the bourgeois (who so loyally fought for the Republican victors). Old inheritance law had been, like tea, imported directly from London, and had given advantage to wealthy British Americans with land. The southern states were the last to reform, but eventually, they too, were forced to evolve. In the Virginia House of Delegates these efforts were spearheaded, in the late 1770s, by Thomas Jefferson, who successfully dismantled two old laws of entail and primogeniture, which were effective legal devices that automatically passed property to the eldest son on the event of a father's death. Entail was particularly valuable to privileged men because it allowed a property owner to stipulate that only a single direct descendant could inherit his land and that the land could not be sold or inherited by anyone outside the family.[13] Large tracts were not broken up, but remained intact, and the same families owned them for years, consolidating power, controlling cities, counties, states and, soon, entire regions.

The end of entail in most states made it more difficult for rich landowning families to transfer their wealth through multiple generations intact, and dramatically increased the importance of marriage as an alternate means of consolidating and increasing family fortunes. As it was in England at the time of Hardwick's Marriage Act, the exchange of young women with money and portable wealth grew important when marriage became the safest and most reliable way for rich families to consolidate their financial interests. The portable wealth of daughters often came in the form of enslaved men and women, who replaced land in many women's dowries. As historian Stephanie E. Jones-Rogers has shown, 41 percent of enslaved people were owned by women, directly linking white women's desirability as wives to the enslavement of black men and women by her and her family.[14] Jefferson's desire to abolish legal barriers to an individual white man's "pursuit of happiness" made a rich man's daughters an even more valuable currency. With ownership of land in flux, fathers turned to their daughters, making the debutante ritual perversely more significant during periods when wealth was held by a greater number of people.

*W*hile more democratic inheritance practices served to emphasize marriage as a barter system for rich men's daughters, the Revolution also transformed how Americans defined the role of women in society. The cosseted merchant or planter wife, with her towering wigs and *bibelots*, became a relic of the colonial period. She represented the yoke of fashion as defined by the English. Against the backdrop of the post-Revolutionary period, this woman was an affront to patriotism. Rich wives who once enjoyed incredible leisure were now expected to do some housework in order to perform democracy. Wives were charged with birthing and rearing citizens in a new republic, and with living up to the virtues most associated with that republicanism—industriousness, humility, moral fortitude, economy, and, most importantly, maternalness. Their daughters, on the other hand, were given much more freedom to be decorative, and the debutante period of their lives was extended.

In the South, the influence of revolutionary ideology increased white women's labor. They could no longer have wet-nurses, particularly not enslaved women, who, with ever-growing racism, began to be seen as morally unfit to nurse the sons of the republic. This newfound premium placed on education and moral virtue did have some advantages for wealthy white women, who themselves benefited from a kind of trickling down of educational opportunity. They were more likely to be academically educated than they were before the war, as it was thought they could not raise their sons without educations themselves. But their roles overall remained narrow. They lost the little freedom they had in the days when the ultimate social authority, the queen, was across the

Atlantic in Britain. While mothers were busy rearing citizen sons, their debutante daughters increasingly filled their social roles, going on successive rounds of visits, attending parties and teas. Free from the drudgery that made a home actually run, a teenage daughter's role could be increasingly that of a showpiece—making it socially acceptable for a daughter to have more freedom than her mother. This period of life was both fun and romantic and many teenage girls, viewing the lives of their mothers, were in no hurry for it to end.

As the primary indicators of their father's social position, they were the people in society with the time and freedom to roam, the license to be idle. Any frivolousness was forgiven in their efforts to find a husband. In this context, how elite families, and those working for that status, shepherded their daughters toward marriage took on a new significance. Many parents now took the step to send their daughters away to school with daughters of like-minded families.

In the early generations of settlement, some elite southerners had sent their children back to England to be educated. Even some daughters went to stay with English families for a period of social education, increasing their marriageability, and making certain that the thin golden thread linking the colonies to the country of origin did not fray. As this was no longer politically possible after the Revolution, an enterprising crop of educators began to set up boarding schools in regional American cities, especially for children of planters living often on isolated plantations. Girls learned geometry and languages, but also took music, needlework, and dancing classes that would "finish" them and ready them for their debutante season. Private plantation balls still occurred, but southern society began to gain greater cohesion now that its children were attending school together. Girls read the same books, wore similar clothes, and were more likely to be introduced at an urban assembly with their friends from school than they were to have only a single private ball at their father's house.

Girls' boarding schools began to pop up across the country beginning in 1814 with The Troy Female Seminary (now Emma Willard) in upstate

New York. The Virginia Female Institute (now Stuart Hall), outside of Charlottesville, and St. Mary's School, in Raleigh, both founded in the early 1840s, were popular with rich planter families and their daughters, who were excited to meet other girls and be in a town. Southern girls began school at around thirteen years old, still definitively children. At around fifteen, girls began to wear a more mature women's clothing. Lizzie Kimberly, a member of a wealthy North Carolina family, left her home in Chapel Hill at fifteen to go to St Mary's in Raleigh. She wrote to her father that she needed "all new clothes," including a corset.[15] Parents generally allowed their daughters' requests, believing that such an investment now would yield greater social mobility.

Graceful but restrictive clothing, which required them to move more slowly, replaced the loose dresses they had worn, which allowed them mostly the same physical freedom as young boys. A long, full skirt with a tight waist signaled a girl was of age and that her limbs, now sexualized, needed to be concealed. Girls were berated when they showed their knees, and told not to stand in certain masculine-seeming positions. Any pose that could be considered "common" was prohibited.[16] At times it must have felt as though it was common to move at all. Corseting inhibited a girl's movement and created the cultural ideal, pacifying the sexual threat of an hourglass figure by rendering it immobile, and concealing the legs in a vast billow of skirting. Clothing and hairstyles were designed to restrict, and also to pose challenges. Could a girl achieve grace when dancing in difficult shoes? Could she keep her elaborately set ringlets up in innumerable pins? She was always on the verge of failure. Restraint further inhibited movement and reinforced passivity. Clothing codes also created and reinforced competition between women. Only certain families could afford the most luxurious materials and employ the lady's maids who had the best hairdressing skills.

Still, while clothes and hairstyles beckoned their daughters, wealthy southern parents, unlike their aristocratic English counterparts, greatly valued women's academic education and believed it differentiated their daughters from other young women with lesser educations, since they did not have titles to set them apart. In 1845, Virginia planter Lloyd Noland wrote to his daughter, Ella, at Mrs. Edwards' Seminary in Leesburg, Virginia, imploring her "not to neglect one moment of your studies. This is the most important time in your life—your character hereafter may now be about to take its *cast*." Four years later, when Ella was eighteen and about to finish school, her mother advised her to retain this focus: "let nothing draw your attention from your studies."[17] This didn't mean academic life was the only focus. Social training was vital. The ideal daughter would embody a "happy union of female gentleness and delicacy, with masculine learning and genius," as William Wirt wrote to his wife Elizabeth in 1810.[18]

When the school years ended, young women began to prepare for their debuts and eventual marriages in a number of ways. They would accompany their mothers on rounds of visits in their immediate communities, prepare their clothing and personal items—even the wealthiest girls did some of their own needlework, because it showed off their hands. After this period of quasi-apprenticeship, a young woman and her parents often planned a route that would allow her to visit not only relatives but also friends from boarding school and their families. She'd be chaperoned on her way between these places, but not usually by one of her parents. Broadening one's circle facilitated potential marriages into families of their friends. At around this time, a young woman would stop using her given name and begin to be called "Miss," further indicating that she had moved away from childhood and was ready to be married.

Debutantes from older, wealthier families almost always traveled to one or more cities along the Eastern Seaboard to make a debut. Ella Noland, whose wealthy parents had chastised her about keeping up her studies, supported her similarly to do her best job with her social education. She was dispatched to spend the winter of 1850–51 in Philadelphia with her mother's sister, Sally Gibson, and her two cousins, Marion and Grace. Though it was unusual to bring out two sisters during the same

social season, it was common practice for extended families to bring out
cousins together if the girls were around the same age. While sisters might
compete in a way that dampened the family's prospects, people thought
that cousins in search of husbands made charming partners. During this
winter season, Ella and Marion came out while Grace, who was younger,
waited a little longer. Ella's aunt was the well-connected wife of a socially
prominent Philadelphia doctor. Under her chaperonage, Ella would have
access to the inner reaches of what was then the social center of the country. Ella's mother Elizabeth wrote to Sally that Ella was "prepared to take
the gay and noisy city by storm . . . as a *great Virginia belle*."[19]

Ella's season followed the same schedule and had numerous similari-
ties with Nancy Shippen's season in pre-Revolutionary Philadelphia.
The city's upper class had weathered the Revolutionary War intact, and
Ella got to know many of the same families who had been in Nancy's
circle. Ella made her debut at Mrs. Willing's ball, an annual winter event
that kicked off the social season. The Willings were an old merchant
and banking family with a history of producing alderman, mayors, jus-
tices, as well as the first president of the Bank of the United States. Mrs.
Willing's ball was the ideal venue at which to enter society. Ella's ledger, included in a letter to her mother, tells us that her dress for the ball
cost $28 ($840 today). She also had an outstanding bill at Levy's, the dry
goods store owned by the prominent Sephardic-American family who
not only outfitted Philadelphia society but were also a vital part of it,
for $41 ($1,230 today) and "small articles" worth another $25 ($750). She
also asked her mother if she could have permission to buy a "spring silk"
to wear out in the evenings, sweetening the request by saying "Aunt S.
thinks I had better get mine." Ella's concern about the cost of these items
is evident when she lets her mother know "it can be charged and my
bill paid at any time before I leave here."[20] The expense proved worth
it for the family. Ella was wearing her "exceedingly handsome" dress of
"light silk suit, a skirt of white silk [sultan] embroidered all over in bouquets of flowers & a beautiful bustle to suit; Grace's coral necklace on

my hair [and] coral earrings & bracelet." After the success at the ball, she received more invitations to other balls and to the weekly assembly. Men remarked on her "cherry lips and rosy cheeks." Soon after, two serious suitors make appearances in her letters. Historian Anya Jabour collected a series of letters written by Ella's friends and mother, wherein they all warn her not to marry too quickly. One friend wrote, "take care of that little heart and do not yield it too readily." Another warned her off coming home too quickly to the "dull life" in the country, writing that the women around her spoke only of "the having of babies and the treatment thereof . . . both of which are topics I suppose as devoid of interest to you as myself." Her mother also cautioned her against marrying too soon. "Good and clever husbands are rare articles nowadays," she advised, "and you are quite too young to encumber yourself with family cares."[21]

Ella did not end up marrying either of her Philadelphia suitors. She returned to Glen Ora, her family's plantation outside of Middleburg, Virginia. Her cousin Marion continued her season in Washington, D.C., and Baltimore. Ella spent the following winter supervising the domestic work in the plantation houses: the seasonal changing of curtains and rugs, the spinning of yarn and its organization, as well as menu choices, canning and preservation of food, and the whitewashing of the house. After this year spent at home, Ella married a physician from a prominent Baltimore family and moved to that city. And it is here that our record of her life wanes.

Not every southern debutante would enjoy her coming out. Penelope Skinner was the only daughter of Joseph B. Skinner, a wealthy North Carolina planter and widower with large plantations near the coast. Because Penelope's mother died when she was a child, she and her brother Tristrim were sent to live with a friend of her father and his family in the foothills of Hillsborough, North Carolina, while her father, known to family as Joe B., managed the family's rice and cotton plantations. This was a common arrangement for planters, especially widowers whose plantations were in the difficult and disease-ridden coastal climates. Penelope and Tristrim attended day schools while living there. After their early schooling, the two decamped to other family friends in Philadelphia, where they both attended French-language boarding schools run by the son of a French count whose father had been Consul General there. From their respective schools, Penelope and Tristrim, who were very close, were only permitted to exchange letters with each other in French, their father's requirement, a practice that was unusual even among the most sophisticated southerners. The letters, collected, edited, and published by scholar Mary Maillard, track the unconventional Penelope's transition from adolescence to debutante to young wife.

Penelope's social life was problematic from the beginning, because her father was known for his "queer ways" and social unpredictability. He discarded invitations at the last minute and barred his children from attending parties that would have made their experience in society run more smoothly. According to Maillard, some friends appreciated Joe B. for the loyal heart hidden under his gruffness, but family letters make clear that he was tolerated by wider society because of his wealth and power. Pen, as she was widely known, was independent and opinionated like her father, but these traits were, of course, less tolerated in a young woman. She was thought unattractive; she had a thin face with a sallow complexion and a boyish figure, all features that were deeply unfashionable in the antebellum period, when people equated beauty with goodness, and often used the terms interchangeably. Penelope was launched into society in 1837, at age nineteen, with her family hoping that her fortune and status would supersede her unconventional looks and temperament.

Penelope first came out in Hillsborough. There is no record of the event at which she was presented, but it appears that it was an uneasy time for her. Letters of the period are vague, but point to Pen having had a dalliance with the son of Justice Nash, her guardian during her early school years.[22] Penelope left Hillsborough not having been an early success, and having offended those close to her. She prepared to try to relaunch herself during the summer season in Williamsburg. There, she was also disliked, and was soon accused of "going after" Robert Dew, the president of the College of William and Mary. It's unclear what Pen's exact transgressions were, but she wrote to Tristrim in despair: "Brother between you & I, I think the Williamsburg people are most tired of me. Mr. S said when I went the last time that it was to catch Mr. Dew & I was treated so singularly at his house that I would not go back there again."[23] She was also thought to have had "a fling" with John Tyler Jr., whose father would soon be president of the United States. Although southern debutantes were judged by how many proposals they received and tried to rack up as many as they could, Penelope's inability to negotiate what was required of a belle—a delicate balance between coquetry and innocence—was not helping her. Her time "on the carpet," as southerners sometimes called the season, wasn't working out. People believed that in trying to catch a husband, she had erred on the side of pursuer rather than pursued, and she knew it. Though she was a keen observer of people, her inability to meet the requirements elite society had created for its belles led people to judge her harshly.

After her failed season in Williamsburg, Penelope returned home to the family plantation to care for her father, who suffered from bouts of fever—likely malaria. She collapsed into depression, writing to Tristrim that she had "the blues prodigious bad." While there, she entertained suitors but wrote to her brother saying, "Father is so strict & particular that the young men will I fear soon begin not to come here at all." Penelope, determined to marry to escape her depression and isolation, entered into an engagement with James French, a man her family didn't know and were concerned about. In the South, engagements were casual, and often entered into casually to enhance the desirability of the young women. Many were not kept. Young women didn't speak about them publicly until families did their discreet vetting. Young women understood that their fathers could intervene and stop their engagements at any time. Given this, the process of investigating French was initially an open discussion between the three Skinners. Penelope asked Tristrim to inquire about him at school, and her father wrote to friends to see who could speak to his character. But as Penelope became more deeply entangled and her father began to hear from friends that nobody knew Mr. French, he began to worry over his character and vanity. He implored Tristrim to keep secret his doubts about Pen's fiancé. "Nobody must know I have written to you about him—and nobody shall know what you write to me not even your Sister."[24] He continued, emphasizing that he would make the final decision about the potential marriage, "I must make up my mind, and you must be free—frank—and [unreadable]—in all you know or can hear—and these are our secrets." Ultimately, her father and brother convinced Penelope that French was not the man for her. Shortly thereafter, she began to deny they had an engagement to friends.

Pen was concerned about what she called "the old stock" remaining "on the carpet" in the face of "new stock" coming on the market, as she described the younger crop of debutantes to Tristrim. She quickly entered into another engagement in July 1839, one that her friends considered "rather desperate." Penelope had accepted a proposal from John Beverley Christian, the brother-in-law of president-to-be John Tyler, who was a judge and widower with five children. Her neighbors and friends were shocked by the speed of the engagement and disturbed by the extreme age difference—nearly thirty years. It's not clear if Penelope received open pressure from her friends and family but she broke off this engagement, too.

In October 1839, Penelope became engaged for a third time, to a man only identified as Mr. S. in her letters. She told her brother about the engagement in a way that revealed that even she doubted she'd go through with it, saying the wedding is being talked about by everyone and it would be "a pity to disappoint" her friends and neighbors. She asked Tristrim to "never tell anything to Pa." As Penelope continued to violate the norms of elite southern society, those who had previously loved her began to criticize her openly in their letters to friends. Judge

Frederick Nash, whom Pen had fallen out with after allegedly dallying with his son, wrote of this engagement:

> So Pen is to be married at last. She told me the wedding would take place in January—Perhaps she is marrying the man she ought— close, selfish & parsimonious. . . . She will need a Mark & she will get one—who will soon [illegible] her that his will is her law—I sincerely pitty him. She no more loves him, than she does me—in truth I do not believe she is capable of loving any one but herself.[25]

When Penelope stopped hearing from Mr. S. in November, it slowly became clear that the wedding would not take place in January. After the original wedding date, her father received a letter from Mr. S. in which he canceled the engagement. At the time, Pen's circle thought that she might have rejected him, but also that her father may have intervened to cancel this engagement, too. Historian Mary Maillard has hypothesized that Penelope's lack of female support, owing both to her mother's early death and dearth of female relatives, prevented her from moving through her debutante years gracefully. She was not surrounded by women who could help her understand the nuances of the female role in the courtship process, and who could have let her know when she stepped out of bounds. A community of supportive women was vital to debutantes not just because they needed instruction but also because they needed insulation from their own worst instincts. Penelope was distrustful of women, especially a new crop of debutantes, and had no friends near Edenton Plantation. She felt her father was ruining her chances of marriage with his "queer ways" and tendency to run off her suitors. She confessed to Tristrim that she blamed her father for her state of life. "To have had thirty offers & not be married is awful had it not have been for my father I should have been happy now." She talked of her "enemies" in her letters, accusing them of being "jealous of my reputation as a Belle."

Penelope finally married in March 1840. He was a doctor, Tom Warren, whom she described as being "the only one [able] to put up with Pa." Her father, for reasons unknown, decided not to give the couple a proper wedding. Maillard speculates that he had marriage exhaustion, and that his own social awkwardness contributed to his decision. But because Skinner had thrown a wedding party for his niece just two months before Penelope's wedding, and because he would not permit Tristrim to attend, it seems clear that his anger at Penelope was deep, especially because the marriage was a respectable one, with Warren being well-liked and considered honorable. Her father's decision to cut out the wedding parties offended everyone around Edenton, including relatives who snubbed the Skinner family for months. Penelope records no animosity for these cousins. She simply expressed relief that she was finally married.

If Penelope Skinner made her way through her debutante years leaving a series of faux pas in her wake, this was not the experience of her contemporary, Jane Caroline North. North, known by her nickname "Carey," was a member of a wealthy and socially connected South Carolina family. Like Penelope, Carey was born on a remote plantation. Badwell, in Abbeville County, near the North Carolina border, was a large and prosperous estate with unusual refinements—an allée of white oaks, a springhouse where meat and dairy products could be kept cool, and a sundial, then uncommon. Carey's father, Dr. John Gough North, had died when she was sixteen, and she and her sisters under the care of their mother, remained on the plantation. Though Carey's mother didn't like society and preferred to stay at Badwell, she knew that her daughters needed husbands and when Carey turned seventeen she sent her oldest and most beautiful daughter to spend the winter social season with her mother's extended family in Charleston. Carey remained there for several years.

By the time Carey started keeping a journal in 1851, at twenty-three years old, she had already been out for several seasons in Charleston.

For another young woman, several seasons in circulation might indicate a problem. In Carey's case, it indicated that she and her own family knew her own value. Prolonging the debutante phase was something beautiful and rich young women often wanted to do. Once married, they often quickly became pregnant, which curtailed their social lives and prevented them from attending parties, from traveling, and, depending how remote their new home was, from being in company at all. It was understandable that they'd want to have fun for as long as possible.

Carey, unlike Penelope, was surrounded by women who could teach her how to navigate the complexity of the antebellum marriage market. Her mother's sisters took her to balls, as many as four in a week, held at private houses, and to concerts at the St. Cecilia Society. She also attended dinners and formal afternoon teas. In one of the nation's most exclusive social environments, urban Charleston, Carey wore her social sophistication and good manners as if they were invisible, and she was the perfect product of her elite society. Carey sent letters home to her mother that detail precisely what she wore to many events and how she decided on her clothes so she could communicate that she was going to a variety of parties and progressing in her search for a husband. When visiting an elderly family friend, she wore a subtle "blue cashmere" dress, letting her mother know that she had chosen it so as to be "neat but not remarkable."[26]

In contrast, she wrote three full paragraphs to describe what she wore to a "fancy dress" (costume) ball, which was always the apogee of Charleston's winter social season. Costume balls freed women from the strictures of traditional dress and hairstyles, and allowed debutantes to present themselves at their most seductive. Carey dressed as Titania from Shakespeare's *A Midsummer Night's Dream* and had her costume copied from a book's engraved plate. Her dress was constructed with many layers of diaphanous fabric, so it was both airy and sufficiently modest. It was covered in water lilies and roses at the waist and by garlands along the seams. She wore her hair in a long flowing style capped by a headband with a pair of silver wings attached to each side of her head. She also carried a wand. Carey's hair drew immediate attention, which she recorded happily. "Joe Pyatt turned to me and said 'Miss Caroline, I always thought your hair handsome, but I never knew before it was so long, it is really beautiful.'" It is easy to imagine her pleasure in transgressing that boundary without having to pay a price for it.

When the summer began to ebb and it was no longer too hot to travel, Carey's aunt and uncle took her with them on several long trips around the country. Their first expedition, in August 1851, was to the Virginia hot springs, a series of hotels in western Virginia located near natural sulfur baths where people took the cure, or simply relaxed and enjoyed themselves. These hotels were highly social places and well-known marriage markets, and functioned as a kind of trade route for guardians and their available daughters. For Carey, this was a work trip.

Unlike in Charleston, where you only encountered people you knew, it took some skill to negotiate the hotels at the springs. Historian Michael O'Brien, who collected and edited Carey's letters, recounts a series of incidents when "strange" people began speaking to her and she had to assess whether she needed to extricate herself politely. It was not always easy. Carey writes with relief that she didn't snub a "talkative lady who would not let her alone" on the train. The woman finally came up to her and asked "don't you want to know who I am? You must think it funny a stranger would be so sociable." Carey informed her that she would be happy to know who she was and the stranger replied, "I am Miss Barnwell sister of Mrs. Pinckney (an old Charleston family). I knew you were a North. I knew your father and uncle." Carey wrote in her journal, "I was really glad to find out who she was, for her *talk* was so peculiar that I was certain she was distracted and think so a little still."[27]

Gentlemen posed similar problems. Without knowledge of a man's family, it was hard to assess who he truly was, and young women and their families often came to rely upon one another for information. Carey met a young woman named Iseatta Coles, "an uncommon nice

girl, tall, fair, and with magnificent auburn hair. Withal not pretty, eye-
brows too light, freckled and teeth dark, but one of the most agreeable
girls I have ever met."[28] Assessing other belles was essential and always
contained a tinge of competition, but the two were fast friends, laughing
at their "wretched polkas" with "careening" partners. The two shared
information about respective suitors and strategized together about how
to keep them at bay. A typical example of such a situation came in the
form of a Mr. Goode, the son of the owner of the hotel where they were
staying, who was, in Carey's view, a "self-sufficient, insufficient, stupid
man, full of pretention and folly." When he learned that Carey, Iseatta,
and her brother were searching for a way to visit some friends at a neighboring spring, Mr. Goode offered to get a buggy for them. But he then
said he could possibly find two buggies and stipulated, to Carey's horror, "that he should drive me." This was a major social transgression.
When it turned out that there would only be one buggy, Iseatta and her
brother took it, and Carey was able to avoid going with a man she felt
"had not the delicacy to perceive that his company was disagreeable."
It's hard to know whether Mr. Goode was as bad as Carey said he was,
or she developed that feeling after he crossed this class boundary.[29]

In other situations, Carey's account of her encounters with men at the
springs show her skill at negotiating complex flirtations with men she
didn't necessarily know well. Overall, she tended to be more gentle than
she was with Mr. Goode. At the springs, Carey could exercise her flair
for withdrawing from suitable beaux she didn't see as partners without
causing offense, which she did in most of the cases. Harder, though, was
Iseatta's brother, Stricker, who had developed a strong attachment to
her and finally confessed, "You know I love you, Miss Carey, you know
your power." Carey tried to "laugh off his nonsense" and recounts in
her journal that she "never saw a more absurd person in his manner of
talking" when he confessed his love for her. The Coles family left White
Sulfur Springs a few days later. Before leaving, Stricker told her "Miss
Carey, you have had a great deal of experience, I see you know just how

to amuse yourself, and yet frustrate me at every turn, you saw my design and determined to prevent it, and I know it, you amused yourself all the time." Stricker's description of Carey, and others like it, gave rise to stereotypes about coy and plotting southern belles. But in a culture where saying "no" to men was neither easy nor safe, skillfully dispensing with her friend's brother and not causing true offense was a job well done. She and Iseatta corresponded for the rest of their lives.

Carey's skill at assessing the other circulating belles was essential to her efforts to find a husband, and her journal is filled with her opinions about how other young women looked and behaved. While she admired some women for their beauty and sweetness, and made lifelong friendships, she was not fond of the future Civil War diarist, Mary Boykin Chesnut, although she held that Chesnut was "certainly clever." She records that while the two were on a walk at Saratoga Springs in New York, Chesnut told her, "I always preferred shining in conversation to attracting by dress, or paying much attention to anything of the sort."[30] Carey, who took great pleasure when others lauded her taste and style, likely did not appreciate being undercut in this manner by Chesnut, a fellow member of Charleston's elite and a former debutante. Chesnut married one of the richest planters in the south, confederate colonel Joseph Chesnut, Jr., and was suggesting she did it without deploying any of Carey's superficial charms.

Carey was not alone in determining how she should behave at the springs. She often deferred to her aunt and uncle, who disapproved of certain men, occasionally expressing that they were too solicitous or unctuous or, worse, that she, herself, had let them get too close. Carey relates that her uncle was "not pleased at the devotions of Mr. Vanderhorst, but I don't encourage him and can't help it, both Uncle and Aunt are so particular that I think they attribute more to the foolish man than they ought. He has identified himself with our party but I have nothing to do with it." She makes many references to "his nonsense," her oft-used word for the sort of flowery declarations of love that were most embarrassing to her. Overall, she was exhausted by Mr. Vanderhorst's advances. He was older, and not socially right for Carey, according to her family. When insistent men like him aggressively pursued debutantes, they created problems for young women who were trying to please their family chaperones and yet to draw their own boundaries. Still, men transgressed, especially older men. Carey North wasn't the only woman to record her experiences trying to manage much older suitors.

"Old widowers" and "old bachelors" show up frequently in the letters of southern teenagers. May-December marriage was, in many ways, the southern ideal, for men and young women's parents, at least. A marriage between an established man and a young, presumably fertile woman was both the clearest reflection of antebellum values and had the best chance of perpetuating them. Though these marriages were sought after hungrily by parents, the girls themselves were particularly vicious when it came to their older suitors. Historian Anya Jabour collected a series of accounts in her book *Scarlett's Sisters: Young Women in the Old South*. Girls had different ways of resisting older men. Jabour tells the story of the daughter of a South Carolina planter ridiculing one of her elderly suitors: "He is decidedly the most stupid silly old man that ever lived. The idea of an old bachelor of thirty-six coming to see a girl of sixteen? Preposterous!!" Mary Brown, a North Carolina debutante, wrote triumphantly to a friend that "an old Bachelor" in her neighborhood was unsuccessful in his pursuit of the local young ladies, despite his possession of "that never failing charm, of being very rich." "He has addressed one of our own young ladies," Brown wrote, "but she cannot get her OWN CONSENT to become an Old Mans Darling."[31]

Elizabeth Ruffin Cocke, another planter's daughter who began keeping an exhaustive daily journal in 1828, at age twenty, not only dealt with much older men as a belle but also as the mother of a belle, when one came to call on her daughter's friend Rebecca Dupuy. Just as Cocke and a group of other mothers had "concluded that there would be no [other] visitors," that day, she recounted knowingly, "who should be issued in, but the frisky widower Mr. Thompson of course leaving at home the 5 children; when he proposes an evening walk, Beck just finds out she is not fond of walking, if riding, the same excuse is offered, tho' in the interim between his visits both walking and riding are indulged in." Cocke noted that Thompson favored very young women, remarking with disapproval "he goes to see Adelaide Payne not yet eighteen." Cocke sets herself apart from the parents who favored these matches and sides with their teenage daughters. "He stands very high in the community as a most estimable, excellent man with plenty of money, but none of the girls like him."[32] Yet, parents eagerly foisted these May-December romances on daughters without any real consideration of their future happiness.

The experiences revealed by the letters and diaries of antebellum debutantes make clear that their lives were far more complex than current stereotypes suggest.

The Civil War mummified the agrarian South, and during Reconstruction white people began to speak and write about how idyllic their world had been, fashioning idealized images of family life after the humiliating experience of the Civil War. Images of debutantes at balls on plantations not yet destroyed, with enslaved people in their rightful places, soothed a region stuck in time and in memory. After the Civil War, the debutante in the South ceased to resemble a dynamic character or real person and became either a seductive and calculating belle like Scarlett O'Hara or a demure and dignified Melanie Hamilton, her foil in *Gone with the Wind*.

Many of the large-scale southern debutante balls that exist today were organized in the 1880s, a generation after the Civil War, and are rooted in this experience of loss and the desire to reimagine the past. Southern planters attempted to return to the social hierarchy that placed them above both former slaves and poor whites, and were committed to keeping the southern lady on her pedestal, ready to serve her family and courtly husband. A spate of rituals grew in this time, including Mayday festivals and carnival balls, onto which debutante presentations were often grafted. Elite families brought low by war read chivalrous literature, and taught their daughters to embrace its passive medieval ideal—be a lady in a tower. Calmly wait for your knight and savior. Protecting the lady became an organizing princi-pal of southern society during Reconstruction, and helped to justify attacks on black men and women. The southern lady was a martyr, sacrificing all to retain her values.

The debutante herself was fed a steady diet of Sir Walter Scott, not only in school but also at home, where families read medieval stories together. Mark Twain famously blamed the antebellum obsession with Walter Scott for the Civil War. "Rank and caste down there, and also reverence for rank and caste, and pride and pleasure in them," were responsible, he said. The theme of sacrifice was crucial, and was sup-ported by the reading habits of women in the South. Scott and other chivalrous writers were permitted at schools, but girls' schools limited which other novels girls could read, particularly novels that questioned courtship and marriage conventions. In an Augusta, Georgia, girls' school, Jane Austen and the Bronte sisters were kept under lock and key until as late as 1890, and girls could read their novels only with permis-sion and after the school day was finished. The stories of Scott exalted a world that was simple and pure and where good and evil were obvious. Southerners strongly identified with a noble history of sacrifice extolled by writers of chivalrous literature and it helped them to align with sacri-fice to elide and justify all their behavior. Particularly missing from any discussion was any acknowledgment of slavery.

Scott, however, was not the only popular novelist read by southern-ers. Families read Tennyson's *Idylls of the King*, particularly his telling of the story of *Tristan and Isolde*. Guinevere and Isolde failed to restrain themselves and an entire social order collapsed, which reinforced the southern ideal of individual sacrifice for the group. Elaine d'Astolat, the model for Tennyson's *Lady of Shallot*, was the most major of the minor characters in the Arthurian legend, which is itself a fitting description of the daughter role in Victorian life. Elaine died of her unrequited love for Lancelot and drifted down the river to Camelot with a lily in her hand and flowers woven into her hair by her loyal maids. *The Lady of Shallot* was one of the most popular poems during Reconstruction. Elaine d'Astolat was a pure martyr to her love for Lancelot, who was bound to his chaste vow to Guinevere. Elaine died of unrequited love rather than sullying herself and bringing down her family.

As northerners moved into the South and made money, the southern lady ideal evolved to encompass genteel poverty. Whatever burdens society presented, she absorbed them and made them into the most desirable qualities to have. If "carpetbaggers" came and made more money, then money, once a hallmark of the planter class, became repugnant. Genteel poverty slowly became both cultural ideal and ready excuse— southerners would deemphasize wealth and magnify lineage to dissociate themselves from wealthy northerners, a practice that continues today.

A culture of piety around faux poverty developed, allowing the old southern families to disdain riches, while solidifying them into a caste that could not be penetrated by carpet-bagging northerners or newly rich southern whites. In truth, they remained rich and in control of their communities. Debutante balls held during Reconstruction were sometimes shabby affairs, but none of the wrong sort could get in. In their impenetrability, they advanced the region's ongoing separatist aims. Wealthy white daughters who weren't from the "right" families increasingly left the South. As the region folded in upon itself, going elsewhere to make a debut would be the only option for women with money and aspiration. Many found greater class mobility at the hot springs resorts, which began to grow as national social centers, and bridged the gap between the closed-off South, and the intimidating and glamorous debutante scene in New York.

There was no debutante scene to speak of in rural America, and this was fine when there were no residents of rural America who wanted debutante daughters. But the desire to be genteel had spread to dusty farms, where young girls read the same fashion news as young girls in coastal cities, if a few months later. The ballrooms of Charleston or New York weren't open to these girls, but there was a new and enticing option. The spas where Carey North encountered wealthy but questionable characters in the 1830s gradually grew in popularity and became a meeting place for a developing national elite. Beginning in the late eighteenth century, but accelerating rapidly in the nineteenth with improved rail networks, the spas at Saratoga Springs, New York, and White Sulphur Springs, Virginia (now in West Virginia), attracted an ever-larger number of visitors. Americans had always visited spas to seek cures—including the Puritans and the Quakers. Elite colonists who returned to visit Europe, or were educated there, often took in the European spas, particularly at Bath and Baden-Baden, as part of an edifying social tour. The regular influx of newspapers from Europe contained news not just of assemblies in London but also of recreation at these elegant resort communities. The hotels there held balls, and it was possible to make a debut there, bypassing the strictures of regional cities and their restrictive local elites. People did visit to seek cures for ailments, but visiting the spa was primarily a social experience, and the national elite congregated at spas during the summer months. They provided an overall genteel experience, complete with shops and musical and dancing evenings. In short, they became desirable leisure places, where one could display one's refinement, compete with others over the best clothing, and find a husband.

The atmosphere of the springs was one of social chaos. For a nineteenth-century society with sharp gender divisions, social life at the hot springs was a heady experience of mixed-gender activity. The great rooms and parlors of the hotels were filled with people sitting and drinking tea and watching others go by. Lobbies, courtyards, gardens, restaurants, and sitting rooms all allowed men and women to mix—there was no way to fully separate the sexes. Whereas in normal urban environments, women were not permitted to interact with men casually, at the hot springs it was normal to do so. This naturally increased its desirability as a location where one could forge one's own way. Some people came to the spas in a delicate state, and the vulnerability of healing provided cover for all sorts of trickery. Presidents and other dignitaries visited but so did gamblers and ambitious cads—like the son of a South Carolina senator who charmed all of Saratoga with his elegant manners and beautiful dancing. He was nearly engaged to a beautiful young woman when, during the middle of a dance, a steamboat captain happened to enter the hotel's ballroom and exposed the man as his ship's steward.

The problem of inter-class mingling grew as it became more affordable to visit the spas. Both Saratoga and White Sulphur Springs created committees to address this problem, and they began to act as intermediaries who made all introductions, ensuring no upper-class girl need speak to any middle-class boy. In Saratoga, the "Committee of Management" was run by Nathaniel Parker Willis, a publisher and social climber who made a living writing about the rich and their leisure pursuits.[33] In White Sulphur Springs, Colonel William Pope ran the "Billing, Wooing and Cooing Society." Modeled on a similar system in place at Bath, Colonel Pope acted as a master of ceremonies at all balls, and protected "the dear sweet ladies from villains and imposters, who deceive them at the Springs by an appearance of wealth." He posted a guideline to proper manners in wooing, a series of rules for the "encouragement and promotion of marriage" called the "Articles of Flirtation," and took on 1,700 young men and women who proved they had the necessary pedigree. With parents either not present or unable to confidently judge the refinement of young men and women beyond the purview of their own home social scenes, Pope played the important role of *in loco parentis*. Young men and women signed Col. Pope's "Articles of Flirtation" and could refer back to them to see if they were behaving properly. The establishment of a standard was deemed necessary, and would have made it even more enjoyable to participate in the joyous act of exclusion.[34]

The mothers who took their daughters to the spas to find husbands had a particularly grim reputation. Though these matrons virtuously claimed to be present so that that they could exercise the "severest supervision" over their daughters, and "stand on alert to see that [their daughters] don't fall in love with anybody not well established in business or well to do in the world," their true role was as hard-nosed negotiators. The mothers were objects of ridicule at balls because of their shameless questions about the opposite sex. For them, one observer wrote "money is everything." The mothers mingling together above the ballroom watching their daughters seemed to "resemble climbing plants, who throw out their tendrils, and in their blindness are unable to distinguish a pillar of state from a decaying worm-eaten post."[35]

Elderly men who had outlived their inheritances dressed themselves in their finery and went to the springs to find young heiresses to reverse their fortunes. Observer James Kirke Paulding witnessed "many instances of this fraud, which would be truly lamentable, did not the woman who sells herself in this manner deserve her fate." Paulding had no sympathy for the status-seeking woman, an opinion that was widely shared. Charles Astor Bristed, scion of the New York Astors, criticized "young dandies" who went to the springs not to be married but to victimize "innocent debutante[s], and leave [them] more or less brokenhearted."[36] Bristed and Paulding criticized the marriage markets at the springs from the vantage point of the established elite, and lamented the encroachment of the newly rich and their feral manners, which softened their anxiety about the successes of the new rich.

CHAPTER 4

The Four Hundred and Beyond

OLD NEW YORK

B y the mid-nineteenth century, the American social landscape was unrecognizable from what had initially developed a hundred years earlier. Philadelphia, Charleston, and Boston, which had been eighteenth-century social centers, had, over time, developed their own impenetrable aristocracies, creating castes in those cities that had made them provincial and largely irrelevant on the world stage. Their own debutante rituals continued like a record caught on skip. The same families stayed in power in those cities and used debuts to reaffirm and justify that power, but the debutante presentations were cordoned off to outsiders and, as those cities lost their significance, outsiders neither knew nor cared that they were being excluded. Though the upper classes in those cities had localized economic power, nobody with a real social hunger could have satisfied their aspiration in them.

Debutante events happening in Washington, D.C., didn't have any kind of unifying national character to distinguish them from any other city's, and their purpose wasn't to bring together young women on a national stage. Most politicians were from socially prominent families, and their daughters needed peers to socialize with. But political posts were impermanent and the family would likely not remain in Washington, making it necessary for most girls to debut in their home cities, too. In London, society had followed the schedule of parliamentary session, but was organized under the larger umbrella of a monarchy whose authority to set fashion was unimpeachable. There was no central social authority like this in the early republic. However, economic power had started filling this gap, and it had begun to shift from Philadelphia and Washington toward New York.

The reasons for New York's economic ascendancy were numerous. Philadelphia, the center of banking in the colonies and immediately afterward, funded the Revolutionary War and was the location of the first federally chartered bank and stock exchange. The Delaware, however, could freeze over in the winter, stalling trade. New York Harbor was superior as it was much deeper and more navigable and thus less likely to freeze over. By the 1790s, New York had overtaken Philadelphia in the value of goods imported. Finally, the building of the Erie Canal connected New York to the Great Lakes and to vast and untapped resources in the rest of the country. Where trade flows so do information and people, making New York the first point of entry for new fashions, music, dance, food, and ideas. In 1819, the first-ever transatlantic passenger service was established in New York, and the city became the main point of entry for immigrants, many of whom settled in there and contributed to a dramatic rise in population and inexpensive workforce. By 1830, all major American banks kept their deposits on Wall Street. When Philadelphia lost the charter of the United States central bank in 1836 and Abraham Lincoln signed two banking acts in the 1860s that required that all US banks keep 15 percent of their lawful deposits in New York, the city lost all competition for financial preeminence.

Social power followed financial power, but although the city was a growing economic force in the antebellum North, no codified debutante system had yet developed there. Most of what we know of private balls and debutante presentations in this period comes from write-ups of the events by attendees. People tended to insert verse right into their letters—the poetic epistle remained popular. After a New York ball, a young debutante named Anne Macmaster sent a letter to a friend abroad that included some verses that described her evening.

> Of Beaux there were plenty, some new ones 'tis true,
> But I won't mention names, no, not even to you.
> I was lucky in getting good partners, however,
> Above all, the two Emmetts, so lively and clever.[1]

Period satire also reveals some of the standards young women were obliged to adhere to, even if the system was still fluid, and society's dependence on its members' collective understanding of norms. Custom dictated that debutantes could not dance with the same man twice in one evening, nor turn anyone down. Young women depended on men knowing where they stood on the social ladder, and their understanding of minute social distinctions. Young men without title or money, men who were new to the assembly, or out-of-town visitors, or poor but respectable relations, would know not to ask eligible young women to dance. When a new arrival didn't know the manners of the establishment, however, there were no socially acceptable ways to let him know. Literary satire filled that void. In his satirical literary magazine, *Salmagundi*, Washington Irving created the recurring character of Will Wizard, a classic bore who dressed for the assembly in clothes "so tight that he seemed to have grown up in them." Washington places Wizard in all sorts of situations in which a well-mannered person would know how to behave. In one scene, a friend who accompanies Will to a ball "drew him into a corner where [they] might observe the company without being prominent objects [themselves]." But Will found his way onto the dance floor anyway, dancing "strenuously and with abandon." Will Wizard was both funny to read about and a caution to socially ignorant young men. As historian Eric Homberger points out, balls existed to make marriages through repeated introduction of young women to men. If there were too many Will Wizards in attendance, they could not serve their primary function.[2]

For years, New York mothers had quietly launched daughters at the City Assemblies. The subscription price of the dances had worked to keep out most undesirables. However, by 1820, presenting a debutante there was something every wealthy person in New York could afford. The assemblies began to fall into decline. Groups of young men did get together occasionally to throw Bachelors' Balls, to which they sold tickets to only people they knew. Though popular with newly married couples, it was considered unseemly for young girls to make their debut at parties hosted by groups of bachelors. Dance technique fell into decline with less demand for dancing masters, and very few people still attempted the complex group and partnered dances that had made colonial assemblies riveting to watch, and proving grounds for young ladies. New York's upper class were so interconnected by both family and business ties that correct behavior was easy to predict and transgressions were difficult to endure or forgive. It was a world, as novelist Edith Wharton described it, that was "balanced so precariously that its harmony could be shattered by a whisper."

Until the Civil War, this society held fast. The stability of the social environment was due largely to the social machinations of women, and was a testament to the durability of intermarriage and Anglo-Dutch roots. But the commercial sector, run entirely by men, tolerated any white entrepreneur who could make money, regardless of his origins. After the Civil War, a rush of newly rich families from the Midwest, South, and West made their slow way east in search of people they felt were more like themselves. They had made new fortunes in railways, fur trapping, coal, iron, department stores, textiles, and harvesters that freed workers from the fields. Or, more darkly, they had profited from the industries of war—trading in armaments, cloth, medical supplies, and preserved meats to feed the soldiers. But the services they came to want after they made their money didn't exist in their small towns.

There were no musical diversions, nor opera, nor ballet, no dressmakers, no perfumers, and no culture. There was nothing to buy. And when it came time for their daughters to marry, there weren't any men they wanted their daughters to marry. So they went to New York.

When they arrived, there were not many people who welcomed them eagerly, and it was challenging for them to enter the uppermost reaches of society. While they could buy a ticket to the City Assemblies, it had lost prestige, due in no small part to the addition of newly rich people among its ranks, and the subsequent retrenchment of the old guard. The gradual erosion of common standards of manners after a critical mass of newcomers arrives usually leads to calls for tighter controls over rituals as self-appointed social authorities work to enact their own agendas.

These social leaders, some natural and some self-appointed, began to take greater control of the New York debutante process. By the end of the nineteenth century, the debutante system had transformed from a small and reliable system that got people married to a fully functioning industry with an interconnected web of services to support it. This elaborate system required enough wealthy people willing to participate regularly and recognized social leaders to steer the social calendar.

The sociologist Emile Durkheim pointed out that calendars not only express the rhythm of shared activities but also codify them—those who controlled the calendar controlled which events and activities were socially acceptable and which were not. The most social part of the season had always loosely taken place in the period between Thanksgiving and Lent, but the calendar was not absolutely reliable until the blue-blooded Caroline Astor and the socially ambitious Ward McAllister took command of it.

Caroline Schermerhorn Astor was a perfect mix of old New York and new. While both her parents descended from the Dutch settlers who made fortunes in the seventeenth and eighteenth centuries, her husband's family, the nouveau riche Astors, were an enormous conglomerate who had made their money first in fur trapping and then later with vast real-estate holdings. Their money made her own look as quaint and old as the Brooklyn Heights street that still bears the Schermerhorn family's name. Caroline's marriage to William Backhouse Astor (Caroline made him drop the "Backhouse"—period slang for toilet) was a time-honored trade, his money for her status. Tall, dark, with a fleshy face, Caroline was determined to control New York society, and her husband provided her with something rare to help, a private ball-room. After removing her rival Astor sister-in-law from her perch at the top of society through sheer force of will, Caroline set about refining the society she kept around her. Caroline found her perfect courtier, Ward McAllister, in the late 1860s. Together the two created dancing schools, teas, and musical events that prepared young women for their debutante season and revived the old assemblies, but made them more exclusive. This was a significant moment for the debutante ritual as an instrument of social change in the United States because, for the first time, two Americans were consciously attempting to transform [codify might be better] society into a system with recognizable barriers that best reflected their own interests and supported their own power. In order to accomplish their mission to change society, it would be necessary that McAllister and Astor first set about to change the debutante ritual, the entrée into society.

Ward McAllister was from a socially prominent but largely penniless Savannah family of lawyers and judges. With no prospects in Georgia, he went west, and became a successful lawyer in California during the Gold Rush. With his copious earnings, he left California and headed to Europe, where he undertook a grand tour. He went to all the major European cities, but made a particular effort to go to the spas at Pau, Baden-Baden, and Bath. There he was able to study the manners of the European nobility at leisure, whose behavior he wanted to model. After he returned, he married Sarah Gibbons, a daughter of the man who gave Cornelius Vanderbilt his first boat, and began to use her wealth to add vital fuel to his social connections. Unlike Isaac Brown, McAllister was an insider, and with his wife's New York connections and wealth he needed no other career.

McAllister was also related to the Astors through his cousin Samuel Ward, a prominent lobbyist and gourmand, who had married a granddaughter of John Jacob Astor and moved in New York's highest social circles. Ward was a habitué of Delmonico's, the fashionable restaurant of the nineteenth century, where McAllister would later hold his debutante presentations. Without his wife's fortune, McAllister could not have participated at this level of society, a fact he always had in the back of his mind as he set out to make himself into the ultimate social authority, as similarly indispensable as Isaac Brown. McAllister devoted himself entirely to the small details of society. He was a fierce materialist who applied his painstaking work ethic to "the mean admiration of mean things," as Thackeray defined snobbery.[3] His pronouncements were legendary, and he was only too delighted to provide them for public consumption, writing newspaper columns, really more pronouncements, whenever he could. In a column about the 1893 World's Columbian Exposition, he urged that, if Chicago society hostesses wanted be taken seriously, they should hire French chefs and "not frappé their wine too much." He became a national arbiter by dispensing advice on everything from food to how to best ignore someone on the street. Like Martha Stewart, he was a valued keeper of arcane detail, but also a snob. He warned:

If you want to be fashionable, be always in the company of fashionable people . . . if you see a fossil of a man, shabbily dressed, relying solely upon his pedigree dating back to time immemorial, who has the aspirations of a duke and the fortunes of a footman, do not cut him; it is better to cross the street and avoid meeting him. It is well to be in with the nobs who are born to their position, but the support of the swells is more advantageous, for society is sustained and carried on by the swells. A gentleman can always walk, but he cannot afford to have a shabby equipage. When you entertain, do it in an easy natural way, as if it was an everyday occurrence, not the event of your life.[4]

Interspersed with his pretension, McAllister had expertise—a deep knowledge of food, and real-life experience with the European aristocracy that nearly all Americans lacked. His particular combination of vicious snobbery and service journalism appealed to a Gilded Age society who were compelled to consume, but hungry for guidance because they did not trust their own taste. As is generally the case for people who make society a career, his most devoted acolytes were those he sought most to exclude.

Because McAllister and Astor were distantly related, they had many opportunities to discuss what rich people always discuss at parties—the decline of standards, social climbers, and possible solutions to those problems. The two felt that if society were better organized and they had control over it, the barriers they created would prevent its degradation. In his grand vision for an American society that resembled Europe's, McAllister plumbed history for ways to reorganize it, with a primary role for him at its helm, of course. The most important ritual of society, the ritual that had the power to both create and break down old barriers through uniting families, was the début. McAllister came to the conclusion that they had to revive dancing assemblies, which had always facilitated marriages, and which loomed romantically in the memories of people who harkened for better days. They had done their job to speed the gentrification of early New York society, and once gentrified, this society ended them and closed its doors, so as not to let anyone else in.

Other people had attempted to revive these balls in the past. In the 1830s, one enterprising group organized a large ball at a downtown hotel, with the idea to bring back the "old noblesse of the assemblies." An observer described two thousand candles glowing in the ballroom and eight hundred guests dancing. Newspaper reports give a picture of the debutantes as "the beautiful Miss H, one of the fair daughters of a widow lady up town." And "the ravishing daughters of Mr. W., the Wall St financier," who "adorned the room by their presence, hanging carelessly on their father's arm." But this was a one-off event, and not a reliable system for introducing daughters to society. In the antebellum years, it seemed New York society could not figure out how to launch its daughters on any kind of grand scale, and did not really want to—preferring the propriety of sealed drawing rooms. New assemblies were launched and failed with regularity. Another series at the Delmonico Hotel was held in the 1840s and typified the problem. It was forced to disband when "a Wall Street banker, not even a native American" crashed their party only to find himself "left in solitary grandeur." When another group hosted a subscription and called itself the Cheap and Hungries, and had the gall to operate through secret invitation, well that was the final straw.[5]

In 1866, McAllister and Astor decided to hold their first series of debutante parties at Delmonico's. These were large balls. Several hundred attended and were enthusiastically embraced by what McAllister called "General Society." The attendees were not the social leaders, but nobody to cause any embarrassment, either. These parties were a success, but too much of one, and McAllister and Astor decided that this was a wider net than they cared to cast.

Then in 1870, a venerable old New York family broke with the long-standing tradition of introducing a daughter at home before presenting her at an assembly. Instead of holding a tea, Archibald Gracie King (whose family gave the city Gracie Mansion, the mayoral residence) hosted his daughter May's debut in the ballroom of Delmonico's. Eight hundred guests attended, and the host brought out his best madeira. Young men expressed "great satisfaction" with the mirrors that lined the banquet hall, and they "admired their reflections as they swept by in waltz."[6] May Denning King's ancestry was unquestionably good. She descended from old New York, including super-chaperone Lady Kitty Duer, who had hosted the Trumbull girls sixty years previously. The fact that May's ball was in a restaurant did not impede her social successes. She was married that fall into the prominent Van Rensselaer family. Hostesses began to wonder why they had ever held parties in private townhouses in the first place. Society was best left to the professionals. Girls could first have an intimate debut at home, after which they'd be launched into wider society at a ball. But the debut could now take place in a restaurant without any harm to the family's reputation.

With the great success of May King's ball, both McAllister and Delmonico's had the imprimatur they needed. McAllister decided to create a series of cotillion suppers at Delmonico's, where dinner and dancing would happen in the same place. People customarily dined at private dinners before departing for a larger ball. Having the suppers at the restaurant had another advantage; it allowed the rich families of Gilded Age New York to be written about by proto-paparazzi who lurked outside the restaurant. The Delmonico family was discreet, but they, too, had relationships with the press, whom they could tip off. The parties at the Delmonico provided the necessary cover of correctness, while also allowing society greater self-display.

In addition to the larger parties that she and McAllister put together, Mrs. Astor held smaller dancing evenings in the ballroom of her house on Washington Place. At that time, according to McAllister, sounding every bit the courtier, "her small dances were most carefully chosen; they were the acme of exclusive-ness [sic]. On this she prided herself." Astor also arranged and controlled during the winters of 1870 and 1871 smaller balls for three hundred subscribers at Delmonico's. These parties were strictly for matchmaking purposes, being "confined to the young men and maidens, with the exception, perhaps, of a dozen of the young married couples; a few elderly married ladies were invited as matrons."[7]

They came to be called "The Blue Rooms," after the decoration of the rooms in which they were held. These evenings provided a key advantage to young women from the most privileged families, giving them a definitive head start over other women in the race to find husbands.

Dance had always been used to filter people—breaking down groups into ever more refined company—so it was only natural to use it once again to separate wheat from chaff. McAllister joined forces with Astor, and combined her dances with his. McAllister consciously based these cotillion suppers on the Almack's model, appointing patronesses who worked under Mrs. Astor's aegis. The two sent forth their requirements, and those requirements radiated outward to their lesser functionaries. At these events, McAllister seated himself at the head of the table among his new patronesses and "whispered confidential forecasts about the social fate of newcomers." The parties proved a success.

So that young women and men would not be awkward at these parties, which had a higher standard of dancing, McAllister and Astor created the Family Circle Dancing Classes. McAllister himself had an ungainly daughter about whom he worried ceaselessly. These dancing classes were the first that were organized specifically to funnel directly into the cotillion parties (the common debutante feeder today). They were held in private houses during the first season, but later at Delmonico's and at the largest dancing school in the city, Dodworth's. The difference between these classes and simply signing up at a school is that you were required to apply first. Whereas previously anyone who could afford a dancing master was almost by definition genteel or on their way there, the new dancing school application process would take care of those irritating Midwesterners. These people might be able to enter Dodworth's and attend a dancing class. They might be able to afford to attend a ball at the City Hotel. But they would not get into these most particular dancing classes. Mrs. Astor vetted the people she knew, and McAllister himself looked into the pedigree of every applicant and had final say over who was accepted.

A young lady attending one of McAllister's dancing classes was tutored in more than simply how to move her body on the dance floor. Her teachers were charged with infusing her every gesture with the social values of New York's upper class. Dancing masters emphasized grace and silence, and were in some ways members of the extended family, working in their service, even while they were performing the manual labor of a skilled service professional. Parents had already coaxed their children, through years of praise and disapproval, in how to perform upper-class mannerisms, and gave them the outward confidence of a ruling group unbothered by self-reflection or anxiety. One reason that nouveaux-riches families worked so hard to get their children into dancing schools was so their children's behavior could become natural, and that gestures of the coal-blackened parent would not transform into lifelong affects that prevented the social rise of the child. The idea was to become upper class, which meant absenting any remaining working-class manners or affect.

Many wanted to attend McAllister's dancing school, and he had the singular pleasure of rejecting them. Now that access to wider society functions was under greater control, McAllister set about organizing the upper echelons. In the winter of 1872–3, he established the Patriarchs, a committee of twenty-five men "who had the right to create and lead Society." McAllister cannily placed his trust in others, who in return were loyal, not wanting to be cast out from the narrow social circle into the wide. In his characteristically modest way, McAllister told his Patriarchs he had invested them with a kind of "sacred trust." Each Patriarch could invite four ladies and five gentlemen to a ball. Caroline Astor was the muse of the Patriarchs, with McAllister calling her his "Mystic Rose" and invoking her spirit when it was time to send out invitations.

McAllister's goal was to define and create society—to exclude others so judiciously that everyone present in the room would know right away that they were part of an anointed group. To that end, he also created a list of people, which he called the "the Four Hundred," famously based on the number of people who would fit into Mrs. Astor's ballroom. For McAllister, this was the number of people in New York who really mattered. "If you go outside that number," he warned, "you strike people who are either not at ease in a ballroom or else make other people not at ease." A cursory glance at McAllister's first list is amusing—it contained not only paragons of old New York, but also a flash of nouveau riche industrialists and some of McAllister's friends from down south.

But McAllister did have competitors, at least in his role as eminence gris. As early as 1870–80, a handful of well-connected young men in New York made a good living from giving the newly rich advice about their problems, and paving their way into the best drawing rooms or clubs. They were nicknamed "little brothers of the rich," a term that was also an anti-gay slur—applied by both men and women to diminish the power of gay men as social arbiters. (The position of gay men in society was an unspoken secret, debated in diaries, revealed by jilted wives in posthumous books, or known only to the two people in the marriage.)

That Ward McAllister chose the Patriarchs from old and new money suggests a particular cleverness on his part. He carefully selected people from both types of families so he could create an impenetrable new super-society. McAllister's *Four Hundred* were to be an unassailable group, ostensibly united by some kind of utopian combination of behavior, breeding, and a kind of vague "goodness." Conveniently, these qualities could shift when McAllister changed his mind about who fit. The ideal definition of society, for McAllister, was "the people I say society comprises." After all, if you are making a new society, you need to be able to include yourself. McAllister's definition of society was necessarily broad, or else he could not be in it himself. And Mrs. Astor needed McAllister, too, as a worker under her command, and as a flatterer. They accomplished their reorganization of the structure of society just a few years after the Civil War ended and that structure—a dance between figureheads with status and true believers to do the work—has persisted since McAllister's time.

If McAllister and Astor created a new and more orderly structure into which young women were launched, their mothers managed their daughters' days with similar enthusiasm for social control. In the eighteenth century, the debutante phase had been a taste of freedom before marriage, sometimes so delicious that girls wanted to prolong it, but this was not the case in nineteenth-century society, where women were increasingly treated as if they would shatter if bumped. Once they made their debuts, debutantes were still kept largely at home. They visited other houses not on their own, as debutante Nancy Shippen had done in eighteenth-century Philadelphia, but with their mothers or a suitable chaperone. Debutantes were not given their own calling cards; instead, a girl's name was added to her mother's card. After a debutante was out for a year, she was given her own card for certain visits, but not for very formal events—for those she remained on her mother's card. This control over public behavior served to increase a debutante's value, which was derived in part from her isolation and purity. The more money and status her family had, the more likely it was that a young woman would be more highly controlled.

When the mother and the debutante were getting ready for the girl's debut, the two went together to call on every woman who would be invited to the debutante reception or tea. Huybertie Pruyn was a young woman from an old Dutch family in Albany who came down to the city with her sister Harriet to make her debut in 1891. The Pruyn family was prominent—then-president Grover Cleveland and future Supreme Court justice Oliver Wendell Holmes Jr. were frequent dinner guests. Mrs. Pruyn took her daughters abroad to be presented to Queen Victoria. They also attended Royal Ascot and the Henley Regatta, spent their weekends at the large country houses of aristocrats, and mixed with people like Oscar Wilde.

Huybertie describes the calls she made with her mother as an end-less tedium.

> It was slow work . . . Mother had a book with the list and on some blocks we went to almost every house. Owen [the driver] would climb off the box and take the cards and then we would watch like cats to see the door open and try to glean hope from the way the cards were taken. Often the maid would leave the door open and go on a search party for her mistress and from the noises we heard while waiting in the parlor—it seemed as if the poor woman had been routed out of bed and was slamming doors and drawers in her effort to get herself clothed. Louise [Huybertie's cousin, who came out with her] and I fumed at the delays and at the general misery of the afternoons and of having to smile sweetly as one after another would say—"Well, how do you like being out?" My diary says on December 1st, "This afternoon Mother took Louise and me on our stupid old visits—we made 14 and 10 were out—it is terrible—Louise and I sit and grin and say nothing."[8]

The tedium, however, was an important sign of respect and willingness to step into roles they might not have fully rehearsed. Mrs. Burton Harrison, a popular minor novelist and social commentator during the Gilded Age, describes its ideal debutante as a girl who would have been brought up almost in total seclusion until the age of eighteen, during which she would be "trained by experts in every detail of the accomplishments specified." She would attend weekly dancing classes that were "controlled by a bevy of matrons" who "carefully select those who are invited to join." When it was time for a girl to make her debut it was "the mamma [who] determines the time when a proper celebration would occur and her daughter shall be accepted by the world as a full matured woman . . ." The main aim of this ceremony was to "convey the information to the world that the young lady has been graduated in all the accomplishments and knowledge necessary for her use as a woman in society."[9] That use was marriage.

To toe a line between inconspicuous and self-effacing and accomplish the work of getting married was exceptionally challenging for all but the wealthiest, most beautiful girls. This was complicated by the fact that, unlike their British counterparts, many elite American girls had received educations. They often read Greek and Latin in addition to speaking fluent French and German, and were well versed in both philosophy and mathematics. Their season required that they give all this up and pliantly stand beside their parents.

If a girl was making her debut first at her family's house, the evening began with a reception, which would be followed by a supper, and then some dancing. At the beginning of the reception, the debutante would stand to the left of her mother as the guests entered so that she could be presented to the ladies and her elders. While the debutante was presented to older women, the younger gentlemen were presented *to* her, a signal of deference and the hierarchy of the ritual, and a nod to the idea that she might choose one of them, even if this was not practically the case. Edith Wharton wrote of how peculiar it was that friends of her brother, boys she had regarded "like elder brothers" when they had dined at her parents' house, suddenly became formal in her presence. When they asked her to dance at her debut, held at a family friends' Fifth Avenue mansion, she "cowered" in her dress, cut low for the first time, and was too frightened to say yes, "unable to exchange a word with these friendly young men." For many women being "put into" a dress, as Wharton described it, was both a heightened experience of one's own body and a detached one.

When it was time for the dinner to begin, it was a brother's, or male relative's, if there were no brother, duty to escort the debutante to the table and to seat her ceremonially at her father's left side. When people began to dance, it was the debutante's mother who was expected to choose a dancing partner for her daughter from among close friends or relatives. This was all organized well in advance. After her first dance, the debutante was to dance only once with any one partner. The highly choreographed evening mirrored the values of the ritual's architects—deference and hierarchy. They emphasized a debutante's innocence but not without a nod toward her position as a product. She did not dance with available men more than once lest she decrease her own value in the market by signaling her interest in any and, thus, lowering the competition for her.

If a family did not have enough money or space for an elaborate coming out at home, it was considered perfectly correct to present a daughter at an afternoon tea. Members of in-groups in society often created their own rules to support old families in difficult economic circumstances, and the afternoon tea, held at 4 or 5 p.m., was a good way to accommodate genteel poverty, or at least genteel descent. A tea had one course only, and people could move between sitting and standing. They could navigate through cake stands to serve themselves while speaking to a wider variety of fellow guests. There was no pressure to find a dance partner, and dress was less elaborate, though still required a formal gown (even in the afternoon). Though a wide variety of food was served, it was laid out on various buffets rather than served by servants. There were delicate sandwiches like cucumber and cress, cheeses, an array of scones, and small cakes like Victoria sponge or Battenberg, after English tradition. The most important feature of the food at a debutante tea was that at least some of it had to be dry to the touch. Copious amounts of butter ruined women's gloves and forced them to remove them when etiquette held that they shouldn't. Serving the tea itself was a formal ritual that required a great deal of elegant and fussy equipment— a large kettle, creamers, pots, delicate cups, and water heated to a precise temperature, just short of boiling. Writers of etiquette manuals also tended to recommend teas because of the increased likelihood of young men being able to attend. Unlike an evening reception, where one was expected to stay for many hours, teas allowed for dropping in. Young men in New York tended to work at their companies, or as lawyers, like

Newland Archer in *The Age of Innocence*, and did not just tend to their affairs like an English country squire. A man could stop by briefly at a tea in Greenwich Village on the way home from his office, and still spend an evening at the theater or even at home.

Afternoon teas had originated after the Panic of 1870, when people in reduced circumstances, but still wanting to socialize, began to have "kettledrums" based on a practice that originated with British officers in India who, in the absence of proper furniture, gathered around the traditional Indian nagara to have tea. The terms "kettledrum" and afternoon tea were sometimes used interchangeably in Gilded Age New York, but over time the kettledrum became more raucous than a tea. At a kettledrum, parents put a large silver bowl or "kettle" in the middle of a large room, usually the parlor. Unattached young men crowded around the bowl and used spoons to make a din that would cover any flirtatious conversation. If someone who was drumming wanted to speak to a debutante at the party, he would leave the kettle and offer the woman a cup of tea. The young lady accepted with a spoon, signaling that the young man could court her. They spoke for as long as they both held their teacups, at which point the young man would return to the kettle and keep up the din. Perhaps it is not necessary to say that this type of debut had its detractors, who wondered how any real conversation could occur with the constant clanging. The kettledrum reached a farcical point when a Mrs. Clark of Fifth Avenue held one for her pugs and invited all the elite dogs in the neighborhood. The kettledrum, with its ritualistic noise, brought a new bluntness to the debutante transaction.

After a young girl came out at a reception or tea at her parents' house, she would attend the Patriarch's Ball, or another large evening dance, where she'd make her more public, formal debut. Some debutantes, particularly if the family was economizing, decided against participation in a ball. Introduction into the wider marriage market was the main aim of this ritual for most families, and they made various calculations on whether to spend the money based on their daughter's beauty or general appeal. If the family had a good name and no money, they might borrow money or enlist a richer relation to tend to their poorer but gorgeous daughter, with the hope that her name and beauty would appeal to a rich suitor.

Introduction into the wider marriage market and into a society that could be judged and delineated by outside entities like the press, who regularly published lists of who attended and what they wore to the party, was itself a rite of passage, and one to be nervous about. Huybertie Pruyn recalled her night at the Patriarch's Ball, which, in her terror, she had to be "dragged to." Her mother had handled her daughter's trepidation in the usual upper-class way, by keeping her entirely in the dark, only telling her she would attend at the very last minute. Her debut was to begin at Delmonico's where she would meet her escort, her "second cousin, at least 55 years old." She fought the hairdresser over her hair, insisting that it stay in its unfashionable knot, rather than be worn in the unfamiliar, alluring "psyche knot" that was popular in the day. Presumably her mother had arranged for her dress without her knowing as well. Bertie also met the center of it all, Ward McAllister. When she returned home to Albany, she scrawled in her diary "He is a F.O.O.L., we would not tolerate him here. I enjoyed it all as a sort of show circus, but I would not care to go again."[10]

The debutante needed to perfectly reflect the values of society—to "equip herself in the shining armor of conventionality," stepping neither "to the right, nor to the left of the line prescribed by custom." She must "above all repress her preferences in the matter of companionship, and mete out civility in equal share to all who are presented to her." In doing this, the debutante signaled to her parents that she would not choose her own mate, by demonstrating her own preference. Through the process of the season, a girl's parents would vet her possible husbands, watching their behavior and judging their interactions. If a girl signaled too much toward one gentleman, she would be labeled a flirt, but on the other hand, if she did not attract enough attention, she'd be labeled a failure.

The etiquette around giving and receiving flowers demonstrates this delicate exchange well. The code of flowers was a serious one and most Victorian families had a book on the language of flowers in their library. In *The Age of Innocence*, Newland Archer sent his fiancé, May Welland, lilies of the valley, tiny buds with a clean scent that for Victorians, conveyed purity, modesty, and simplicity. But to Ellen Olenska, his true love, he sent yellow roses, the message of which was more complex. When Archer saw them at the florist he felt "there was something too rich, too strong, in their fiery beauty," for May. But for Victorians, yellow roses had an ambiguous meaning, they could also mean jealousy or infidelity. They represented the full measure of life and effectively conveyed Archer's feelings, which he had not yet admitted to himself.

For young debutantes, flowers were a measure of popularity. Debutantes would carry bouquets they received from men during their morning walks, effectively displaying their success. Some girls would carry as many as eighteen bouquets at a time. Some girls received such large and elaborate displays that they were almost like art installations or small lawns, and still they had to be carried. Women's families would reciprocate by inviting the young man to dinner or by extending an invitation to sit in their opera box. Debutantes received so many bouquets that elite families assigned a dollar value that, once reached, would require a response. This problem eventually led older girls to stop carrying bouquets in public. There was no other way, however, for younger girls to establish their popularity, so they continued the practice. When newspapers reported on debutante receptions, readers could gauge a girl's success by the paper's description of the flowers. If the *New York Times* said the party was "weighed down with flowers" the girl was a success. If the paper was forced to actually describe the young woman, or extol any of her individual virtues, she had flopped.

Flowers were not the only measure of success. Debutantes also received favors at balls, most of which were elaborate and precious. The host and hostess of a ball would give favors—at one of Mrs. Astor's balls, she gave out tartan plaid silk sashes, with her monogram and the date of the ball etched in gold. Men also brought individual favors to women: small jewels, ink blotters, and silk sachets were all popular examples. Men also received gifts from their hosts—leather tobacco pouches and gold golf tees were typical—but never from debutantes. For young women from the most prominent families, being asked to sit for a miniature for Peter Marié's collection was the apogee of social success. It was generally assumed that a perennial bachelor with a good name and extensive fortune might be gay, though the better the name, the less likely the reasons would be gossip. Such was the case for Peter Marié, a habitué of debutante parties, who was at the debuts of both Bertie Pruyn and Mrs. Astor's daughter, Carrie. Peter Marié's position in society, unlike that of Isaac Brown or Ward McAllister, was undisputed. His family had made its money in trade in the French West Indies and he was heir to their large fortune. An eternal bachelor with manners deemed to be old-fashioned even in a society that loved to look backward, he was what was then known as a "diner-out," a person welcome at any table, at any time. He also gave parties, like the one described in his invitation for February 14, 1870, as "an intellectual tea" on St. Valentine's Day, after the manner of the Hotel Rambouillet. He continued with a friendly warning: "No guest can hope for tea, until he has undergone the reading of one of Mr. Peter Marié's poems." His own wry sense of himself won people over. When he was a houseguest, he was allowed to take over the proceedings, offering prizes "in contests ranging from foot-races to essay-writing on the subject of 'What is Charm?'"[11] Marié was also a well-known collector of exquisite items—fans, snuff boxes, card cases, and other bijouterie. His dearest belongings were tiny and perfect, and it is easy to imagine him at his beautiful house in Washington Square, surrounded by the sort of small jeweled mysteries that lent their gleam to the precise, but narrow, world he inhabited.

Marié had another collection for which he is still known, a "platonic seraglio" of 300 miniatures painted by the best artists of the time, to illustrate "every type of feminine beauty" although his catalog of beauty was drawn only from the debutante daughters and new wives of the best families in New York. For two generations, women sat for Mr. Marié's miniaturists, and this was the apogee of their social careers. Eleanor Roosevelt opened her autobiography with the declaration: "My mother was one of the most beautiful women I have ever seen. Old Peter Marié, who gave choice parties and whose approval stamped young girls and young matrons a success, called my mother a queen, and bowed before her charm and beauty, and to her this was important." At the Patriarch's Ball, Bertie was introduced to Peter Marié, saying she "felt instantly that I was far from measuring up the necessary standards of being included in his museum."[12] These paintings were totems. Historically, miniatures were used to introduce people at a great distance—noblemen sent miniatures of their marriageable daughters to suitors. For a male socialite who did not marry, a collection of paintings of young women shows an achievement beyond any made by a man finding a wife.

Much in the way that Joseph Shippen's "Lines Written in an Assembly Room" served to provide both social taxonomy and legitimacy for eighteenth-century colonists by memorializing young debutantes of the period in verse, Peter Marié's large collection of debutante miniatures presented a particular vision of the women of New York in this period, and that vision, like Shippen's, values conformity above all. The value of the woman depicted derives not only from her family, but also from her ability to conform to the culture's vision of female beauty, itself wrapped up in demure uniformity and family name. Peter Marié's miniatures were a triumph of group identity and repetition. Eleanor Roosevelt's mother Anna's success in making it into Marié's collection was the perfect victory—recognition within a tiny sphere, the only one that mattered. The ideal beauty of New York society was like Edith Wharton's May Welland, who was valued most of all for her sameness, and an occasional victory at archery, or a triumph at a dinner, only highlighted that sameness.

These miniatures are now in the collection of the New-York Historical Society, though Marié wanted them to go to the Metropolitan Museum, which rejected his bequest. Met director Luigi di Cesnola explained the newsworthy rejection to the *New York Times*: "There are two difficulties about the miniatures. In the first place, some of them are not art, and in the second place, they are not, considered as a whole, of the historical value that was claimed for them. It was said that the collection was of the most beautiful women in the United States," he added. "That is not true, for beautiful women are not confined to the 'four hundred,' and I could go out on Broadway and find women as beautiful as any in the collection." The rejection of Marié's miniatures signified that society was moving in another direction, and moving beyond the confines of downtown Manhattan.

CHAPTER 5

Transatlantic Crossings

Clarissa Jerome was miserable. Alone in her enormous new mansion overlooking Madison Square Park, surrounded by layers and layers of beautiful things, she was a victim of the closed social structure of old New York society. She could not call on anyone without first being called on. She was not welcome at the many afternoons of tea and evenings of music and dancing held in the city. There was nowhere respectable for her to go without an invitation, and nobody cared to extend her one. Clarissa's husband Leonard was a successful stock speculator, railway financier, and an impassioned lover of opera and its pretty singers. As a millionaire and horse-racing enthusiast, Leonard was quickly accepted by the men of New York and rapidly became one of their own, working with them to found the horse-racing prize, the Belmont Stakes, and the New York Academy of Music. Leonard ran around with August Belmont, the model for Edith Wharton's shady Julius Beaufort in *The Age of Innocence*—banker, gourmand, bon vivant, serial adulterer, and secret Jew. If Clarissa and Leonard had had sons, their children would have melted right into society, just like their father. Rich bachelors were never unpopular. They tended to turn into hardworking husbands who provided a steady stream of money to keep their wives in Worth dresses and who bothered nobody as they only rarely appeared at social events with their wives.

But Leonard and Clarissa Jerome didn't have sons. They had three gorgeous daughters, with natural manners, beautiful faces, good educations, and large dowries—girls who posed an active threat to the daughters of old New York. After many days and nights spent at home watching her girls sitting around in their correct dresses, and because they, too, were uninvited to birthday parties and teas, Clarissa made a decision. The Jerome girls had no future in a New York run by Ward McAllister and Caroline Astor unless they found a way around the system. Together the couple came to the conclusion, abetted, too, by Leonard's constant infidelity, that he would stay in New York and work and Clarissa would take the girls to make their debuts in Paris, where the Empress Eugénie, who had an American grandfather, welcomed young, rich, American women. When the girls returned from Europe, with the undisputed imprimatur of having been presented to a monarch, they would have entrée to New York society, and perhaps titled British husbands as well. The Jeromes were among the first wave of nouveau riche families to take this route toward bringing their daughters into society, but many followed, trading the United States for Europe, and especially for England, where their fortunes enticed impoverished blue bloods. These women married European men, and while their primary houses might have been in Europe, they traveled a predictable social circuit, at prescribed times of year. By uniting rich families in different countries through marriage, they eventually created a more modern and international upper class, an upper class that still functions in essentially the same way today as it did in the latter half of the nineteenth century.

Clarissa and her daughters arrived in Paris in 1867, when the city was in the throes of Baron Haussmann's reconfiguration of its urban grid. Haussmann replaced narrow medieval streets with wide boulevards fit for strolling and people-watching. The Jeromes lived close to the city center and the best shopping. The girls were not quite ready to be out in society and took lessons at a fashionable school to prepare. From her apartment on the Boulevard Malseherbes, Clarissa planned her daughter Clara's debut, which would take place at a ball held by the emperor and empress at the Tuileries Palace. The Jeromes visited Charles Worth, the empress's dressmaker, to obtain the necessary wardrobe. Worth's atelier was a social center of upper-class Paris and was frequented by women who lived in a world where different morning, afternoon, and evening gowns were the bare minimum of acceptability. Worth had just introduced a dress with a slightly shorter skirt for ease of walking— perfect for the partner of a rich flâneur as they strolled without aim in Haussmann's Paris. In 1868, Worth engineered a skirt "with no crinoline or hoops at all but the rather more attractive bustle." The House of Worth was the first to use live models, and each lady, while sitting with her lady's maid in one of the luxurious fitting rooms, waited for the great designer himself to swoop in at the last moment to give her choice his imprimatur. While she waited, a server presented a plate of foie gras and a glass of Sauternes, to ease decisions.

On the evening of her debut, Clara wore her first low-cut Worth frock and went to the palace with her mother. When she returned, she told her younger sisters Jennie and Leonie about her confusion at having to walk up the grand staircase between the cent-gardes (the emperor's magnificently uniformed soldiers), telling them that no procession was formed but "when the company was assembled the doors were flung open and 'sa Majesté l'Empereur!' was announced." She said that then after a pause came the announcement of the arrival of the empress, who "appeared a resplendent figure in green velvet with a crown of emeralds and diamonds spiked with pearls on her small and beautifully shaped head." Clara told her sisters about the demands of court ceremony and etiquette and the degrees of bowing and curtseying required as the guests proceeded to the ballroom.[1] Though her mother had believed she might turn her daughter into a comtesse or duchesse, that dream was quickly cut short by the invasion of Paris by the Prussian army in 1870, shortly after Clara's debut. The family left on the last train from Paris at the time of the conquest, and made their way to London and into rooms at Brown's Hotel. Other rich American families had fled Paris with French aristocrats whom they had befriended there and who would smooth their way into English society. And so it happened that a group of rich, beautiful American heiresses found themselves in London right in time for the opening of the social season in May.

English society had grown in size and scope since Queen Charlotte had expanded debutante presentations in the 1780s, though formal presentation at court had still remained limited to a very few young women. But Queen Victoria differed greatly from her predecessors in that she had no problem with the middle classes—and was delighted by the solid burghers who made money for her realm. She preferred them to the fast-living actors and impoverished romantic poets who had populated the salons of Regency London. In the mid-nineteenth century, Queen Victoria began to allow daughters of favored members of the gentry and even some daughters of the haute bourgeoisie to be presented at St. James Palace. The wealthy bourgeois heiresses and the braying, chinless aristocrats who pursued them were targeted by satirists like Anthony Trollope, who, in *The Way We Live Now* (1874), associated a general social decline with the decline of the aristocracy, whom he saw as feckless and desperate. In the Victorian satirical magazine *Punch*, anonymous authors ridiculed the debutante on a near weekly basis, using well-known contemporary poetry to skewer the aspirants. In "The Charge of the Court Brigade," a long riff on Tennyson's Crimean War elegy "The Charge of the Light Brigade," courtiers crashed into each other, and girls and their suitors were left in tangles as they tried to get the best seats.

By mid-century, it was clear that the aristocracy would have to use every resource it had to maintain its edge. One strategy for retaining influence and relevancy was to act as sponsor to a newly rich person who wanted to enter society. Elizabeth Bancroft-Davis, wife of the American ambassador to Britain, writing in 1841, relates meeting George Hudson, railway king, Tory MP and skilled briber, at a concert he gave in his new London house:

These things are managed in a curious way here. A nouveau riche gets several ladies of fashion to patronise their entertainment and invite all the guests even if he has a wife. Lady Parke entertained for the Hudsons, whose guest list included the Duke of Wellington. Lady Parke stood at the entrance of the splendid suite of rooms to receive the guests and introduce them to their host and hostess.[2]

Social events were eventually opened up to a somewhat wider elite that included bureaucrats, bankers, merchants, university dons and influential members of the Anglican Church. Mixing was more common after the institution of a Civil Service examination in 1854, which ended absolute patronage as the primary means used to get government appointments. Public schooling became the necessary adjunct to political and social life, and ambitious mothers were soon fine with enterprising young men with no background apart from the right schooling. William Gladstone, who was prime minister four times between 1868–1898, was born into a successful merchant family. By attending Eton College, he gained the necessary manners and connections to go along with his fortune. He married Catherine Glynne, the daughter of a baronet who grew up at Hawardan Castle. Nancy Mitford has one of her fictional characters in *Don't Tell Alfred*, an heiress with unreliable parents, married off to Alfred, an entirely respectable university don.

Yet British mothers who organized parties were confronting new problems that they had to work around. In the eighteenth century, once you were accepted to an institution such as Almack's, you would be received at all the important parties. You were vetted and could talk to anyone. In the nineteenth century, however, the careful regulation of parties was vital. In the 1850s, male attendees had to sign their name and rank on a debutante's dance card, and girls were prohibited from dancing more than three dances with one gentleman in a night. Chaperonage was increasingly strict as well—an unmarried woman under thirty could not go anywhere or be in a room even in her own house with an unrelated man, whether married or single, unless she was accompanied by a married gentlewoman or a female servant. An unmarried gentle-woman, no matter how old, could not be a proper chaperone to a dance. Even if she did not marry, she was always nominally attached to this social system.[3]

The only possible silver lining to this obsessive focus on marriage was that, gradually, there were more varieties of possible suitors than before. During the Victorian period, middle-class behavior patterns and mores were grafted onto society at large, replacing the honorific code of the aristocracy with the greater rubric of "gentility," creating space for a more mutable definition of manners. Fortunately for the Jeromes and others, appropriate behavior was reported in such far-flung places as America. Society became more mobile, too; with British control over its empire strengthening, there was a feeling that London society was *the* society to join, and socially ambitious people flocked to London from all continents. The developments in photography of the 1860s and '70s only served to bolster this image of London, as glittering portraits of debutantes and society parties were published around the world. Aristocratic women and their debutante daughters quickly learned how to manipulate the new interest in publicity and exploited their social connections for financial and social gain by acting as patrons to fashionable clothing and lingerie shops and even appearing in advertisements.

London society was becoming too broad to define, as political theorist Beatrice Webb recalled in the 1880s:

> From my particular point of observation London society appeared as a shifting mass of miscellaneous and uncertain membership, it was essentially a body that could not be defined, not by its circumference, which could not be traced but by its centre or centres; centres of social circles representing or epitomizing certain dominant forces within the British governing class. There was the Court, representing national tradition and customs; there was the

Cabinet and ex-Cabinet, representing political power; there was a mysterious group of millionaire financiers representing money; there was the racing set. All persons who habitually entertained and who were entertained by the members of any one of these key groups could claim to belong to London society. These four inner circles crossed and re-crossed each other owing to an element of common membership.[4]

Webb's description is borne out by statistics. In 1841, 90 percent of the women presented at court were from the titled, landowning class. In 1871 it was 68 percent. By 1891 the proportion had dropped to less than 50 percent for the first time in history, and never again exceeded it. Debutantes were drawn from the rich of different backgrounds, "even trade is not debarred," remarked one contemporary observer.[5]

In the early nineteenth century most people had known where they stood socially, and the careers of the ambitious were seen more as moralistic warning than as how-to manual. But as the century wore on, upper-class society became both more nebulous and more porous. The Court was no longer the only means to access real political power. Society's emphasis, thus, shifted toward its own more decorative functions—debutante presentations, the races at Ascot and regatta at Cowes, and assorted charitable events. As society wielded less real power and its drawing rooms were no longer a place for political negotiations, it became more accessible, too, for those who desired its symbolic power most.

By the end of the nineteenth century, a reversal had occurred, wherein members of society sought out the newly rich and powerful instead of merely tolerating them. Some aristocratic women in dire financial straits even advertised their services, as is the case in one taken from a London paper in 1895: "A lady in the smartest society in London wishes to chaperone a young lady. Terms 1000 pounds for one year. Highest references given and required." Those most likely to use the services of such a woman were ambitious Americans, like the Jeromes, who used a series of Englishwomen to smooth their arrival.

Americans were welcome in London, in large part because of the Prince of Wales, later King Edward VII, who had visited New York City in 1860, during a state visit to Canada. He was bored of the endless banquets given in his honor, so asked if New Yorkers might throw him a real party, a ball. The crowds at one given at the Academy of Music in Greenwich Village were so many that the floor collapsed right as he arrived, and a team of carpenters, led by Isaac Brown, repaired it while the 4,000 guests waited and looked at each other in embarrassment. Floor collapse notwithstanding, the prince loved the relaxed manners of American women, and his successful visit was understood by Americans to have made it acceptable for a cultural rapprochement and relationship to develop between the two countries. In fact, the prince would later serve as matchmaker and fixer in a number of Anglo-American marriages, including in Jennie Jerome's. Victorian bourgeois values were less distant and more familiar to Americans—the cultures had more in common than they had had in the earlier part of the nineteenth century because of the growth of industry, and the middle classes in both countries along with it, leaving them more on the same footing. The English, who believed all Americans were the same and primarily defined by their money, also didn't discriminate regionally within America. The idea that there was a better society in one part of America than in another was an absurdity to them.

For American families wanting to penetrate English society, Cowes was the best first stop. The seaside town allowed for less formal interaction. Because it was on an island, the queen was able to keep out the press. Free from onlookers, the aristocracy could relax. The Jeromes went down for some sailing, and, of course, to advance the marriage prospects of their two elder daughters. Clara and Jennie, the latter of whom was an exceptional pianist, played piano and sang duets, wearing their Worth gowns, of course, while British men watched astonished.

For aristocratic English girls, education was suspect, and American women exhibited the kind of seductive charm generally reserved for courtesans and actresses. American parents, in contrast, looked at education as another opportunity to display their daughters' wealth and sophistication. The Jerome girls were not only rich, but they were also smart and impish, and played piano and sang beautifully. They began to receive invitations.

Never shy about making an entrance, on August 12, 1871, Jennie and sister Clara, dressed in white tulle dresses decorated with fresh flowers, boarded a launch to attend a ball in honor of the Prince and Princess of Wales on the HMS *Ariadne*. At the ball, Lord Randolph Churchill, third son of Duke and Duchess of Marlborough, spotted Jennie across the room. He asked for an introduction, and the two danced a quadrille together. Jennie and Randolph fell instantly in love and they became engaged a week later, to their parents' great dismay. The Jeromes wanted more for their daughter—as a third son, Randolph would not become the duke. The duke and duchess, against the marriage as well, did not want their son marrying an American, particularly after the duke made inquiries into the origins of Leonard Jerome's fortune. The Prince of Wales, who was fond of both Jennie and Randolph, intervened on the couple's behalf, and marriage negotiations began. Randolph could bring very little to the marriage. His father would settle his debts but he would only have £1,100 a year. The young couple would have to live off their marriage settlement, the sum of which was up to Jennie's father, Leonard. He offered £40,000, which would produce £2,000 annually, but insisted on providing his daughter with an additional allowance of £1,000 per year for her personal use. Lord Randolph's lawyers were outraged and wrote:

> The Duke says that such a settlement cannot as far as you are personally concerned be considered as any settlement at all for . . . Miss Jerome would be made quite independent of you in a pecuniary point of view, which in my experience is most unusual. . . .

Although in America a married woman's property may be absolutely and entirely her own, I would remark that upon marrying an Englishman, she loses her American nationality and becomes an Englishwoman so that I think that the settlement should be according to the law and custom here.[6]

Leonard replied that he felt the English custom of making a wife completely dependent on her husband "most unwise." In America, the money that a woman brought to her marriage was her own to control, but in English marriages, it was expected that the bride's money be handed over to her husband, to do with it as he saw fit.

Randolph's father, the seventh duke, pressured Leonard Jerome so intensely in part because the duke was a man in financial trouble. As Disraeli put it, he was "not rich, for a duke." He had five daughters to marry off and also had the upkeep of Blenheim, a palace, to consider. Already, he had sold a vast tract of land to Lord Rothschild, as well as various family treasures. Randolph had the tastes of a man with a considerably greater fortune and a gambling habit he would not be able to sustain for much longer. In the end, Leonard conceded to all the Churchill's financial demands except for one. He gave Jennie her own allowance. The modest marriage took place in 1874 at the British Embassy in Paris. Eight months later, the couple had their first son, Winston.

While younger brother Randolph was finally settled with Jennie, the dilemma of his older brother, the Marquess of Blandford, who was heir to the dukedom, perfectly illustrates the problem the British aristocracy was facing at the close of the nineteenth century. The marquess, known simply as Blandford, would be left little because his father, the seventh duke, had not been able to eke out a living. The Blenheim estate netted only £37,000 a year. First the elder duke sold off land. Starting in 1875, he sold the family jewelry, followed by the contents of the Sunderland library. The famed Blenheim enamels followed. With the estate in tatters, there would be only £7,000/year for Blandford, with the expensive palace to maintain.

Blenheim devoured money. It took one man one year to wash all the windows. When he finished, he began anew. The palace had fourteen acres of roof that needed near-constant retreading. When Blandford, now the eighth duke, inherited it from his father, he was forced to sell eighteen Rubens, two Titians, two Rembrandts, and other works by Poussin, Watteau, Claude Lorrain, and Van Dyck, the proceeds of which cleared £400,000. And this was still not enough to run Blenheim.

It became very clear that the eighth duke would need to go to New York. Though most English aristocrats were welcomed eagerly, this one was not. Blandford's reputation was abysmal. He had had multiple scandalous affairs; he had tried to blackmail the Prince of Wales and was, for years, persona non grata in British society. There was no young debutante for this duke, but with the help of a social fixer he met Lily Hammersley, a rich thirty-four-year-old widow with $100,000 a year and $1 million of her own. Lily was not a beauty. Jennie's husband Randolph Churchill wrote to his mother that Lily's "mustache and beard are becoming serious." The *New York Times* stated it plainly: "It has been generally understood that Mrs. Hammersley married the Duke for his title and the Duke married her for her money."

Lily Hammersley's money helped save Blenheim for a little while, but by the time their son, the ninth duke, who went by Sunny, inherited the palace, it would become clear that a more extreme solution was necessary. He trained his eye on the huge fortunes of the Vanderbilt heiresses, cousins Gertrude and Consuelo. While Gertrude was permitted to attend school, and had more experience in society, Consuelo was schooled entirely at home. Her mother Alva lunched with her children every day, taking the time to interrogate them about what they were learning. When the family traveled for months at a time on their 275-foot yacht, the children saw the world, and wrote essays about every sight on the way. Consuelo was an intelligent and curious pupil but was deeply sheltered. The peculiar combination of erudition and isolation in her childhood produced a sixteen-year-old who told her governess that she wanted to translate *Thus Spake Zarathustra* into English, but who had no idea there were already twenty-seven English translations.[7] By the time she made her debut in 1894, most of the United States knew that Consuelo's dowry was worth $20 million (around $500 million today) and the press followed her every move. When they could not see what she was doing, they filled in the blanks with their own ideas of her story.

Consuelo made her debut in Paris, at a private *bal blanc* (named for the virginal dresses, it became a *bal rose* when young married women were in attendance), given by the Duc and Duchesse de Gramont for their own daughter. She wore a dress by Worth made of layers of white tulle, and white gloves that "came almost to [her] shoulders." She wore just a ribbon around her famous long neck, and no jewelry, as it was customary for debutantes, especially in France, to be totally unadorned, a persistent reference to virginity that left them feeling both childish and dowdy. Consuelo later wrote:

> A *bal blanc* had to live up to its name of purity and innocence; it could not inspire the mild flirtations of a pink ball where young married women were included. The men who attended them, no doubt with the intention of selecting a future spouse, were expected to behave with circumspection. There was no opportunity for conversation. A debutante was invited to dance and once the dance was over she was escorted back to her mama. Rows of chaperones lined the walls, discussing the merits of their charges. The young girls stood diffidently beside them. The terror of not being asked to dance, the humiliation of being a wallflower, ruined the pleasures of a ball for those who were ill-favored. With the politeness inherent in the French, a galaxy of partners presented their respects to me and I was soon at ease and happy.[8]

There could be no wallflower's life for a girl of Consuelo's beauty and a fortune of around $20,000,000. In the week following her French debut, Consuelo learned from her mother than she had received five proposals of marriage. She was allowed to consider one of the proposals, which had come from a German prince. She described wryly how her mother's "intention to marry me to an English duke had, for a moment, faltered." But the idea of Consuelo being sequestered in a provincial German town was appealing to neither mother nor daughter.

Her mother soon reverted to her initial plan, and she and Consuelo proceeded to London, where Alva initiated her plans to launch her daughter. The two paid their first visit in London to Lady Paget, a rich American heiress at one time, she was a friend of both Jennie Jerome, now Lady Randolph Churchill, and Conseulo Yznaga, a Cuban-American heiress from Louisiana who was now the Duchess of Manchester. (The latter was the inspiration for Edith Wharton's Conchita Closson in *The Buccaneers*, her unfinished novel about transatlantic marriage.) Minnie Stevens Paget's father had owned a hotel in New York, and it was rumored that her ambitious mother had once been a prostitute. Lady Paget had achieved resounding social success in her marriage to an English peer and close friend to the Prince of Wales. Over time and through unrelenting effort, she had fashioned herself into London's queen gossip and social fixer and was said to have inspired Henry James's pointedly named Fanny Assingham in *The Golden Bowl*, a character who sets off all the various *mésalliances* in the novel through her ceaseless plotting. Lady Paget was rumored to accept money for doing social favors, including introducing people to the Prince of Wales.

The fact that Alva wanted to have Paget bring Consuelo "out" was a nod to Alva's mercenary aims. Consuelo, for her part, was horrified, describing Lady Paget as "Becky Sharp incarnate." On their first meeting, Consuelo related her discomfort at being sized up: "The simple dress I was wearing, my shyness and diffidence, which in France were regarded as natural in a debutante, appeared to awaken her ridicule."

Paget remarked to Alva, "If I am to bring her out, she must be able to compete at least as far as clothes are concerned with far better-looking girls."[9] Consuelo's obvious ability to compete and win, because of her money and good looks, make Lady Paget's comment quite interesting— she was an older woman with less social status asserting her authority over a young girl she needed to use to improve her status.

Lady Paget, because of her reputation for arranging introductions and harboring rich American debutantes, was also sought out by aristocrats who wanted her to make a match for them. When Consuelo met the Duke of Marlborough at a dinner at Lady Paget's house, she was aware, having been placed on his right, what the intentions for the evening were. But nothing happened that she knew of. In her autobiography, Consuelo relates that she received three other proposals of marriage from "uninteresting Englishmen," which she found "disillusioning." She wrote "they were so evidently dictated by a desire for my dowry," they dispelled "whatever thoughts of romance might come my way."[10]

In the early autumn of 1894, Consuelo was relieved that she and her family would return to America in November. She had expected that she would arrive to a flurry of social activity because it would be the beginning of the social season in New York. She had grown to like balls and parties and longed to see her friends, from whom she had been separated for months. She described her relief that the "dangers of a foreign alliance" were for the moment "in abeyance." She did not understand that she was allowed to return to her own life only because her marriage was already settled. The reason Alva Vanderbilt had remained in Europe for as long as she could was so that she might ride out the repercussions of her own divorce in company that was less likely to experience its immediate fallout, but Consuelo was dismayed to discover, upon her return, that, though she still received invitations to balls and teas, her mother was paranoid about whom Consuelo met and spoke to. Not only because she wanted Consuelo to remain on her side in the split but also because she feared that her impressionable young daughter might ruin the plans she had made for Consuelo's marriage.

Consuelo and Alva were to return to Europe in March 1895 for the summer season, but even before their departure for Europe, Consuelo had threatened to topple Alva's plan by becoming engaged to a family friend, John Winthrop Rutherfurd, a denizen of Mrs. Astor's New York. He was part of her social scene, was generally well-liked, and had excellent prospects. For anyone but Consuelo, or Alva's vision of her, he would have been a dream partner. He was tall, handsome, athletic, and charming. He proposed to Consuelo after the two of them managed to outpace her mother on their bicycles. He was able to convince her to marry him while they sped down Riverside Drive—entering into a secret engagement before she left for Europe the next morning. They vowed to keep the engagement from her mother, who would never consent to it. He did follow her to Paris, but was turned away when he called. His letters, too, were confiscated. Consuelo was miserable, and her mother berated her for her "martyrdom." Consuelo wrote of how she tried on clothes procured for her coming time in London "like an automaton," talked of "deadly" debutante balls and the dull feeling she had when she danced with anyone. Soon they would go to London, at which point Consuelo felt that she was being "steered into a vortex."[11]

The visit to England was short and notable because the Vanderbilts visited Blenheim. The ninth duke did not formally propose to Consuelo on this visit, but the nature of her visit to his ancestral house was clear. The duke, who lived at the house alone, had his two sisters come down for the house party. He gave Consuelo a tour of his estates on horseback, and she was enchanted with the countryside and surrounding villages. She knew that keeping up this kind of estate, still feudal, would require torrents of money.

The Vanderbilts left Blenheim, having secured a US visit from the duke. He would come to their house in Newport in September. This was an ingenious plan on Alva's part. Newport was a Vanderbilt stronghold, and Alva would be persona non grata there because of her impending divorce (despite it having resulted from her husband's adultery). In hosting the Duke of Marlborough, she had engineered her own permanent place in Newport society. While Newport might have been able to ignore Alva, and many would have liked to, local socialites couldn't pass up the chance to fete the scion of one of England's most illustrious aristocratic families. The fact that he would be staying at Marble House, with Consuelo and Alva, meant they would need to form a line to kiss Alva's ring. It's hard not to see Alva's machinations on behalf of her daughter's marriage as an effort to save herself from the social embarrassment of her own divorce.

When they returned to Newport in July for its season, which ran from then to September, Consuelo's sympathetic father was out of reach and, as he sailed around the world with his mistress, Consuelo felt a prisoner in her mother's house. She was under constant supervision by her mother and governess. The porter was instructed to not allow her to leave on her own. When her friends called, they were told she wasn't at home. Alva thought she had made certain that Consuelo would not be able to meet her fiancé, but finally, by chance, they met at a ball. They were able to have a quick dance before her mother hauled her away. Consuelo, reassured of her feelings, planned to implore her mother to allow her to marry the man she loved. Society was, after all, long past favoring arranged marriages, and didn't condone a forced one. After hurling invective at Consuelo's fiancé, Alva told her daughter that she would select a husband for Consuelo, her decision "founded on considerations [you] are too young to appreciate." Consuelo speculated that, after a lifetime of obedience, her stubborn stance startled her mother. Alva said she would shoot any man who she believed would ruin Alva's life, not worrying about Consuelo's. They argued until dawn in what their biographer Amanda Stuart MacKenzie called "the most famous mother-daughter row of the Gilded Age," when an exhausted Consuelo finally left for her room.[12]

The next morning, servants informed Consuelo that her mother was ill. A friend of her mother's who was staying with the family came to Consuelo's room to tell her that her "callous indifference" to Alva's feelings had caused her to have a heart attack and implored the girl not to finish her off by insisting on her ridiculous marriage. "Your mother will never relent," she said, "And I warn you there will be a catastrophe if you persist. The doctor has said that another scene may easily bring on a heart attack and he will not be responsible for the result. You can ask the doctor if you do not believe me!" In "utter misery" Consuelo directed her mother's friend to inform her fiancé that she could not marry him. "Brought up to obey, I surrendered more easily to my mother's dictates than others . . . might have done."

Consuelo took solace in her governess's descriptions of life in England, of the many different opportunities she would have to do some social good. She wrote philosophically that "history records many marriages of convenience" explaining that they were "still in vogue in Europe," finally saying that these prevailing attitudes made her mother feel she had made a "reasonable decision concerning my future." Her mother gave a ball for the duke, "the most beautiful fete ever seen in Newport" according to the papers of the day. The favors for the cotillion included old French etchings, fans, mirrors, watch-cases, and sashes of ribbon, all from the Louis XIV period. Amid trips to the casino and beach, to parties and teas, Marlborough proposed to Consuelo and she accepted. When she told her brother he unkindly responded, "he's only marrying you for your money." He didn't know she had been in love with Winthrop Rutherfurd and thought her cynical. She burst into tears.

Consuelo had no input into her trousseau and made no decisions about her ceremony. Her mother chose her eight bridesmaids from the daughters of her own friends. Of her father's family, only Consuelo's grandmother was invited, but naturally refused to attend a wedding from which the rest of her family had been excluded. The degree to which this wedding was Alva's show was evident, but few people stayed away, beguiled as they were by an opportunity to visit Marble House.

Reporters called the house incessantly and invented stories about the level of excess and bad taste. They falsely wrote that Alva had commissioned diamond-studded gold garters for her daughter, which led Consuelo to wonder how "she would live down these vulgarities." When her wedding dress arrived, Consuelo realized that her mother had ordered it at Worth when they were in Paris, before they even met Marlborough, so sure was she of her plan's success.

Consuelo spent the morning of her wedding locked in her room crying. She felt "like an automaton, I donned the lovely lingerie with its real lace and white stockings and shoes. My maid helped me into the beautiful dress, with its Brussels lace cascading over white satin. It had a high collar and tight long sleeves. The court train, embroidered with seed pearls and silver, fell from my shoulders in billowing whiteness. My maid fitted my veil to my head with a wreath of orange blossoms; it fell over my face to my knees. I felt cold and numb as I went downstairs to meet my father and the bridesmaids who were waiting for me." Consuelo cried so much that she needed her face cleansed numerous times before she could walk down the aisle. She cried through the ceremony and was grateful for her veil. When the couple left the church, throngs of onlookers rushed at them and women grabbed at flowers from her bouquet. She was the Duchess of Marlborough, despite her own best efforts.

Between Jennie's marriage to Randolph and the First World War, more than 500 American heiresses married titled Europeans, and an estimated $220,000,000 (more than $4 billion in today's dollars) followed them to Europe.[13] While in the British press, American girls were initially eyed with suspicion, they were eventually revered and celebrated for bringing money to Britain. The general feeling of American newspapers of this period toward titled marriages was grim. They lapped up social news with an enthusiasm that bordered on embarrassing, but they also regularly exaggerated the financial component of titled marriages.

Whereas once these marriages had been cause for pride, and a measure of American acceptability, people began to view any English proposal with skepticism.

There was a growing sentiment in the United States that American capital was being wasted on dowries used for the upkeep of European aristocratic households. Newspapers wrote coyly that the wealthy classes in the United States had an unhealthy, undemocratic obsession with acquiring hereditary titles. Commentators believed that millionaire fathers were depriving others in the United States from enjoying the fruits of their endeavors, that they were preventing a trickle-down of their own wealth by sending it overseas. American debutantes were to be considered a national resource, like mineral deposits, and their money should go to American men, not foreigners. Women making titled marriages were accused of upsetting American social and economic values and became symbolic enemies of both capitalism and nationalism. As the first wave of these marriages began to collapse in divorce around the turn of the century, the public's opinons about them only soured further.

Heiresses who chose to marry domestically were feted as progressive and patriotic. When Gertrude Vanderbilt married Harry Payne Whitney, a member of a wealthy Massachusetts family that owned railroads and bred horses, newspapers cheered. At the wedding reception, the bandleader, without prompting, played "The Star-Spangled Banner." Commentators even suggested a protectionist tariff. In 1908, British magazine *The Tatler* reported, "Those who are always carping at the tendency on the part of our young peers to take unto themselves wives from among the heiresses of America will be glad to hear that there is a suggestion in the United States that a graduated tax, increasing according to the size of the lady's fortune, should be levied on all rich American brides who marry titled foreigners."

But the patriotic expectation that wealth would remain in one place was unrealistic. In mid-Victorian Britain even a small landowner had been able to keep pace with new manufacturing wealth. But from the later nineteenth century on, only the most enormous landed aristocratic fortune could remotely compete with that of a middling industrialist. And not a single British fortune approached the level of the new American superrich.[14] Once fodder for satirists everywhere, American women on the international scene were now admired and considered sophisticated, and most had the education, manner, and clothing to support the claim. In 1910, *Town Topics*, a gossip magazine, could write, "It was easy to pick out the American girls. They dress so well and know exactly how to put on their clothes." This sort of press coverage was a strategic mercenary decision that forced reporters to find ways to admire these women. Similarly, the press no longer treated Anglo-American weddings as socially unbalanced, but rather looked to elevate the American girl. When Beatrice Mills, daughter of the financier and thoroughbred racehorse owner Ogden Mills and heiress Ruth Livingston Mills, married the Earl of Granard in 1909, *The Tatler* wrote, "her mother, who was a Livingston[e], belongs to the ancienne noblesse of the United States." And they were only half-joking.

By the turn of the twentieth century, society in England and the United States was well integrated, particularly at the top levels of society. Titled marriages between American debutantes and English aristocrats had played their part in the consolidation of bourgeois values in both countries. With more exposure to American money, British culture gradually transformed into something resembling what it is today— a modern society led by successful capitalists. Even if those business leaders came from the aristocracy, it was their business interests that were most important. Whereas once the debutante's fortune was used to rebuild the house, in this next generation, it would more likely be applied toward finding a good career in business, to buy a seat on a city board, or lending credibility to an English commercial concern. With England increasingly commercial, the aristocracy lost some of its gloss. Easier travel meant that young girls were raised as much abroad as

Queen Charlotte, wife of King George III, created the first large-scale debutante ball in 1768 to benefit the London maternity hospital that bore her name. *Royal Collection Trust / © Her Majesty Queen Elizabeth II 2019.*

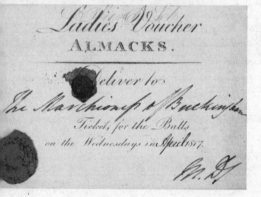

An admittance voucher was needed to enter Almack's Assembly Rooms. *Stowe Papers. The Huntington Library, San Marino, CA.*

widely distributed image at the time, this engraving depicts the first quadrille at Almack's, danced y patronesses Lady Jersey and Lady Worcester and their partners. *From The New York Public Library.*

The challenge of mastering the quadrille made group practice with a dancing master essential. Geor Cruikshank's series of satirical engravings are a catalogue of the potential ballroom disasters that amused onlookers. *From The New York Public Library.*

Lack of awareness of one's partner, or unfamiliarity with steps or music, could lead to embarrassin encounters like this one. *From The New York Public Library.*

Physically mismatched partners were a cause of both consternation and amusement in ballrooms. In this case, two tall women are obliged to move through dance figures with a man much shorter than themselves. *From The New York Public Library.*

The back-to-back disaster was no less humiliating. Spectators relished these events, which were ripe for popular caricatures like Cruikshank's. *From The New York Public Library.*

Invitations to the Veiled Prophet
Ball always have an esoteric theme.
© Missouri Historical Society.

Susie Slayback, daugh-
ter of Alonzo Slayback,
the founder of the Veiled
Prophet Society, was the
first queen of the ball.
© Missouri Historical Society.

Edith Wharton, member of an old New York family, was painted for socialite Peter Marié's collection of miniatures of upper-class women. Fernand Paillet, Mrs. Edward Wharton (1862–1937), 1890, watercolor on ivory, 2 ½ × 2 inches, Peter Marié Collection, 1905.266, New-York Historical Society, Gift of the Estate of Peter Marié. *Photography © New-York Historical Society.*

Anna Roosevelt, mother of Eleanor Roosevelt, felt being painted for Marié's collection to be one of the most important events in her life. Katherine Arthur Behenna, Mrs. Elliott Roosevelt (1863–1892), 1893, watercolor on ivory, diameter 2 ½ inches, Peter Marié Collection, 1905.216, New-York Historical Society, Gift of the Estate of Peter Marié. *Photography © New-York Historical Society.*

Mary Leiter, a Chicago heiress whose father was cofounder of Marshall Field, later married Lord C *zon, becoming the Vicereine of India.* Fernand Paillet, Mary Victoria Leiter (1870–1906), 1889, watercolor on iv 2 ⅜ × 2 inches, Peter Marié Collection, 1905.53, New-York Historical Society, Gift of the Estate of Peter Marié. *Photography © New-York Historical Society.*

The Minturn sisters, daughters of shipping magnate Robert Minturn, were almost never referred individually. Theirs is the only group portrait in Peter Marié's collection. The Daughters of Robert Mint 1899, watercolor on ivory, 3 ⅞ inches × 5 inches, Peter Marié Collection, 1905.161, New-York Historical Society, Gift o Estate of Peter Marié. *Photography © New-York Historical Society.*

Heiress Consuelo Vanderbilt, before her marriage to the Duke of Marlborough.
Library of Congress, Prints & Photographs Division, LC-DIG-ggbain-25016.

A 1920s debutante gown by the Parisian fashion house Boué Soeurs is a dramatic and modern departure from Gilded Age styles that highlighted the waist. Boue Soeurs gown. Boué Soeurs (French). Court Presentation Ensemble. 1928. White silk new with silver cord embroidery, white silk chiffon, blue silk lamé, polychrome silk ribbon flowers. The Metropolitan Museum of Art, Gift of Mrs. George Henry O'Neil, 1968. © *The Metropolitan Museum of Art. Image source: Art Resource, NY.*

It was common for women to sit for photographs of themselves in their court dress at a London studio before their presentation. © Lafayette / Victoria and Albert Museum, London.

in the States. It was also now possible to live in more than one place and to move more quickly on a social circuit. Upper-class life in the United States resembled upper-class life in Europe. Titled marriages had provided the impetus for this change, making it more acceptable for rich people in search of society to socialize together. By the turn of the century, it seemed ordinary that American debutantes with huge fortunes would marry aristocrats. May Goelet, a real-estate heiress who took the mantle of "America's richest girl" once Consuelo and Gertrude Vanderbilt were married, embodied the new model.

May was raised in a constant circuit between New York, Newport, London, Hamburg, and the Riviera, sailing with her mother on their steam yacht with French and Italian teachers, a riding instructor and a fencing master in tow. May was so rich that the broke ninth Duke of Manchester announced his fake engagement to her just to calm his creditors. She was kept in seclusion until serving as one of Consuelo Vanderbilt's bridesmaids in 1895. Her first debut, in London at a private ball, followed in 1897. Her New York debut, a ball at Sherry's hotel in 1900, was thrown by her aunt Mrs. Cornelius Vanderbilt Jr. May spent several seasons in London deciding whom to marry. In addition to being enormously rich, she was a good dancer, personable, and popular. When she finally settled on the Duke of Roxburghe, the two married at St. Thomas's in Manhattan. Two hundred people had to be ejected from the church gallery by the police. Ten thousand people, mostly women, surrounded the church to try to get a glimpse of her. May brought $20,000,000 (roughly $1 billion today) to her 1903 marriage.

Similarly, Cornelia Martin, a banking heiress with socially ambitious parents, was barely American, growing up mostly at Balmaccan, her family's estate on Loch Ness, and in London. Rushed into marriage at just sixteen to the Earl of Craven, Cornelia, like May, was a new sort of American debutante, one who did not need to be taught international etiquette because it was present from birth. Whether one made one's first debut in London or New York mattered less and less. In a few short years, in the extreme upper reaches of society, it wouldn't matter at all. The American social season began to take on a predictable shape, with families spending the early fall in the Berkshires, the winter and early spring in New York, the late spring in Paris (to get one's wardrobe in order), and then going to London for the late spring regattas. In the summer, international society converged on Newport, where the newly rich built "cottages" at a rapid pace. Newport had originated as a bohemian coastal retreat, but after the Civil War it was invaded by wealthy New Yorkers, first the Knickerbockers and then the nouveau riche. Newport was social aggregator of sorts—a place where prominent families from all over the country converged to escape hot weather and summer doldrums. Rich matrons ran the city's social life, and many men, especially married men, only spent weekends there. In America, men, even the richest, worked.

Newport in many ways was the ideal venue for debutantes because men from all over the world congregated there with marriage in mind. But this was not a place for the wanly aspirational. The patronesses of Newport society engineered its etiquette to be both ever changing yet utterly inflexible with the specific goal of exclusion. A family needed to be prepared to spend massive amounts of money to provide the bare necessities Newport etiquette required. May King Van Rensselaer, whose ball at Delmonico's transformed how women debuted, became, in her later years, a Gilded Age social commentator. She wrote about Newport:

It is an axiom of Newport that it takes at least four years to get in. Each season the persistent social climber makes some advance through a barrage of snubs. The seasoned member of the Newport colony enters into the cruel game of quashing the pride of the stranger with great glee. Eventually, if he will bear all this, the candidate receives an invitation which indicates that he has finally been accepted by whatever particular set he has besieged. Then he turns about and snubs those remaining petitioners as harshly as he himself was snubbed. For the privilege of being a guest at certain houses and the license to affront those not yet in, he has spent perhaps a million dollars.[15]

Elizabeth Drexel Lehr, a Philadelphia banking heiress, describes the bare minimum wardrobe requirements of Newport:

Such clothes! How they swished and rustled! Petticoats of satin, of lace, of taffeta, petticoats embellished with elaborate designs of cupids playing gilded lyres, true love knots interspersed with doves embellished in seed pearls. Parasols to match every dress, enormous flopping feather hats assorted to every costume. White gloves to the elbow, three or four new pairs every day, priceless lace ruffles at throat and wrists, yards of lace flouncing on under-skirts, thousands of dollars worth dragged over the Casino terrace. Different dresses for each occasion, eighty or ninety in a season, worn once or twice and put aside.[16]

Time spent in resort towns like Newport, Bar Harbor, or Lenox served to consolidate social life. These resort towns also led to a greater fusion of old and new money. Even a girl with an astonishingly vulgar family didn't need to go to Europe to buy herself acceptance. The international aristocracy that titled marriages helped to form created a more modern society, one based on shared financial status and lifestyle choices, and cemented by the participation in a regular social circuit. Parents could choose to hold their daughters' debuts in the regions that suited them best. When debutantes from different cities met each other, they formed relationships, then later visited each other. They brought their daughters out together, creating intergenerational relationships that bolstered a more uniform class identity.

In England, the death of Edward VII in 1910 ushered in a new era of decorum, which furthered the similarity between American and British values. King George V, now ruling, resembled his grandmother Victoria in favoring bourgeois neatness over aristocratic indulgences. Unlike his father, Edward VII, George was not a sensualist and his wife, Mary of Teck, was famously regal and stiff. Their son Edward VIII's abdication, to marry American divorcée and former Baltimore debutante Wallis Simpson, called the monarchy itself into question. When Edward's younger brother, Albert, Duke of York, reluctantly took the throne as George VI in 1936, his wife, the former Elizabeth Bowes-Lyon, was the first queen not born of royal blood since Henry VIII married Anne Boleyn. In Elizabeth, a low-key country girl who favored riding and other country pursuits, English debutantes had their first queen who was truly like them.

In the United States, the debut continued but entered into a period of confusion, wherein all the different types of ritual were happening at the same time, with each faction asserting its superiority. In 1900, the *New York Times* published a piece that spoke to that confusion.

> The Assembly Ball is now the sole relic of the departed days of the New York society—the one and only general ball where the various leading sets meet on the same floor and in the same social atmosphere. The question of abandoning them was seriously discussed two years ago, but so many were the protests received that it was determined to continue them, and last season's balls were so successful that they have taken on a new lease of life and may now be continued indefinitely. New York, with its changing social conditions and its multiplicity of sets, finds it more difficult to maintain and keep alive a series of subscription balls than do smaller communities. The oldest and really most aristocratic subscription balls of the country are those of the St. Cecilia Society of Charleston, SC. Second only to the St Cecilia in age and prestige are the famous Assembly Balls of Philadelphia.[17]

Still, some old New York families persisted in launching their daughters in the old way. When a debutante outlived her place in society, it sometimes resulted in tragedy—Lily Bart, Wharton's heroine in *The House of Mirth*, is a ready example. But there were glamour-free Lily Barts, too, young women who did not quite make it to marriage before their fortunes changed. Though she danced in the same ballrooms as Jennie Jerome and Consuelo Vanderbilt, nobody remembers Pauline Robinson, whose story is a perfect cautionary tale.

Pauline Robinson's family made their money in real estate, holdings that they later reinforced with modest but strategic early investments in railroads. Pauline was a member of older, established New York society, a group of families with names now recognizable mostly because they remain on street signs. Pauline made her debut at age eighteen at the winter Patriarch's Ball in 1899 and kept six years of debutante scrapbooks.[18] It was common for debutantes to keep records of their seasons, but it was not common to have so many of them—because the girls usually married after one or two years. Pauline's problematic six are a meticulous account of New York society at the turn of the twentieth century. Large and dark-haired with heavy features, by modern standards Pauline was not a beauty, but her pale skin and dark, hooded eyes were not so far removed from the Gibson Girl ideal. Pauline Robinson was a dutiful cog in a machine that was slowly disintegrating around her.

Pauline described every dinner she attended, saving calling cards and invitations, press clippings about parties and ticket stubs from plays and concerts. She wrote down the name and seating plans for pre-ball dinners. She recorded the names of the patronesses of each ball, made notes of each manager, but never shared her own opinion. In the world Pauline lived in, a name communicated everything anyone needed to know. She was expressing her opinion just by making a list. Pauline was the embodiment of what a New York debutante should be. Precise, compliant, predictable, and demure, she edited her scrapbooks to the point of curation, carefully removing any trace of personality until she perfectly embodied a cultural ideal.

Pauline attended forty-nine parties between January 1 and February 27, 1900. She made five trips to the theater and, in that entire time, sent only five regrets, a testament to the importance of constantly being present, particularly for a young woman who would not make any stir on her own. Her social schedule was grueling, with numerous events on nearly every evening. On a typical night she would dress with the help of a lady's maid into a long, pale gown. She would make her way to dinner at around 8 p.m. During the debutante season, the hosts were often the only married couple in attendance, presiding over a party of twelve diners, composed of a mixture of debutantes and single men. Similar dinners happened all over town and would precede a ball held at Sherry's, a hotel similar to the Delmonico, where social mixing took place. In the later part of her second-year debutante scrapbook, one sees that Pauline started attending weddings, including some major ones like the marriage of J. P. Morgan's daughter. She herself appears at the edge of photos of Vanderbilt descendants at Shelburne Farms, in Vermont, and with Marshall Field's daughters on Jekyll Island. She continued to attend debuts and parties for several years, and she continued to appear in photos, but she never married. Her family's money dried up by the First World War after some bad investments. She could not marry down without degrading the family name, so she did what Lily Bart could not bear to—she supported herself by teaching fine needlework, and died after the Second World War, a sewing instructor.

The closed world of Edith Wharton novels was changing rapidly. By the early twentieth century, a society once led by aristocrats had definitively fractured into several smaller groups with differing, though sometimes overlapping, values. There was a group of families that resembled an aristocracy, who espoused privacy, attended private school, and made debuts together, but did not seek out publicity. Then there was something that resembled what we might consider society today. Its members might have some connection to the prior group, but they cultivated publicity. The people organizing these debutante presentations tended to court the press, but they did so behind the scenes, and the families knew to feign horror when the press showed up outside of events. Then there were the celebrities, and the people who were able to comingle with them because of their great success in business, sport, or the arts. These people did not yet have a debutante ritual, though soon their daughters would be sought after as debutantes. Traditional aristocratic values continued to hold some shabby glamour (especially for traditional aristocrats), and those values were invoked at key cultural or personal moments, to bolster one's status, or keep another person at bay. Aristocratic values continued to hold a kind of glamour—an amorphous, unimpeachable authority—and were occasionally trotted out by people like the British writer Nancy Mitford, in her still-discussed essay on class difference in linguistic usage, in which she divided common words into the categories U and non-U (upper class and non-upper class) and set off a feverish discussion about usage and bias in English society. Occasional eruptions of this sort of class-consciousness became less frequent as time passed, and the social authority of power individuals waned.

There were no more Mrs. Astors. The great age of the arbiter in her style or Ward McAllister's style had ended. The sheer force of will required, the mix of wealth, family, social ambition, fearless aggressiveness, and inside social information, research and originality, as well as the wise manipulation of publicity, was replaced by an organized social structure that in many ways had been created by Astor and McAllister but eventually devoured them whole. This structure followed the basic rhythms arbiters had championed. The system they created was replicable in every town, with smaller debutante systems paying homage to the prestigious one in New York. Many little fiefdoms fanned out, governed by now-nameless dowagers with no less sway in their area than

Mrs. Astor, who made their small regional changes—changing punch to champagne and back again—but still acted as madams to get their girls married.

Observers would say that the final end of the old ways was World War I, which fractured traditional British aristocratic social structure not only because of the unrelenting death of young, marriageable men, but also because it was almost impossible to serve on the front with another man, facing death together, only to return and ask them to work in service. In this period, British aristocrats realized they could no longer afford to keep their estates and servants, if even available, nor the cost of modernizing. Formerly grand families skulked off to country cottages, selling their belongings to millionaires. Large-scale private events, like those held in Mrs. Astor's ballroom, vanished. Developers knocked down mansions and built large apartment buildings. The new rich did not entertain at home as often in their smaller apartments, but rather traveled with trunks filled with the items they needed. Families with fortunes made in railroads, gold mining, shipping, and telegraph lines, which seemed parvenu to the elite of the 1880s, were now written about in the press with the "immemorial dignity of the real estate and China trade of the 1830s." With the faster pace, and less centralized social structure, fewer people paid heed to the queenly women who had been leaders of society in the Gilded Age. If one was tyrannical, you could escape her tyranny by going to coastal France. Some of these women outlived the society that created and supported them. Alice Gwynne Vanderbilt, widow of Commodore Vanderbilt's grandson, was still ensconced at the Breakers, entertaining smaller and smaller groups of elderly women until her death, at eighty-nine, in the 1930s.[19] Once known simply as "the Mrs. Vanderbilt," the Depression era press called her "the loneliest figure in American society," although it is doubtful she knew that anyone viewed her this way.

CHAPTER 6

The Bright Young People

AN OLD RITUAL AT THE DAWN OF THE MODERN

World War I did away with the last vestiges of Victorian aristocratic culture, though social changes are always felt in waves by the people who are living through them. Those born in the early part of the nineteenth century still lived on as family elders, and in their bearing contained the beliefs and feeling of people raised in simpler and slower times. From 1809 to 1879, 88 percent of British millionaires were from the landowning class. That figure dropped to 33 percent between 1880–1914. Industrialists, many of them from overseas, displaced the aristocracy by buying their estates, often including their furniture, libraries, jewelry and pictures. Much of the aristocracy decamped for London, which changed their social lives and activities.

Dramatic cultural shifts like these first become evident in the raising of daughters. As their families' most valuable commodities, daughters were vessels for the expectations of generations and were obliged to elegantly carry forth the culture's shifting manners while still holding families together during unstable periods. The debutante ritual had always functioned by screening the manners of newcomers to see if they were able to follow their money into an extant upper class. In the 1920s, the British aristocracy was forced to face that they were no longer able to keep control over their own ritual, or at least not one with any of the grandeur they were used to. The war had decimated both the servant class and a large percentage of aristocratic young men. Many debutantes had lost at least one brother, and it was not unusual for a family to have lost more than one. Without men to seek out for marriage, the old definition of a debutante began to collapse. The ritual rapidly began to morph into something that looked very different than it had before the war.

Debutante presentations stopped during the war and resumed in 1921. The upper classes tried to maintain some of the spectacle. Lady Airlie, one of Queen Mary's ladies-in-waiting, described the debutantes as "a heterogeneous crowd of all ages, some straight out of the schoolroom, others weather-beaten from years of driving ambulances in France."[1] The upper classes soon tried to repurpose society to reflect nostalgic fantasy and emphasize their financial role in bolstering all classes of British society. One aristocratic woman held that the war heralded a rebirth of the season:

> The season, as part of our national fabric, was refurnished and reborn . . . the English set out to stabilize their national currency, which consists not only of gilt edged securities but the social system which radiates from their monarchy . . . So when Parliament is sitting, the opera in full swing, the world entertaining the great world, the season is of importance not only as the axis of our social stability but as the basis of trade prosperity . . . The season is the property of the nation and for that reason, because it is the barometer of prosperity—more than from any social distinction it confers—the world holds on gallantly though purses are slender, taxes high, and estates a burden. The people must live, the shops must sell, the shops must buy, produce and manufacture, and unemployment must be narrowed down.[2]

In truth, very little trickled down to the masses, and even less money circulated out of London. While the rituals of monarchy and aristocracy would fuel tourism later in the century, travel was not yet common and was not yet a factor in economic life in Britain.

In the early 1920s, most debutantes, who came out at private balls, alone or together, still came from upper-class landowning families, some of whom had economized or set aside money for a debut. Writer Nancy Mitford and her sisters were presented at great cost to their parents, who were barely holding on to their vast but ill-managed and low-yielding estates. Elizabeth Ponsonby was presented to the queen in 1925. Her father, Sir Arthur Ponsonby, had been Queen Victoria's private secretary and was later the Secretary of State for Foreign Affairs, and her mother the daughter of a lord. Despite this background, her father's letters during the 1920s are riddled with financial worries.[3] Parents' efforts to present their daughters despite the expense speaks to how significant the ritual still was as a status marker. A formal presentation remained the best way to maintain social relevance because the ritual retained its ties to money and status.

Aristocratic families also may have wanted to continue the season because they felt a new urgency about their own decreasing clout. In the postwar years, more titled families had lost their wealth than ever before in English history. Many had fallen into genteel poverty. While their need for money bumped up against their belief that most work was vulgar, maintaining social status was the impetus for the upper-class belief that the season was a patriotic necessity worthy of financial and social sacrifice to provide the ritual for this new generation. It inspired a variety of social sacrifices, in their view at least, including, inviting men from a wider range of backgrounds to their daughters' debutante parties.

Daughters who inherited their parents' generation's sentiment also invested the debutante ritual with hallowed meaning. One former debutante admitted that, although she occasionally questioned a system which made a business out of the pleasure exercised in a continual round of balls, jaunts, hunting, and country-house visits, she, at eighteen, considered it important. "By just dancing myself dizzy, looking as nice as

I could, or exploring myself anew through some fresh pair of eyes, I felt I was furthering some momentous, indeed some almost devout purpose."[4] For her parents, she was.

There was little time, money, or need for young women to be in London before their debutante season, and many British debutantes departed for London directly from their countryside schoolrooms. British parents often continued the practice of not fully educating their daughters. Nancy Mitford, who came out at a ball in November, 1922, and was presented at court the following June, wrote extensively about how little she and her sisters knew of basic academic facts. Their educations were tended to by a parade of governesses, with their mother filling in between their tutors' comings and goings. The Mitfords learned arithmetic, French, and reading, but not much else. This was not an unfamiliar model for many aristocratic families, who felt that daughters should not be too clever lest it herald curiosity and the problems that creates. What daughters needed was a social education, which they had already attained to some extent just by living on a country estate and absorbing the manners of family and friends.

Debutantes who were more educated also found that an education was not an asset in the marriage market. Mary Pakenham, the daughter of the Earl of Longford, was raised in a similar fashion to the Mitfords, but had a governess who had higher standards, and who successfully gave her a better education. After their instruction at home was deemed finished, Mary and her sister Pansy were dispatched to a school where they thought they would continue their studies. The Pakenhams learned when they arrived that they were only expected to stay one semester so as to improve their social graces before moving to London in 1926 for their debutante season. In her memoir, *Brought Up and Brought Out*, Mary Pakenham wrote that "for years French and Latin and Italian and Euclid and Algebra and History and the rest had been thrust at me, and I had never known them well enough. And now suddenly I found I knew them much too well." She explained that she was expected to be completely ignorant, recounting that when she was able to fool an eldest son of an aristocrat into thinking she was unread, she won praise from him. "Why you're not at all what I thought!" he said. "I thought you were the sort of person who read books!"[5]

Pakenham described the experience of arriving in London without the required sophistication as the most mystifying period of her life, writing: "I do not think that at any period I was so completely at a loss as to what was going on around me, and what was expected of me, as at the time when I was a debutante." She was shocked to find out that she was "expected to remain in complete idleness from breakfast until it was time to go out to dinner." She had been to the rare countryside dance in childhood but was slow to understand the idea that going to ballrooms was now her work. She compared herself to a shift-worker, and described coming home exhausted from a late night working (at finding a husband).

Pakenham includes that it was important for all debutantes to retain the dowdiness of the countryside lest they be viewed as "unpresentably fast." Until the late twenties, British debutantes took care to remain out of the press. And, she wrote "it was considered dubious, if not positively vulgar, to allow a studio portrait of oneself in an illustrated weekly." Still, she noted, girls slyly made an effort to casually pass in front of photographers at events—and if he found out a girl's name from a friend, "well, one couldn't prevent that." Debutantes like Pakenham were acutely aware of how their dresses contrasted with the chic, loose, and fashionable dresses of their more liberated peers. "Fashions did not help us," she wrote. "Slimness was all the rage—bad news for an 18 year old with an unformed figure." Their evening dresses were generally made of unforgiving georgette with very tight skirts, unflattering to girls who had not yet shed their childish softness. They "were all cut the same, with a high-ish back and front like an old fashioned sleeveless vest." Debutantes did not wear lipstick, especially not the vampy shades that were fashionable. They fashioned eye kohl and brow powder by rubbing their fingers along the grates of fireplaces. They pinched their lips and cheeks to put color in their faces.

In previous centuries, mothers would either accompany their daughters to London, or send them to trusted family members who acted as chaperones. By the twentieth century, these codes had relaxed. Though debutantes would live with family until they were out, they traveled together to and from parties, where there were far fewer chaperones in attendance. About six weeks before a ball, the debutante and her mother would receive word from another mother who was bringing a daughter out. "I hear you have another daughter out . . . I will take the greatest care of her." Under the other mother's care, the debutante would then attend a ball at the house of someone she might not know personally. If she were in London, or at a neighboring house in the country, she could make a short trip. If she were farther away, she might stay for several days for what was known as a house party, when there would be other guests for the several days surrounding a ball, or larger party.

The hostess often wore a dress that was likely in style at the time of her own coming out. She wore long white gloves, sometimes carried a big fan and had a tiara perched on "elaborately coiffed but already falling down grey hair." Pakenham describes the main participants as stock characters in a familiar play. "There was generally a rather sheepish daughter pretending that the party was nothing to do with her, just a harmless whim of her mother's, and a son who arrived very late with his hair on end, and a father who would have liked to have been jovial if he had dared."

When a dinner preceded a ball, men waited in the hallway and were handed a ticket that would tell them who they were meant to take down to dinner. Girls were not told in advance who their escorts were. The dining rooms were L-shaped and decorated with maidenhair ferns and roses or carnations. The same band played and the same announcer was at the door, the caterer was the same and their plates the same. As in prior generations, worry over not being asked to dance led debutantes

to work hard toward getting married. One expressed the stress suc-
cinctly—"It's bad enough to be put up for auction, but to be put off for
auction and find no takers . . ." She did not need to finish her thought.

Debutantes did not have to be presented at court to participate in
a season, but for those who did participate, it was her season's most
important event. The only real change for court presentation was in the
debutantes' dresses, which did evolve with the times. By the twenties,
most debutantes wore looser, drop-waisted dresses with some beading, a longer and more demure version of the flapper style of the 1920s.
The dresses were still pale, white or pastel. The obligation to wear three
white feathers attached to a mid-length veil, to carry a small bouquet,
and to perform the curtsy remained, along with all traditional rules of
protocol, the same. One major innovation was that debutantes arrived
in cars rather than carriages, though they were still escorted by their
fathers, who would wear court clothing that reflected their station.

Most of all, the formula of the season ensured that participants learned
their roles. Sameness provided arbiters with a standard for assessment,
allowing them to pronounce behavior correct or incorrect based on a
known standard. The survival of a ritual depends as much on the slight
deviations that can be critiqued as much as on perfect repetition. Aristocrats who once freely spent their money without fear of bankruptcy
now began to value discretion because they were not financially sound
enough to value the accumulation of beautiful, useless things. They
barely had enough money to hang onto them. People tried to keep up
the appearance of having much money for as long as they could. Postwar financial instability led to a series of economic tremors that changed
the debutante ritual. After one market downturn, cocktail parties, formerly attended only by Bohemians, and strictly forbidden to debutantes,
became common among everyone, even older women, simply because
they were inexpensive to host. Chaperoning, too, went out of style, as
society became more casual and free, and debutantes were allowed to
travel by themselves through a wider swath of London. Pakenham writes

that because of the economic uncertainty "mothers told their daughters to have as good a time as they could before the big crash came."

When status outlasts money, parents make unusual decisions. They began to allow their daughters more freedom after their first debutante season was over. Pakenham's younger sister Pansy Pakenham and her friend Evelyn Gardner (later Evelyn Waugh's first wife—yes, Evelyn and Evelyn), were allowed to share a flat and work in dress shops after their debutante season. They mostly modeled the clothes, which was considered sufficiently ornamental to remain within the bounds of propriety. The debutante world began to bleed into artistic and literary London, creating the hybrid world of the Bright Young People, a term coined by the tabloid press for a diffuse group of aristocrats and socialites who went back and forth between their aristocratic drawing rooms and permissive, bohemian London. At night they threw costume parties, danced at clubs, smoked cigarettes, took cocaine, and drank until passing out, sometimes in the street. The Bright Young People whom Waugh characterized in his novels would have been of less interest to the tabloid press if their ranks didn't also include aristocratic daughters and sons who created a dramatic frisson for the public by flouting the behavior they learned as children. In the eclectic world of the Bright Young People, the worlds of debutantes, socialites, and celebrities began to fuse.

A parallel transformation was taking place in the United States. When the United States entered the war in 1917, a generation of American women went to work, and many didn't want to leave their livelihoods when the war ended. Even if they had wanted to leave the workforce to get married, the war and the flu pandemic that followed it killed almost an entire generation of young men, leaving young women without husbands and with companies in need of workers. The mechanization and automation of killing ended an insular naiveté in the United States, which resumed a policy of isolationism, leaving in its wake a sense that life was so fleeting that many reacted by trying to enjoy it before it passed. The aftermath of war also left a smoldering feminism, abetted by the freedom to vote, which women received the year after the war ended, after eighty years of struggle. Both women and men had better educational opportunities, and that created a larger and more powerful middle class. Changes in divorce laws allowed women to leave their marriages with at least some of their property, which further collapsed the necessity of staying in a marriage, and allowed women to leave desperate situations in which they previously would have remained trapped. Prohibition further liberated women by allowing them to drink in speakeasies with men. Before this period, women would not have been able to be in bars, alone or with friends, without losing their reputations. Now nobody could talk about it without getting in trouble themselves.

In this period, the model for ideal womanhood changed drastically. The Gibson Girl's voluptuous respectability was replaced by the boyish and wiry "flapper," whose short dresses and bobbed hair embodied frantic youth, and made her seem feral to an older, quieter generation. Still, Fitzgerald's definition of a flapper could equally be applied to the debutante: "Lovely, expensive and about nineteen."

Most cities had groups of flapper-debutantes. In Chicago, they were known as "The Four," a name this media-savvy quartet had given itself. The group traveled in a pack, and its members included Ginevra King, F. Scott Fitzgerald's first love, later the model for Daisy Buchanan, and Edith Cummings, an heiress and the greatest golfer of her day. Their fathers had grown rich in the Midwest boom years that followed the Civil War. They made their debuts in massive, recently built Lake Forest mansions. They were debutantes, still, but a new variety.

In a 1925 article in *The New Yorker*, communications and mining heiress Ellin Mackay wrote, "the game has lost its savor; there is no longer the same breathless interest in which a young lady will be fortunate enough to secure for herself the particular matrimonial prize that is at large." Mackay had come out just over a year before she wrote her article, and her debut was not low-key. Her father scheduled her party for December 23, at the tail end of the debutante season, a day you would choose only if you knew you had great social power, and threw her the largest and most expensive ball of the 1922–23 social season. It would have been inconceivable for a debutante to write a piece in any paper or magazine in the previous generation, particularly one that picked apart her own world, but Ellin was an atypical debutante.

Ellin's father was the chairman of the Postal Telegraph and Cable Corporation, founded by his father, and also the heir to her father's huge mining concern. Ellin's grandfather, John William Mackay, had emigrated from Ireland to work in the California silver and gold mines that were collectively known as the Comstock Lode. He and three of his fellow Irishmen formed a partnership and, in 1873, they hit the largest silver ore deposit yet discovered, known as "the big bonanza," which made them incomprehensibly rich. Ellin's father was born a year later. Like the Jeromes, John William Mackay and his wife Louise, newly rich and Catholic, were shunned by New York society. John Mackay chose the same solution as Leonard Jerome—he bought his wife a mansion in Paris. She lived there with their children, entertaining French aristocrats, glamorous expatriates, and social leaders, while he remained in the United States diversifying his businesses by building some of the first transatlantic cables and becoming one of the first telegraph moguls. Ellin's father, Clarence, was brought up between Paris and New York and met her mother, former debutante and socialite Katherine Duer, on a transatlantic steamship crossing in 1897.

Katherine Duer was a member of the same old New York family as Lady Kitty Duer, who had introduced the Trumbull girls to New York society in 1801. The couple married in 1898. Mackay's parents gave them Harbor Hill, an enormous Long Island estate designed by Stanford White, as a wedding present. The two settled into their house. Katherine, an early and ardent suffragist and passionate advocate of public schooling, became the first woman to sit on a local school board.

Clarence and Katherine had three children as well as a difficult marriage. When he became ill with cancer, Katherine fell in love with the doctor who was treating him and left him and their three children for the doctor. The court formally awarded custody of the children to Clarence, and Ellin rarely saw her mother, who had moved to Paris.

The Mackay family was one of the richest in the United States by the time it came for Ellin to make her debut. The debutante ritual is typically overseen by mothers, grandmothers, and aunts, but when the newspapers announced Ellin's, only her father's name appeared. Held at the Ritz-Carlton in New York, Ellin curtsied in front of one thousand guests, including fellow tycoons John D. Rockefeller, Harry Payne Whitney, Marshall Field, and numerous members of the Pulitzer, Astor, and Havemeyer families. The *New York Times* wrote that the ballroom was designed to give the effect of a California garden, like her grandparents would have had in mining days, with white oleander, orange trees, and garlands of bay branches.

Mackay began to write for *The New Yorker* shortly after her debut—she produced columns that shocked both the public and her editors, but sold magazines and made her a sensation within her social circle. Her friends dismissed her pieces as "saucy but amusing." She defended her generation's abandonment of the Junior League and "polite society" for dancing the Charleston. "It is not because fashionable young ladies are picturesquely depraved that they go to cabarets," she wrote. "They go to find privacy." Privacy was unimaginable for young women before the 1920s, but now they could hide among paying guests in a crowded club. But Mackay, perhaps channeling the experience of her mother's unconventional departure, looked at herself and her contemporaries as fully modern, noting: "Modern girls are . . . not so keenly aware, as were their parents, of the vast difference between a brilliant match and a mésalliance."

In 1926, Mackay made good on her desire for a freer life, ignoring her billionaire-father's objections and marrying the composer Irving Berlin, a Russian-American Jew fifteen years her senior. Her decision to marry

Berlin was made easier by the fact that he was a wealthy man at the height of his fame. Her father disowned her, and the two did not speak for five years. There was room in her marriage for her writing—Mackay had a column in *The Saturday Evening Post* and published three novels and several story collections. The marriage lasted sixty-two years, until her death in 1988.

For every happy ending like Mackay and Berlin's, there were others that were more complicated. Zelda Sayre, the daughter of a prominent judge and his socialite wife, was an accomplished dancer with no care for gender convention, regularly dressing like a boy, drinking, smoking, and keeping whatever hours she pleased. Instead of trying to control Zelda, which would have been pointless, her family watched her warily. When, as a debutante, she met the socially undistinguished F. Scott Fitzgerald at a country club dance in Montgomery, her family urged her to stay away from him. Fitzgerald, stationed there with the US Army, was freshly bruised by his girlfriend Ginevra King's rejection. He became enamored of Zelda and proposed to her. She rejected him at first because, unconventionality notwithstanding, she thought he was beneath her. They were soon separated by the war. When they reunited in New York, and he achieved success with *This Side of Paradise*, she relented and married him. Zelda and Scott's tumultuous and sometimes violent relationship, with its alcohol and drug abuse, itinerancy, and creative fire, has since embodied both the dynamism and darkness of the Jazz Age. Zelda and Ellin were transitional figures, debutantes who benefited from their social status but for whom convention was too stifling. Though they both held the interest of the press, neither wanted celebrity for its own sake. They were unusual in this regard.

The infusion of celebrity into the upper reaches of society began with the flappers and bright young things who created a bridge between society and bohemia. During the height of the Great Depression this relationship solidified, and the adventures of a series of debutantes, who mingled with artists and musicians, provided the American public with both a much-needed frisson and a reliable source for moral outrage. Debutante parties reached their zenith in this period, when the traditional coming of age ritual gelled with modern mass culture. Because the press published photos and stories in national newspapers, young women began believing that becoming a debutante was a good way to become a celebrity and reap all the benefits of that status. Fame might have retained a whiff of vulgarity—the upper classes always maintained barriers by defining and rejecting vulgarity. But if a debutante became famous by happenstance, while participating in an enduring rite of passage required of women of her background, she could enjoy its rewards while maintaining that it wasn't intentional. For upper-class women, avoiding being seen as the ones who called attention to themselves was important and a "who me?" performance was a common way to feign a lack of ambition. Fame was immense and tempting, could promise financial independence, bolster self-esteem, and provide a kind of career for both debutantes and their ambitious mothers as well. Debutantes were perfectly suited to walking the thin line between manners and ambition.

The debutante ritual continued in its traditional manner within the social life of cities like Charleston, New Orleans, and St. Louis, where the same white families maintained power through intermarriage and had fewer meritocratic challengers. But in New York, the debutante ritual began to lose its traditional utility to meet spouses. An editorial that ran in *Fortune* in 1938 put it plainly:

> From the society into which a New York girl makes her debut today, adults and especially men—marriageable or otherwise—have almost completely disappeared. So have they in Boston, where debutantes are now presented to the Harvard undergraduate body, minus freshmen. They have disappeared because the social game costs time and money. It flourishes where there is most leisure for caste and least pressure for cash. Which means the social game is possible for men in Charleston, say, but a hardship for harried New Yorkers.[6]

College began to replace a social season as an intermediary step between childhood and adulthood. By the 1930s, between 10–15 percent of upper- and middle-class women went to college, a possibility that barely existed in the nineteenth century. According to one survey completed in the 1930s, only 30 percent of the season's debutantes married within a year of their debut, and about 20 percent in the following year. If debutantes weren't using the ritual to find husbands, what were they using it for?

CHAPTER 7

Café Society, Celebrity, and Conformity

1930s–1980s

Against the backdrop of widespread financial struggle of the Great Depression, the sagas of heiresses like Barbara Woolworth Hutton and Brenda Frazier were especially enticing. The press followed the richest debutantes hungrily and regularly reported their smallest activities. During the height of the 1938 debutante season, December 16, 1937–January 7, 1938, *Fortune* estimated that the average New York debutante "danced for 140 hours, or seventy miles. She ate eighteen plates of scrambled eggs and bacon, drank twelve quarts of champagne and sat through twenty hours of beauty treatments."[1] Other magazines upped their coverage of debutantes. While *Vogue* and *Town and Country* had been covering high society for years, their subscription base had always skewed toward the knowing insider, with a smattering of truly ambitious outsiders reading to learn all they could. *Life* was more openly populist, but after *Time* owner Henry Luce bought it in 1936, the magazine began to feature debutantes, not only because covering them made for better sales, but because Luce himself was debutante-obsessed. In the first year of *Life*, he hired debutantes for his office staff, an aesthetic and social choice, which apparently didn't work out well. Snide contemporaries said that the girls were always losing memos, and didn't know they had to come in every day. Whether this was true or just mean gossip was not clear.

Life Magazine covered its first of many debutante parties in 1937, by sending a reporter to Philadelphia to cover the presentation of one of the Widener daughters. The Wideners were a Main-Line Philadelphia family who made their fortune selling meat to the Union Army, and added to it with investments in both U.S. Steel and Standard Oil. That the Wideners allowed *Life* to attend their ball is significant, and indicative of the old guard's changing view of press coverage.

Like the Wideners, most of the older society was opening its parties to the press, either buckling to the pressure, as they would have it believed, or competitively crossing a threshold as standards changed and threatened to exclude them. But unless they had spent time studying arcane specifics, average people did not have a definition of the "old society" that would have pleased any of its members, even if it did include a few debutantes. If asked, they were likely to name a member of what was known as "café society," a group that flourished in the post-prohibition years when one no longer had to do one's drinking in secret. This group of international pleasure seekers congregated together at various balls, charity events, and at a set of restaurants (The Stork Club, El Morocco) where the press would wait to photograph them. Café society included everyone from Hollywood actors, singers, to minor royalty, its spirit well-embodied in the marriage of the actress Rita Hayworth to Prince Aly Khan, the socialite son of Sultan Muhammad Shah Aga Khan, spiritual leader of a breakaway sect of Shiite Muslims. The term was coined by the writer Lucius Beebe, who followed their doings in his column "This is New York" in the *New York Herald Tribune*. Café society sold newspapers in a way traditional society never did, and the celebrity debutante became a key figure in this this press-friendly group. Brenda Frazier, "deb of the decade," and the first celebrity debutante, was their queen.

Without Brenda Frazier, neither Paris Hilton nor Kim Kardashian would exist. Frazier was the first "celebutante." Walter Winchell, an early and powerful gossip columnist, invented the word for her, meaning a person who achieved fame with no talent to speak of apart from a willingness to do and spend anything for publicity. Frazier was a national sensation as much as Hilton was in the 2000s or Kardashian is now, and her exploits were every bit as scandalous then as any "accidentally" released sex tape. Brenda Diana Duff Frazier was a Canadian-American heiress to grain and banking fortunes. Her mother, who had named her daughter after herself, was the daughter of a minor British peer who had friends within the British royal family. Her grandfather, Sir Frederick Williams-Taylor, had cornered the wheat market in the late nineteenth century and had been knighted for his contribution to Anglo-Canadian trade. Her father, Frank Duff Frazier, was from a wealthy family in Boston and had a drinking problem and a penchant for actresses and "tarts," though "only nice tarts, ones who aren't lewd at all," he once wrote. Brenda's maternal grandfather was so horrified at the social careerism and irresponsibility of her parents that he created a trust for Brenda, the principal of which her parents could not access except to support her. The Fraziers' marriage was instantly miserable, and the terms of the trust led to a long custody battle that was presided over by the same judge who presided over the case of Gloria Vanderbilt, another heiress viewed in the press as a poor little rich girl.

Brenda's mother was socially ambitious. It was too late for her to shine so she trained her focus on her daughter. Once awarded custody, she began to dress her daughter in heavy makeup and furs despite her daughter being just twelve. At thirteen, Brenda regularly stayed out all night waltzing at the St. Regis. She was a chain-smoking, hard-drinking little girl dressed in floor-length chiffon and masses of jewelry. Her mother also insisted that Brenda be presented as a debutante at court when she was just fourteen, two years younger than the very youngest British debutantes. Brenda had dramatic dark hair showing off her widow's peak, white skin, and soft, womanly features that set her apart from the icy blonde vogue of postwar beauties like Marlene Dietrich and

Greta Garbo. Men found her warm and appealing, disturbingly so, even at fourteen years old.[2] Photographs of her at the time recall the unsettling photos of contestants in little girls' beauty pageants.

After her English debut, Brenda returned to the States and entered Miss Porter's, in Farmington, Connecticut, which was then a girls' finishing school and allowed students to leave at any time for social engagements. Very few girls studied or earned diplomas, and few graduated. Instead they just departed when their parents deemed they were ready to move on socially. Brenda then spent a year in Munich, where noblewomen impoverished by the First World War and Weimar inflation had opened their homes to elite foreigners so the girls could get some international polish. While her daughter was in Europe, Brenda Sr. was already feverishly planning her daughter's huge coming-out ball. Brenda, who liked the freedom she had in Munich, was reluctant to return. When she objected to a large ball, her mother, unmoved, replied: "You'll be very sorry if you don't have a debut. You'll be much happier if you do." When she returned to the United States, Brenda was, at the behest of her mother, increasingly social. She attended charity lunches and teas during the day and parties at night until she collapsed from illness or exhaustion. She was also getting reams of publicity, much of it bad. Brenda began to appear in ads, with the idea that it made her appear like a real working woman. She endorsed department stores, soaps, perfumes, and even appeared in a Studebaker ad, even though she didn't know how to drive (her family had a driver). This, of course, only led to greater backlash for Brenda, and more publicity for the brand.

Brenda's mother, like most people with social aspirations, pretended to hate the publicity, but actively encouraged photographers, columnists, and other interested parties from behind the scene. In just a few months, the clipping agency Brenda's mother hired sent her 5,000 articles mentioning Brenda from papers all over the world. The more publicity Brenda received, the less likely it was that she'd have any part in the more establishment debutante presentations. When she applied to one debutante ball, the Junior Assemblies, where the old New York families present their daughters (still), they rejected her. The Debutante Cotillion and Christmas Ball, known as "the Infirmary," after the charity it benefited—the New York Infirmary—was slightly less difficult to get into. Founded in 1933, it is one of the older New York balls still in existence. Much like Hilton, who skipped right over old guard debutante presentations, her limited options for a group presentation were of little concern to Brenda.

Society reporters blamed her rejections on a particular incident wherein Brenda was photographed dunking a doughnut into her coffee, an inelegant move that shocked the women of Manhattan's old guard. The ever-eager doughnut industry seized on the photo for an ad, which ran nationally. Shell Oil ran an ad, too, also using Brenda's image, saying that only machines oiled with Shell produced doughnut-dunking as skilled as Brenda's. Even etiquette expert Emily Post weighed in pronouncing Brenda Frazier's doughnut-dunking entirely correct, but it didn't help her already publicity-tarnished image. But even this doughnut-dunk was a simulacrum—Claudette Colbert had already done it in the screwball classic *It Happened One Night*. She played spoiled heiress Ellie Andrew, who broke her hunger strike by dunking a doughnut in coffee.

Much of the establishment remained elusive for Brenda—one polo-playing Vanderbilt remembered that many families wouldn't let their children attend Brenda's party because she was nouveau riche, and a particularly fast kind of nouveau riche. When he asked his friends if they were going, they'd say "well, the foods going to be good, it's going to be a great party, but daddy doesn't want me to go." Brenda's mother cleverly scheduled her debut to begin at 11:30 p.m. so it wouldn't compete with the earlier, and more staid, presentations of other debutantes with more traditional social connections. Even her father worked with his ex-wife on the ball. Frazier rented out rooms at the Ritz for tired guests with the provision that they could bring their servants to mend broken buttons and hems and help serve food. Brenda, meanwhile, was violently ill with the flu, and skipped multiple dinners in her honor to stay in bed until the last minute, wearing even more makeup than usual to hide the fact that she was sick.

Two thousand people came to Brenda's debut, including denizens of both old and café society. The presence of Condé Nast and Henry Luce spoke to the power of debutante parties to generate press. Actor Douglas Fairbanks Jr., heiress Doris Duke, and scads of Vanderbilts and Rothschilds all attended the party. There were also several crashers, including a young female reporter from a Brooklyn paper who sneaked in and briefly became a celebrity herself, giving numerous interviews about what it was like inside Brenda's party. Brenda wrote later that the party was a misery for her, but she put on a good show. Newspaper accounts didn't mention her illness, only that she danced beautifully with many admirers.

Brenda's party did not have a theme like many of the others in that period of time, but it did overflow with flowers. Brenda wore a white silk strapless princess dress made by Bendel's, then an elite store that specialized in women's dresses. She carried a spray of orchids in the style of a bridal bouquet. Brenda's mother violated long-established etiquette that held that one never wore a tiara inside a hotel, and she wore not only the tiara but many strands of pearls. Not wanting to let down the hungry tabloid press, Brenda Sr. had requested that all the women invited to the party wear their most impressive jewelry. She also leaked that the ball cost $100,000 instead of the $20,000 it did cost. The party was a success, and was written up in national and international papers. Brenda was, at last, formally presented to society, and the *San Francisco Chronicle* expressed what many probably felt in a banner headline "BRENDA IS FINALLY OUT, NOW WE CAN ALL RELAX."

In the aftermath of Brenda's debutante ball, the various agents of the remaining old society began a process of retrenchment. Brenda and her ilk were too vulgar. Much like Ward McAllister and Mrs. Astor had wanted to keep out the new rich (who had now become the old rich), established WASP mothers wanted to remove the Brenda Fraziers of the city and restore some dignity and control over their own time-honored social-climbing process. But the social season had become more unruly and scattered. Instead of one ultimate authority, there were many. Some said the season began with the autumn ball in Tuxedo Park, New York, America's first gated community, a few hours north of the city, where girls had made group debuts since 1886. Others said skip that, and just go to the winter parties and the series of charity events in the city.

Whereas in the eighteenth or nineteenth centuries, debutantes attended dancing school or learned from dancing masters at home, the dance lessons were never so codified as they became in the early twentieth century. A series of dancing classes, which began as early as grade four or five, helped various arbiters and patronesses to cull through the potential herd of "presubdebs" and "subdebs," as the younger teenage girls were called. Ambitious mothers started placing their children in socially acceptable schools (Brearley, Chapin, Westover, Hewitt, Miss Porter's) that worked as funnels into the debutante events so they could meet girls whose mothers were on dance committees, and be channeled into the elite dancing schools. The Metropolitan Dancing Class, held at the Metropolitan Club, was the direct feeder into the most exclusive of debutante presentations, the Junior Assemblies (where one hundred girls were presented), detailed later in this chapter. Only sixteen girls were selected from 400 applicants because the rest of the spaces were already taken up by legacy families, or by children of the patronesses' friends.

Lists of debutantes were regularly printed in the press. While the tougher arbiters said that "real" debutantes were only the women who made up the Junior Assembly—another reference to the standard of Mrs. Astor's ballroom—most of the press would print the 300–400 names of everyone who made a debut. Of course, these did not include a single black debutante making her debut at a cotillion in Harlem. In truth, with money, exclusivity was a myth for white debutantes. Through taking a number of judicious steps, a mother could easily have her daughter presented at a variety of balls. None was so restricted or exclusive that a press agent couldn't be hired to smooth the way in.

Most debutante organizations in the Northeast and West were ostensibly philanthropic, with the proceeds earned supporting various charities. Charitable presentations and benefits were particularly important in places where an older society was trying to beat back the new—and could not exclude based on cost alone. In the South and Texas, where many social societies were still run by men, and privately controlled, the balls had no need to justify themselves because their supporters didn't balk at exclusivity and their communities couldn't.

The preeminent debutante fixer for the anti-Brenda crowd was Juliana Cutting, the granddaughter of banker Robert Livingston Cutting. Miss Cutting, as she was forever known, made her debut in 1890 at Sherry's. When the family fortune vanished before she was able to marry, she needed to increase her income. In 1922, she set herself up as a ballroom dancing instructor, and soon after, as a social secretary. Miss Cutting had strict recommendations and required her clients to comply with them. To keep a party going, she had "a boy and a half to a girl if a dinner dance, and two to one if a supper dance." She kept a famed blue book of 2,000 acceptable young men, known as Miss Cutting's List, and put only one hundred girls on her list of debutantes each season. Boys who had a debutante sister had a blue star next to their names. From her suite of offices in the Bankers Trust building, she oversaw hundreds of social functions, arranging not only debutante balls but all sorts of parties, like weddings and galas for visiting royalty. By the 1930s, she had a cadre of assistants and was a resounding business success.

Miss Cutting was the consummate chaperone. A strict disciplinarian, she tolerated no misbehavior. Intolerant of all things fun, anyone who did any carousing would be immediately removed from her lists. She kept precise records on the debutantes and boys invited to her parties, and rated them A, B, C, or D based on their pedigree, wealth, and charm. She spent several hours each day reevaluating and re-ranking the debutantes and their escorts, who were called stags (because they attended the parties without dates). Miss Cutting was above all a businesswoman. One did not have to pay to look at her calendar, which showed debutante parties scheduled three years in advance, but a look at her lists of boys and girls started at $50 and ranged skyward toward $500, depending on which list one wanted to see. Miss Cutting was democratic in her way. You did not have to be on the A list to look at her A list, which she typed out herself onto pale blue sheaves of paper. You only had to pay for it. Because nobody knew exactly where they might appear, dealing with Miss Cutting meant you might be paying to discover your own diminished social status, or to find out you were not as low as you thought, a strange experience either way. Most girls having large debutante parties bought all of Miss Cutting's lists, and many hired her to organize their parties. She charged what was generally considered to be an astronomical fee, akin to what the most expensive planners in New York and Los Angeles earn today. For 20 percent of an event's total cost, she would send out invitations, hire an orchestra, do the decorating, find the flowers and rent a ballroom. She also received commissions from the people she recommended. It could make or break a stationer, florist, or caterer to be in Miss Cutting's good (or bad) graces. When a reporter asked her whether all debutantes sought her advice, Miss Cutting replied, "well, they'd better."

Miss Cutting had her male equivalent in Ted Peckham, who began an escort agency when he saw how many women were going out for the evening by themselves. His escorts were impoverished aristocrats who knew the manners of society but could no longer afford to keep themselves in it. These "ballroom boys," who ranged from college-age to about thirty, were paid $10 until midnight and $15 every two hours thereafter to entertain debutantes and their mothers at parties. These men were not permitted to make any advances toward their dates, and if the woman reported that one did, the man was dropped from Peckham's list. The debutante season had begun to support its own industry back in the eighteenth century, but it was seasonal and itinerant, and many of the roles still fell to relatives like maiden aunts for chaperonage, and to ladies' maids for tasks like hairdressing. The rigor and reach of Miss Cutting and Mr. Peckham had not been seen before—these were professional people who paid other professionals to keep the debutante system flowing.

Despite this increased professionalism, it was seen as both impractical and unseemly to keep debutante presentations going during World War II, especially after the bombing of Pearl Harbor, when American men, mostly young, left to fight abroad. With many women entering the workforce, debutante presentations were increasingly viewed as trivial, and there were few if any escorts. The celebrity debutantes who provided relief during the Great Depression were not followed by others attempting to do what they did. Brenda Frazier, Doris Duke, Millicent Rogers, and Barbara Hutton were child stars with ambitious parents who wanted to launch them onto a world stage. Though increasingly dismissed after World War II, their era was the first time in history when the world paid any heed to a group of teenage girls.

Historians and sociologists have long recognized male adolescence, and were able to study it largely because of the extensive history of apprenticeships for boys and the multitude of records kept by men. Young middle- and upper-class men gradually were given more independence, or earned it, under the watchful eyes of fathers or guardians who funneled them into professions or prepared them for running estates. Girls followed a different trajectory, and few thought their development mattered. "Teenage" wasn't widely recognized as a singular life stage until the 1930s and '40s, when the department stores, who had previously made children's clothing in larger sizes for teenagers, began to market clothing to this specific age group. The *New York Times* first used the word "teen-age" in 1942. By then, this delineation had caught on in larger society, and sociologists began to study this life stage.

The instability of the war had led to a hunger for social rituals, and there was a new level of respect for the rules and regulations of society. Returning white soldiers were able to go to college and get loans and mortgages using the G.I. Bill, and the families they had expanded the middle classes into a previously unknown size and influence, furthering racial stratification. The baby boom hastened the rise of a mass teen culture, where style directives came as much from that microcosm of tidiness, the suburb, as an urban environment. More people who wanted a country club life could have it, and in the suburbs the debutante ritual flowered on a smaller scale, with tiny imitations of more cosmopolitan parties. These opportunities to enter an intermediary social group— an upper middle—were new. The upper middle class differed from the upper class in scale and level of wealth and from the middle in its embrace of aspiration.

Large private debuts were scarce after the Second World War. Large cotillions, where debutantes were introduced one by one on the same evening, took their place in the '50s. In these conformist years, the debutante ritual spread throughout all races and classes. There were more presentations than ever throughout the country, although in many places on a much smaller scale. Suburbs and small cities had their own hierarchies, even if they took cues from the past and from larger social centers.

The postwar economic boom and subsequent de-cloistering of girls raised concerns about teenage girls and their sexuality, brought on by oft-reported stories of the rise in teen prostitution during World War II. Teenage girls were now consistently in the news, and corporations began to launch magazines that were specifically geared toward this emerging consumer market. *Seventeen*'s first issue, published in September 1944, sold out quickly—400,000 copies in six days. Circulation exceeded one million copies by February 1947 and two-and-a-half million by July 1949. The magazine declared that through copies shared with friends and family, it reached over half of the six million teenage girls in the United States. The magazine's readers were mostly white middle- and upper-middle-class girls; 63 percent of their fathers worked as business executives, business owners, professionals, or in white-collar occupations and an additional 19 percent earned their living as skilled workers.[3] Almost immediately after launching, the magazine began to prepare packets for advertisers that detailed the buying power of its readership, and offered lessons in how business might cater to this yet-to-be-tapped market. The pamphlets made by *Seventeen* encouraged advertisers to abandon the glamour-girl with her vampy makeup and fishnets, the Brenda Frazier figure, and to replace her with ads featuring teens that were more wholesome and less sophisticated.

There were no more debutantes in ads for cigarettes, alcohol, or hotels. *Seventeen* did deliver a regular spate of stories about debutantes, showing various dress options and covering parties. The magazine reformed the debutante into a character with mass appeal who was blonde, innocent-looking, and wore little makeup. In order to sell as many dresses as possible, the debutante's lifestyle had to look more like what we'd now see in a prom-specific issue of the magazine. *Seventeen* had a democratizing effect in that it disseminated trends to a larger public, but the trends it chose to diffuse also raised social expectations and created a new world of insecurities that could be soothed only by purchasing the products sold by its advertisers. The 1950s debutante—the wholesome Sandra Dee-like model—was available to teenage girls with enough money to buy the products advertised in the magazine, excluding most Jews and Catholics, of course, and all young women of color. And it was definitively unavailable to those who did not.

The press had a role in reshaping this ritual to make it more democratic, and those who were parents themselves likely had a stake in their daughters remaining obedient to the beats of normative culture. At the same time as the ritual became more democratic, with debutante parties popping up in smaller towns across the country, the myth of its exclusivity hooked a hungry public and sold ads. Cosmetics companies marketed "debutante" lines of face creams and powders, some in pale blue tins with pink flowers, using virginal blondes in their ads. The debutante could still sell products. And not just Brenda Frazier, but a well-behaved debutante, which, despite what the patronesses would tell you, could be almost any teenage girl with the ingenuity to participate.

In order to maintain an air of exclusivity in an increasingly democratic environment, the older debutante organizations repurposed themselves to focus more heavily on charity work. The Junior League, an exclusive service organization that admitted legacy members and a limited number of their friends, had been founded in 1901, when nineteen-year-old railroad heiress Mary Harriman became tired of watching the flowers that suitors brought to coming-out balls wilt and decided to bring hers to hospitals where people could enjoy them. Her friends followed suit and they came together to create a club. Their first volunteer services were focused on supporting hospitals and immigrant families. The League became an outlet for upper-class women who wanted to work but could not do so respectably. Eleanor Roosevelt had been an enthusiastic member.

The Junior League began its own debutante ball in 1952, held every year on Thanksgiving Eve at the Pierre Hotel. The League was a pioneer in tying together social aspiration with charity, a model that gained currency as expensive pleasures for their own sake became suspect in a more democratic environment, and one that had social checks from the press. In 1948, the Junior League of Manhattan sold its luxurious headquarters, which was elegantly furnished and contained a pool and squash court, to the Catholic archdiocese for $600,000, a move designed to get the club out of the newspaper.[4] The women also wanted to reclaim their social exclusivity and privacy. It was not enough to sell the building. The League also put out a pamphlet called "How to Get Off the

Society Page" and sent it to each local chapter, charging chapter leaders to pressure the press in their regions to cover their charitable projects in the general news, but to place less emphasis on names and faces. This didn't please the charities they funded, who depended on names and faces to raise their own profiles, nor the newspapers that covered high society to attract readers.

After they closed their headquarters, the League sent a questionnaire to its members to ask what was to be done about café society, because its relaxed morals, late-night partying, and more casual manners were affecting Junior League events. In the early '50s, the members voted on earlier end times for their dances, and demanded promptness at luncheons and dinners. They created a mothers' committee to watch the girls more closely. They addressed the problems of over-filled stag lines and crashers, limiting the number of boys who could enter. When they attempted some quality control, dowager members complained that there were no men to dance with the debutantes. The League's organizers determined it would now be necessary to exceed Miss Cutting's recommended boy/girl ratio and to have three young men for every debutante, increasing the number of possible partners. The organizers tried to ensure that the girls would have reasonably sober dancing companions, and they tried to minimize crashers, but this made the parties unappealing. The matrons were losing control.

During the early 1960s, old institutions remained desirable to a wide group, but the civil rights movement, and later the growing women's movement, called into question the value of traditional, class-bolstering rituals like the debutante ritual. The slow sexual revolution negated one major precept of the debut—that the girls be virgins. The media, too, grew tired of debutante presentations. Whereas once the press had been a reliable friend, now it was openly ambivalent and sometimes negative. When *Life* covered Henry Ford's granddaughter Anne's 1961 debut in Grosse Pointe, where Ella Fitzgerald sang in front of Meyer Davis's orchestra, they derided it for being so over the top. At a cost of $250,000, it was just too much. In this same issue of *Life*, there was a guide to the kind of debut you could have for different sums of money. Designed to be informative while also sending up the practice, this type of piece would be a typical way that publications would cater to their readers' interest while maintaining moral superiority:

Got $1,000 to spend? Not much hope for you, but you could get her into one of the mass cotillions. For $3,000, you can have a tea dance for 200 people. Involve a charity. You will look good and you can get the government to pay for some of it. [Beginning in 1954, the US tax code allowed a portion of the cost of tickets to be deducted.] Have $25,000? Seems you will be making your debut at a garden party at your parents' Hamptons estate. Good idea! You have the orchestra AND musicians roaming around. Your food is better, but not much . . . 100,000? Don't do it, unless you have an enormous unassailable name. Otherwise, it's just tacky.[5]

Whereas once the press might have ignored or glossed over a truly ugly incident at a debutante party, this was not the case when word leaked out of Fernanda Wanamaker Wetherill's 1963 summer debut at her stepfather's Southampton estate. The great-granddaughter of the department store king John Wanamaker, Fernanda's party was to be all pink, right down to the champagne. Eight hundred guests were expected, including the tenth Duke of Marlborough. The evening started out fine, but when the staid orchestra went home and the rock band for the after-party began to play, the young men in attendance began to destroy the beach house the parents had hired to accommodate overflow guests. According to *New York Magazine*, "the beds were splintered, the chandelier ripped from the ceiling, the crystal and china used for target practice, and the house stoned in a frenzy that broke all but six of the house's 1,600 mullions."[6] In the aftermath, the family inexplicably sold the photos to Henry Luce, who gamely hired a psychoanalyst to analyze the behavior of the riotous bluebloods in an article in *Life* that ran shortly after the party.

That the brawling, riotous teen culture portrayed in *Westside Story* (1961) was penetrating the rarefied world of debutante parties had broader implications for a culture obsessed with propriety. The *Life* article ran with an all caps banner "PARENTS FEAR THEIR CHILDREN." Indeed, the psychoanalyst named the behavior of the boys a "mass psychosis" and described how authority gradually disappeared, and eventually culminated in this rebellion. The psychoanalyst's theory that even the rich could adopt the threatening behavior of a horde alarmed *Life's* frantic readers, mostly middle- and working-class parents who were beginning to confront a fracturing society. It was one thing when teenage chaos was presented by Hollywood, another altogether when it was Ivy Leaguers from America's "best" families. What hope was there for anyone else? The psychoanalyst emphasized that the boys might have subconsciously wanted to destroy "authority," a word notable for its currency then and which we rarely hear now. Inspired by the "primitive beats of the twist band," they took out their aggression on the house itself, a symbol of everything that cosseted and emasculated them. The press talked about the party for weeks. When the affair dragged on without any of the boys being charged, the *New York Times* asked in an editorial, "Do the Rich Have Immunity?" After an extended outcry, a dozen boys and one girl were finally charged. The trial, held nearby in working-class, agricultural Riverhead, drew constant media attention.

In court proceedings, the defendants deflected guilt for their actions. Chandelier-swinger Eaton Brooks said that he was "not ashamed" of what he did. He went on to explain, "We had been drinking for two straight days, with no sleep and a liquid diet. We weren't the same people we are today. I agree that someone has a moral obligation about this damage, but I don't know who is responsible for the atmosphere that caused what happened at the party."

Debutante Fernanda, seemingly unaffected by the chaos at her party, met the press with a fresh Nassau tan, a blue dress, and a double strand of pearls. She told reporters that she had something more important to think about: the offer of a four-year movie contract, beginning with the next James Bond thriller, *Thunderball*. "Frankly," confessed Fernanda, "I'm still toying with the idea. I guess a lot of girls would be excited. But at this point, I'm really not." She hadn't been very excited about her old "job," either. "I never really had any enthusiasm for deb parties. I really didn't get any pleasure out of them at all." Frankly, "this whole deb business is getting me down," she said. In an interview with *New York* in 1991, Fernanda reissues a standard lament of the privileged: "Why does everyone keep wanting to dredge this thing up? I am a perfectly respectable member of society. I garden. I design fabrics. I *do* things. I don't enjoy talking about that party. It was hard on my family."

After 1965 until the time it ceased publication, *Life* barely mentioned debutantes, leaving that to the more upper-crust *Town & Country*. The term "jet set" supplanted the term "café society" and was used to describe a roving band of socialites that had relatively few debutantes, who seemed homespun by comparison. Fashion stories showcased the clothing this jet set needed—the slink of Pucci, the louche sophistication of Yves Saint Laurent—clothes that moved with your body, that were good for getting into trouble in any city. In contrast, the debutante costume had always been ceremonial, but its style froze in the late 1960s. It did not evolve but merged with styles favored by brides. It is still as it was in the sixties—white, stiff, and strapless. Debutantes were removed from time in their immobile dresses, suggesting that a willful acceptance of both quaint innocence and provincial morals was necessary to participate. The ritual no longer aligned with fashion, as debutantes were increasingly isolated into a smaller sector of society.

The 1970s were a nadir for the debutante ritual, but in the years following Reagan's election in 1980, conservative social values were resurgent. Men who made fortunes in junk bonds and hostile takeovers in a newly deregulated market environment yearned to establish themselves and sought out debuts for their daughters. The organizers of these events, relieved after the '70s almost killed off the debut, relaxed their standards. The economic dominance of Japan and the beginnings of outsourcing and moving factories overseas triggered a new nativism that aligned neatly with traditional social rituals. If the wider public thought that the flashy designer clothing with logos displayed openly, extreme makeup, big jewelry, fast cars, and expensive vacations were the zenith of upper-class accessories, they were undeniable nouveau riche "tells" for the people standing in the corners of debutante balls rolling their eyes.

The only debutante to make national news regularly in this period was Cornelia Guest, self-described (with tongue-in-cheek) "deb of the decade." Cornelia is the daughter of socialite C. Z. Guest and Phipps Steel heir Winston Guest, a cousin of Winston Churchill's. Christened an "It Girl" by both Andy Warhol and the *New York Times*, she was the goddaughter of the Duke of Windsor, King Edward VIII before his abdication. In 1982, Cornelia Guest debuted at both the Infirmary and International Balls. The International is a high-profile, expensive, and less exclusive ball (you don't have to come from money, or mimic that style) that launched brashly in 1954 and has retained its slick feeling. Cornelia's parties were covered in *Time*, *Life*, *People*, and the *Washington Post*, among many others. Truman Capote, a Guest family friend, explained to *People* magazine why Guest's party attracted so many celebrities, royals, and powerful people: "Cornelia has a No. 1 name. The Guests are from real patrician stock, unlike the Vanderbilts and Rockefellers, who are descended from crooks." Guest, like her friend Warhol, was an effective manipulator of the press. With her breezy, blonde, and approachable good looks, easy charm, and a combination of proper breeding and modern attitude, she was one of the few celebrity socialites of her era. Unlike her predecessors, who were forced into this world and spent the rest of their lives explaining themselves, Cornelia was refreshing in her enthusiastic embrace of a nouveau riche affect. After her debut, she wrote a tongue-in-cheek look at her world, called *The Debutante's Guide to Life*, a book written in a kind of social bray. She went on to act, including in the recent revival of *Twin Peaks*, to work as a spokesperson for a high-end skincare line, and to create a line of vegan handbags, and a vegan catering company. The *New York Times* still referenced her debutante years in a recent article.

When she crowned herself "deb of the decade," Guest seemed to declare that she would stay in her debut phase for longer than a debutante usually does. She pulled it off through a combination of sheer force of will, legitimate aristocratic connections, and, critically, by never marrying. By the eighties, it was ordinary for women to remain single, even if the cultural pressure to marry remained (and it still does). "Debutante" is a specific phase of life, an intermediary phase between teenage and adult, and you can't stay there for very long without risking being considered cartoonish. Guest put herself in a curious situation by trying to turn "debutante" into a brand during the 1980s, when people weren't yet ready for it. Manipulating an old money background to launch a career is now widespread. Making a career out of doing nothing is now ordinary. Whether Guest minds that she can't shake the debutante label or not is unknown. In 2012, when she was forty-eight, the *New York Times* wrote a piece about her new business titled *A Debutante Grows Up*.

CHAPTER 8

Prophets, Krewes, and Fiesta Queens

THE MODERN SOUTH

Many debutante presentations in the South resemble the presentations that happen in the rest of the country. In cities like Charlotte and Atlanta, where the banking and real-estate industries have brought in an influx of new money, debuts are open to anyone with social connections, even if those connections aren't old. Some balls benefit charities and take place in hotels or other public rooms, and others are held at country clubs. In some older southern cities, however, there are fewer celebrations for daughters of self-made men. Some of the more interesting of the old-line southern debutante presentations are held in Charleston, New Orleans, and San Antonio, all of which are thrown by male secret societies. The St. Cecilia Society has held debutante presentations since the eighteenth century. In its early years it was a music society—St. Cecilia is the patron saint of music—but now it exists only to present debutantes at its annual January ball. In Texas, the parties are large and glitzy, especially at the Fiesta San Antonio, where the all-male Order of the Alamo presents debutantes wearing 100-pound beaded dresses that take a year to make and cost up to $50,000 each. In New Orleans, during Mardi Gras, members of all-white, all-male krewes present their daughters. Other cities with some French heritage, like Mobile, Alabama, also have debutante presentations that are connected with carnival. St. Louis, while not exactly in the South, shares similarities with southern balls in that male members of the Veiled Prophet Society choose the debutantes from among their daughters during the carnival season. This city holds the most unusual debutante ball in the United States, the Veiled Prophet Ball, in conjunction with Fair Saint Louis (formerly the Veiled Prophet Fair) every July.

New Orleans

Mardi Gras debutante presentations in New Orleans began in 1874, around twenty years after the first men's krewes formed to begin holding parades during carnival. Rex, the largest among them, was the first to create a debutante court. Members chose a king based on his social status, and a queen from among the daughters of fellow members. Soon the queen had a retinue of maids in lesser roles to attend to her during the theatrical presentations. Rex also instituted a king's court composed of the men who held the leading civic and economic roles in the city and their daughters. The other men's societies, Comus, Proteus, Mithras, and Momus, joined Rex in the practice, and soon the debutante ritual was inextricably connected to Mardi Gras.

To get an idea of how seriously New Orleans families take their presentations, it helps to know that the debutante season there starts in June and runs until Mardi Gras in February. Many of New Orleans debutantes first come out at Le Debut des Jeunes Filles de la Nouvelle Orleans, the first debutante ball of the season. Their fathers wear white or cream linen suits and present their daughters in the ballroom of the local Hilton. This debut follows the model of a regular presentation, though the linen suits and summer date are a southern twist. The Bachelors' Ball and The Debutante Club, which originated in the 1930s, hold their balls during Thanksgiving, and there is another ball in late December called the Mid-Winter Cotillion, which was founded in the 1840s, and is held at the New Orleans Country Club. Any debutante participating in the

New Orleans season will need to come home from college on numerous occasions to attend these and a series of other parties—everything from simple teas to dinner dances to formal balls—before the season's culmination at one or more Mardi Gras private krewe balls.

The Mystick Krewe of Proteus presents its queen and her court at an elaborate white-tie affair on the evening before Shrove Tuesday. The Proteus Ball has been held on this day, Lundi Gras, since 1882. Like the other old-line parading krewes, Comus, Momus, and Rex, Proteus is a secret society, composed of white men from families who consolidated their power after Reconstruction and who subsequently came to dominate New Orleans both socially and politically. The debutantes are daughters and granddaughters of members of these organizations, and their presentation marks the culmination of a long social season. The Proteus Ball is presided over by a king (a man in his fifties or sixties), a queen (one of his friends' debutante daughters) and their court, a series of maids (other debutantes), male attendants, and pages (the small sons of krewe members). Through family connections, I had acquired an invitation to this ball in 2002, which I would come to think of as the strangest, most interesting party I'd ever attended.

I had flown down from New York on the Sunday before Mardi Gras. Canal Street was filled with majorettes, masqued men, and revelers who flung crawfish heads onto the street. The length of the street was barricaded and loud band music blared. My driver had left me several blocks from my hotel, drawling, "sorry, cher, this is the best I can do," before speeding off into the crowd. Despite not having his help, I made it to my beaux-arts hotel located at the edge of the French Quarter. My first party with the krewe and guests was being held the next day at Antoine's, New Orleans' oldest and most celebrated French-Creole restaurant. Antoine's has been owned by the same family since 1840, and is famous for inventing a number of dishes—Oysters Rockefeller, Eggs Sardou, and the formidable Café Brulôt, a coffee drink made with several types of alcohol, dark brown sugar, whole cloves, and New Orleans's chicory coffee, served flambéed at the end of the meal. It is a concoction that caters efficiently to most, if not all, vices.

There are a number of private rooms in the restaurant, many named for krewes. There were so many of us at the banquet—the Proteus banquet is the largest private event held at Antoine's each year—that we were spread across several different rooms, but the krewe had taken over the restaurant and we were free to walk around the building on our own. The Proteus room was a pale sea blue and covered with memorabilia of past balls, scepters, crowns, and a plaque with the same image of Proteus surrounded by seahorses that was on my invitation. Each year, a week before Mardi Gras, the past queens of Proteus meet together for lunch in this room, and honor their longest reigning queen.

Before the sit-down lunch, when people were milling around with drinks, I was introduced to a woman who, when she was told I was "a writer visiting from New York," wagged her finger like a windshield wiper. "I hope you don't write anything nasty like that Julia Reed did." Reed, a journalist and New Orleans resident, had recently written a short piece about Mardi Gras debutantes for the *New York Times*. Reading the article later, I could see why the woman didn't like it, even though there wasn't a bit of scandal in it. People who attend these parties do so with the understanding that nobody will question what happens to them. Information and secrecy are the currency. The debutantes were hard to differentiate from the other attendees their age, since they were not in their gowns, but you could guess who they were by observing others pay homage to them in a way that adults rarely do with college-age women. To my chagrin, when my polite hosts introduced me, they added, "Kristen is a writer from *New York*," placing strong emphasis on New York. Having coded introductions myself at various times, I knew I was no longer a family friend. When I spoke with some of the debutantes, they were polite, but distant, even as more Sazeracs were consumed. Still, the lunch was charming, ending with Antoine's famous baked Alaska. In New Orleans, all is history.

The ball was being held Monday evening in the New Orleans Marriott ballroom immediately following the Proteus parade, which happens on Lundi Gras. The queen and court were to arrive directly from the evening parade, and, as guests, we were milling around in the ballroom in anticipation of their entrance. While waiting and drinking cocktails in the ballroom, an older man whose daughter had debuted ten years before mentioned that the King of Proteus had been to the St. Louis Cathedral before the parade and prayed to be a good king. Our conversation was interrupted by the announcement that the queen and her court would soon enter. We went to our tables arranged in front of the stage. The queen and her maids and their escorts, as well as two pages, promenaded into the room, making their way toward the stage.

The ballroom had been decorated with an undersea theme, a large backdrop painted with shells, bubbles, seahorses, and a giant painted fish with a carved-out open mouth that the court would pass through on their way to their seats on the dais. The debutantes wore the familiar ivory dresses that look like bridal gowns, but the queen's gown was far more elaborate. Also white, it was both larger and longer, covered in intricate patterns created with Austrian crystals, glass beads, and silver lace. She also had a long robe with an ermine-trimmed train, a paste tiara, and a bedazzled scepter that she waved slowly and regally (she had lessons) at the crowd as they clapped for her. New Orleans dressmakers spend months making queens' gowns and accessories, which can cost upwards of $20,000 and weigh more than seventy pounds. I had read earlier that one dressmaker builds the foundations of her gowns around a back brace. I wondered about these underpinnings as I saw the queen struggle to sit.

When the group was well-situated on the stage, a scrim was lifted to reveal the king, who was dressed in modernized Renaissance garb with a fake beard, bobbed medieval wig, and ermine-trimmed robe, and held a scepter. The other men of the court had fez-shaped hats made of satin in bright primary colors, with a rectangular piece of the same satin fabric attached to the fez at the forehead and hanging down to the collarbone like a backless hood. These hoods, punctured with eye-holes, entirely covered the men's faces. Though the hoods are not white, they still shock me.

What all of this looks like to an outsider means very little to a society that relishes its traditions and mellow decay. While the queen's dress is new, the king's robes are frayed at the edges, their color muted after years of wear. The ceremony itself, the same every year, is the slow dance of a world caught on repeat. The Proteus parade floats use the same chassis from 1882. Everything is recycled, and I found its dilapidation both endearing and familiar. In the lull between cocktails and dinner, I drifted into thinking about my own upbringing and how many of the people I knew growing up were similarly dowdy. Before I had left for New Orleans, I had frantically searched for the pair of white kidskin opera gloves that I'd last used at my friends' debuts in the '90s. I had not worn them since. When I arrived, my hosts told me that they were expected but not required. But I found I felt weird without them. I realized with a stomach-churning feeling that I knew what to do in this secret society where old men in costume paraded around with girls just out of their teens. It's easy to escape into the aesthetic part of a larger social system and to forget that assertive, unchallenged white power often shows up in a battered old Mercedes.

After the tableau and coronation of the queen, men distributed favors to women in the audience. My host brought me a gold seashell charm with a seed pearl onto which the year of the ball was engraved. After this ceremony, the party became a regular ball. While I danced with a series of much older men, clearly instructed by my hosts to take care of me, I asked them what previous balls were like, and how they've changed since they began attending. Most affirmed my view that the balls really hadn't changed, but told me some of the themes, which tended toward the mythical and the orientalist—and numerous retellings of sea gods' stories—not only the stories of Proteus, Poseidon, and Nereus, but also the Arabian Nights. As the night went on, the ball slowly became less formal. People stopped dancing with partners, and began to dance in groups, and eventually became one large mass. People removed shoes, gloves, jackets, and ties. One woman's two-piece gown was detaching in the back as she shook her hips and raised her arms overhead. My hair had long since slid out of its chignon. I jumped back suddenly when I saw a fake mustache on the floor.

In 1992, Dorothy Mae Taylor, the first black member of the New Orleans City Council, introduced an ordinance that would prevent groups that discriminated on the basis of race, gender, religion, sexual orientation, national origin, age, or disability from getting a permit to hold a Mardi Gras parade. Organizations would have to certify their compliance by exposing their member rolls to public scrutiny. Taylor's proposal caused an uproar and hearings that lasted well beyond carnival season. Men called her "the Grinch who stole carnival." After a great deal of deliberation, the city adopted a modified version of her proposal, allowing single-sex clubs to operate with some city oversight, but enforcing integration. The old-line krewes had hidden their member rolls since their origins during Reconstruction; it was part of their mystery and mirrored the masquerade of carnival. The King of Proteus, riding on his float along St. Charles Street, never reveals his identity to the public.

Rex, a large, more public and civic-minded krewe, announced it would comply, and would therefore keep its longstanding dominion over carnival at large (Rex is the king of all carnival). But the Comus, Momus, and Proteus Krewes canceled their parades, deciding to hold only their parties and masked carnival balls. Their membership rolls remained secret. Comus, the oldest krewe, never returned to parading. Momus, whose focus was political satire, sent members to march with another krewe with a political focus but did not continue their parade. Proteus, too, dropped their parade in 1992. The city's antidiscrimination ordinance was gradually weakened, and by 1999 the law only required organizations to sign an affidavit stating they don't discriminate. Proteus resumed its parade in 2000.

In Rebecca Snedeker's powerful documentary exploring her family's history within elite white carnival society, *By Invitation Only* (2006), she captures krewe member and New Orleans businessman Oliver Delery reflecting on the ordinance:

"There's a perception that you have to be a blue-blood to be in this ball or that ball," he said. "A lot of it is the fathers and their friendships. And who they basically hang out with, the different groups." He insisted, "There are no real barriers there to entrance on balls. And all this stuff that the city tried to bring up years ago, open access to everyone. That's a farce. You can't go around just applying for membership in everything. That's not how society works. People aren't like that in regular life. And Mardi Gras is just a part of regular life. That's how we see it. That's about it."

What I watched from my dinner table showed men's power clearly. The debutantes may have been the ostensible focus, but this night was really for the men, who were showcasing their own power and honoring friends through a pantomimed exchange of daughters. I thought about the many northern debutante parties I had attended. Apart from a father-daughter dance, dads were barely a presence. Men's clubs don't run the debutante balls in the Northeast nor in San Francisco, Chicago, or any other of the larger US cities. But in the South, debutante balls tend to fall in the male line. Men's clubs control the debut not only in New Orleans, but also in Dallas, St. Louis, and Charleston. A male hairdresser in Snedeker's documentary puts it plainly. "This is the offering up of the virgins to the young men of the community. It's also an industry." If in the rest of the country there's an invisible presiding male who benefits from the debutante ritual, in New Orleans the men visibly benefit. Snedeker herself offers this: "I think that part of why these traditions are so private is because we know that there is something wrong. Our group identity, the way we have fun together, is linked to this fantasy idea that white is better."

San Antonio

San Antonio's debutante ritual began in 1909, when a wealthy southerner moved west and created the Order of the Alamo, an organization for wealthy white Texan men that commemorated Texas' 1836 victory over Mexico in the Battle of San Jacinto, leading to the independent Republic of Texas. The Order's charter states its two functions. The first was to educate the public about Texan independence and the second was "to choose a queen to preside over a court of 24 unmarried girls and boys." The Order comes together every August to choose its queen in secrecy. The men choose a daughter of one of their peers to reign over Fiesta, San Antonio's spring festival. This debutante ball resembles the Mardi Gras balls in New Orleans not only because the debutante queen is chosen by her father's peers but also in the way that it's intertwined with a larger citywide event. Once the queen is chosen, she can choose her escort, or "prime minister" in the local parlance, from among unmarried members of the group. Interestingly, the first queen and her prime minister married, fulfilling the aim of the organization. The queen's duchesses also get to choose their "dukes."

In the early years of the fiesta, debutantes wore gowns that tracked with the fashions of the period. Early on, the dances had the same theme for several years in a row: flowers first, then fairy motifs, then birds. The themes were beaded onto the debutante's dresses, which were then lightweight with simple designs. But gradually fiesta dresses became more and more elaborate and stopped reflecting fashion in favor of commemorating a family's history within the Order in as grand a way as possible. No more flapper queens in bias-cut slip dresses that were too slight even for undergarments.

By the '40s the dresses' shapes resembled coronation attire, though their fabrics and beading had an unmistakably Texan feel. As the state's oil wealth boomed, so did the cost of fiesta dresses. In recent years, most of these dresses have cost at least $50,000, and each year's court tries to outdo the last.[1] The dresses became so elaborate, so heavy with beads, and with trains so long (twelve feet for duchesses, fifteen feet for queens) that many weigh upwards of eighty-five pounds, and the debutantes were no longer able to lift them without assistance. Some relied upon their escorts, others on weightlifting regimens and daily vitamin B12 injections (really) to be able to cope with their dresses. Others finally gave in and put theirs on rollers. Such strict protocols are necessary because San Antonio debutantes, too, do the Texas dip, but instead of an awkward white dress, they are dragging trains made from hundreds of pounds of beads. In this version of the Texas dip, the debutante doesn't only perform the slow sink down, she touches her forehead all the way to the floor in front of her escort. Then they look up and wait for his permission to rise. Once he gives it, she gets up slowly with his help, and they make their way to a series of risers on a stage and wait for everyone to finish, queen last, at which point the girls are officially out.

In cities like New Orleans or San Antonio, where private men's clubs have long presented their debutantes in conjunction with annual city-wide celebrations, non-Anglo populations in these cities have forcefully objected to this practice. According to an article in *Texas Monthly*, the pushback in San Antonio began in the seventies, when Mexican Americans "were making a new drive for political power." A prominent city councilman, Bernardo Eureste, called the Anglo royalty of Fiesta "a joke." In 1972, a school superintendent banned the annual visit of the Order's king and queen to a predominantly Mexican American school district. The festivities still happen, but there is less engagement with the population at large. Beginning in 1981, the city's gay community has held a "Cornyation," where it crowns a fiesta queen from among a group of elaborately clad drag performers in mock fiesta dresses.[2] While the elite debutante presentations still go on, the fiesta queen now shares her "official" duties—like visiting classrooms and parading—with a more diverse group of fellow queens who are not debutantes but instead represent more inclusive local organizations.

St. Louis

The Veiled Prophet Organization is a secretive all-male St. Louis group that has presented its debutantes at an annual ball since 1878. Its founder, Alonzo Slayback, was a lawyer and confederate colonel who allegedly descended, despite his improbable birthplace of Plum Grove, Missouri, from a French countess and one of Louis XVI's guards. Colonel Slayback cultivated a chivalrous persona that aligned perfectly with the postwar confederate mood. After Appomattox, and in search of redemption, he headed to Mexico to fight for the short-lived Mexican Empire, entering Emperor Maximilian's army shortly before Maximilian was executed by Benito Juarez's firing squad. Slayback returned to the States in 1867 with his only spoil of war, a new and unverifiable title: Duke of Oaxaca. He settled near his brother in St. Louis, and began to practice law.

Alonzo Slayback was a skilled prosecutor and bon vivant, and soon became one of the city's most important men, a stature he gained not only because he was a successful prosecutor, but also because his brother was the city's richest grain merchant. Charles Slayback had lived in New Orleans immediately after the war ended, and returned to St. Louis greatly influenced by the culture of New Orleans. In the ten years preceding the founding of the Veiled Prophet Society, the Slayback brothers amassed further wealth and connections. They became part of a small, intertwined St. Louis elite, made up of the white men who controlled burgeoning industries—meatpacking, bottling, brewing, and other types of distribution.

$\mathscr{S}$t Louis's business leaders had weathered the economic tumult of the 1870s, which began with the Panic of 1873, better than most cities, but had done so at the expense of their workers. In July 1877, after years of docked pay and dangerous working conditions, white and black workers in St. Louis joined a railroad strike that had begun in Virginia and spread along the rails through the industrial hubs of the United States. When the strike arrived in St. Louis, workers from other industries joined it, demanding an eight-hour workday and a ban on child labor. It became the first general strike in the history of the United States. The solidarity of black and white workers in taking control of the city streets frightened St. Louis's upper class, which had depended on factionalism for quiescence. After a week of nonviolent striking, a combined force of 3,000 federal troops and a 5,000-strong deputized special police violently ended the protests, killing eighteen strikers in the process.

The upheaval from the strike slowed down business and created socioeconomic uncertainty in St. Louis for months. Groups of business leaders gathered together to try to figure out how to stabilize the city and their businesses. In late 1877, eighteen prominent businessmen, led by Alonzo Slayback, with the help of his brother, came together to found the Order of the Veiled Prophet. The brothers believed that if they created a carnival atmosphere akin to Mardi Gras, which had enriched New Orleans and other cities like Mobile, they could bring attention and revenue back to St. Louis and allow it to compete with major business centers like Chicago. Charles Slayback had seen debutantes presented during carnival by his marching krewe, and the great interest they drew. Alonzo wove the romantic threads together, naming the society after an orientalist poem "The Veiled Prophet of Khorrasson," by Irish poet Thomas Moore. The poem, widely popular then, was inspired by the life of al-Muqanna, an eighth-century Persian chemist and mystic who, after he had burned his face, wore a veil. The men concocted a legend that claimed al-Muqanna as their leader and as a benefactor of the city itself. At each fair, the prophet would choose his "Belle of the Ball," later called the "Queen of Love and Beauty," making the debutante ritual a key component of St. Louis's civic life.

Historian Thomas Spencer writes that in addition to "attempting to boost trade on the Mississippi and reclaim St. Louis's status as a major modern city," the Veiled Prophet Society had another motive. He continues, "Veiled Prophet members were likely compelled by the Railroad Strike of 1877 to re-institute class hierarchy by demonstrating the power and opulence of the wealthiest and most prominent businessmen in the city, putting working-class strikers in their place."[3] His argument is bolstered by the prophet's depiction: a man clad in a white robe with a pointed hood obscuring his identity. Next to him, balanced upright in his hand is a shotgun. The *Missouri Republican* newspaper described him thusly: "It will be readily observed from the accouterments [his shotgun] of the Prophet that the procession is not likely to be stopped by street cars or anything else." He is also unmistakably a Klansman. The first Veiled Prophet was, not coincidentally, the only prophet whose identity was ever intentionally released to the public. He was James Priest, the city's police commissioner, the man who successfully put down the strike the year before. In this way, the city's elite linked pageantry with social control. His queen was Suzy Slayback, Alonzo's daughter. The Veiled Prophet Fair would be open to the public, but the ball was for the social elite only.

The fair resembled Mardi Gras. It had a large costumed parade, and was held concurrently with the St. Louis Agricultural and Mechanical Fair. At the same time young women were being presented, so were prized cattle and pigs, outsized vegetables, and new mechanical innovations. St. Louis civil rights activists would later say that the Veiled Prophet Fair was designed to distract from the social and racial inequities of St. Louis, quieting a mob with games, as Roman emperors did. Though the crowds could not attend the ball themselves, they did see the Veiled Prophet and his queen on a parade float, and the young women were a draw for fair-goers. Men presented their daughters because their youth, beauty, and wealth affirmed their power as the city's business leaders, especially their power to decide the parameters for what was revealed and what was secret about the parade.

This frisson made the ball an instant success, and soon it superseded the fair in popularity, with local papers giving it more coverage than the fair. For the debutantes, the ball validated their beauty and gave them an important opportunity to display their accomplishments. This meant marching into the venue, the Merchants' Exchange in early years, and performing an elaborate quadrille with their male partners. Suzy Slayback wrote her own account of the ball, in the third person, a convention at the time that allowed for polite distancing. She remembered,

It was indeed a thrill to those who attended the first ball given by the Veiled Prophet at the Merchants Exchange in October 1878, and especially a girl who had never made her debut, to see many well-known and interesting citizens . . .

The society women were exquisitely gowned, and the beauty of St. Louis was represented. The time of crowned Queens did not come for 14 years, but the "belle of the ball" was selected by the Prophet as his most admired partner, his selection for the first queen was Miss Suzy Slayback. He found his partner and escorted her up from her seat onto the floor where he presented her with a very pretty pearl necklace. Her dress was white satin made with a quilted skirt studded with pearl beads and trimmed with lace.[4]

Like many other social organizations that present debutantes, the ball was run by a committee of men who gave out invitations to their friends. The friends then returned them and waited for the committee to vote its approval or its veto. The invitations were sent out and the recipient would almost always come to the ball. In putting on the ball, its organizers had a great ally in the press, who understood that people wanted to read about what they could not see for themselves. The *Missouri Republican* covered the ball in great detail, devoting reams of pages to describing the flowers and dresses. Newspapers were permitted to print the names of debutantes, despite the supposed secrecy. With the increase in literacy during this period, many readers were hungry to read about the lives of the rich. Newspaper articles gave people a window into this world and a subversive opportunity to criticize, if they liked.

In the 1890s, St. Louis newspapers began to print what the debutantes were wearing before the ball happened, suggesting that the organizers understood that a relationship with the press would please both newspapers and their daughters. Women did not have much room for disobedience in this period, and the parameters for what continued respectable behavior were narrow. Since the identity of the Veiled Prophet was a secret, the debutantes were emblems of his power. The daughters were, in essence, acting as proxies for their fathers. The reenactment of a feudal marriage, linking the Prophet, an older, established man, to the daughter of one of his friends, bolstered the St. Louis elite's long history of family alliances, which sustained the tiered social organization. The ball was so popular that it was even shown on television until the 1980s.

Still, the friction that led to its founding appeared at times. Starting in the Depression, boys used pea-shooters to shower dried peas onto the rich people on the parade floats, forcing the organizers to provide large covers that limited the pageantry. That just made it necessary to throw larger items. By the early sixties, parents stopped their daughters from appearing on floats, feeling that it was now too dangerous for them to do so even under the protective covers. The organization even changed the parade route to avoid black neighborhoods, and moved the ball to December, separating it from the July fair entirely. In the mid-sixties, such behavior led the racial and social justice organization

ACTION (Action Committee to Improve Opportunities for Negroes) to begin protesting the ball, making a serious effort to address its racism and that of the Veiled Prophet Organization. On parade day, members of ACTION lay down in the streets where the floats would pass, or chained themselves to floats so they had enough time to hand out flyers. ACTION also staged their own parody of the prophet ball, where they crowned a "Queen of Human Justice," mocking the all-white organization.

In 1972, Percy Green, ACTION's leader, wrote letters to the debutantes, who were mostly away at college, asking them not to participate, and telling them that he hated that they were being forced to participate by their parents. Writer and professor Lucy Ferriss, a debutante in 1972, received Green's letter while she was a student at the University of California at Berkeley. She prints part of it in her memoir, *Unveiling the Prophet: The Misadventures of a Reluctant Debutante*. She writes that the letter indicted the leaders of major St. Louis corporations—including McDonnell Douglas, Budweiser, and Monsanto—for their racist hiring practices. At the end of the letter, Green informs Ferriss that six maids from this year's group were working with ACTION to pull off a surprise at the ball.[5] Ferriss responded with a letter that was part agreement, part condescension. She conveys that she agrees that the ball is racist and sexist, but that her father has been paying for her participation since she was born and she doesn't want to disappoint him. She then makes reference to the ongoing horrors in Vietnam and asks him if he doesn't "have bigger fish to fry." Ferriss's mother, having heard about Green's letters from fellow mothers of debutantes, contacts her urgently, telling her to destroy the letter. When Lucy says she's already written back to Green, her mother resentfully tells her that she should not have invested so much time in her daughter.

What ACTION pulled off in 1972 did shock St. Louis, as Percy Green had promised. Three white female members of ACTION obtained balcony tickets to the ball. One woman created a distraction by yelling "down with the VP" while another, Gena Scott, slid down a cable into the auditorium. Scott said she had fallen and was hurt, but managed to sneak onto the stage, where she pulled the prophet's veil off, unmasking the Monsanto executive underneath. She was quickly removed by the prophet's "Bengal Lancers." The Prophet replaced his own veil, and the ball continued as if nothing had happened. It was not until 1979 that the Veiled Prophet Organization admitted its first black members, who were three doctors. In the early nineties, the Veiled Prophet Fair changed its name to the Fair Saint Louis, in an attempt to shake off its history and broaden its appeal.

Today, the Veiled Prophet Organization is only responsible for the ball, and has admitted the occasional African American and Asian American members whose daughters participate in the debut, following the example of the Junior League and other debutante organizations. Since 2002, the Veiled Prophet debutantes have performed community service projects in the lead-up to the ball. Unlike at some other balls, parents choose their daughters' escorts, meaning that the queen is not the only woman to have an older escort; her maids do as well. Parents try for the highest-profile men they know. In 2016, one young woman was escorted by her father's former boss, Francis Slay (unrelated to the Slaybacks), then sixty years old, and in his sixteenth year as the mayor of St. Louis.

Only the queen wears white at the Veiled Prophet Ball. The maids and debutantes can wear any color they like. This makes the ball look more like a wedding, where the queen/bride has greater significance. The maids, once introduced, would be harder to spot in the crowd if they were not wearing headbands, each with a single feather, a nod to Victorian debutante costume. Debutantes are introduced in ascending order of their father's importance and are escorted down the runway that leads to a stage where the prophet is seated, on a throne, surrounded by his all-male court. One by one, the debutantes curtsy before the seated prophet, who gives them a small gift. The special maids, who are part of the "the Court of Love and Beauty," follow this first group and are seated with their escorts in a demi-lune. At its center are the two thrones, one holding the prophet and one empty. The queen then enters, commanding the runway with her escort. When she reaches its end, she is escorted to the awaiting throne next to the prophet, which is another way this ritual resembles a wedding.

For the Veiled Prophet debutantes, including its African American participants, the ritual is a bonding experience, a way to mark the passage of time, to participate in community service projects. One debutante, Taylor Rose Harris, who was the only African American maid in the 2016 ball, told *St. Louis Magazine* that she felt like a princess, and that her father had been a member of the VP Society since she was a baby. Harris had wanted to come out at the Veiled Prophet for as long as she could remember, but her focus, she said, was on "helping other members of minority groups who have been less fortunate."[6]

Anti-racist organizations still protest the Veiled Prophet Organization, despite its integration. After the killing of teenager Michael Brown in neighboring Ferguson, Missouri, organizations responded with campaigns to unveil the prophet. Black Lives Matter members held a die-in, lying in the streets outside the St. Louis Hyatt where the ball was taking place. Like those white members who worked with ACTION, members gave out their tickets to protesters, who shared photos from inside the event, some of which showed the police commissioner, Sam Dotson, in attendance, linking economic and social power in the city with its brutal policing. When the riot police were called to remove the protesters, Dotson exited the hotel to personally direct them. His attendance served as bookend to the history of the ball, as the very first Veiled Prophet was the city's police commissioner, who had put down a strike that endangered the city's white elite. Many there must have known this history. But inside, there was still a queen to coronate.

CHAPTER 9

Creating a Black Elite

DEBUTANTES IN AFRICAN AMERICAN SOCIETY

While there may have been other balls given by or for black people in colonial America, the first one noted in print was for those rejecting breaking away from Britain. The article appeared in the *New Jersey Gazette* in 1778 and detailed New York's series of "Ethiopian Balls," where free blacks and British officers mingled and danced to the music of black fiddlers and banjo players.[1] The balls were named for the Royal Ethiopian Regiment, a group of free blacks and escaped enslaved men who joined the British in fighting the American revolutionaries (their former owners) after Lord Dunsmore, the royal governor of Virginia, issued a proclamation welcoming them into the British army, offering freedom in exchange for their participation. Both the British officers and their wives, thousands of whom made the trip to America for the duration of the war, attended these balls, together with the black officers and their wives. There are few details about the balls, but we do know that the British officer in command would lead the dance with the wife of the highest-ranking member of the Royal Ethiopian Regiment.

Free African Americans in eastern US cities continued to hold regular balls after the American Revolution during the antebellum period. These balls were modeled on the basic structure of balls given by white Americans, but ball organizers modified their parties to reflect their uniquely African American culture. Composers adapted European dance music to incorporate West African rhythms, and ball decorations often included images of Africa.[2] Much like the "Allmax" tavern in East London that parodied Almack's Assembly Rooms, these early ball organizers openly mocked the exclusivity of white balls. In 1820s New York, black servants held annual balls, arriving in coaches driven by white coachmen. In Philadelphia, where rules about admission to the assembly were printed in the newspapers making them widely known, African Americans began plans for an 1828 ball by telling their committee to "furnish no person with tickets who could not trace his pedigree as far back as his mother." The link to Almack's, still an institution in London, remained strong. When Charles Dickens visited Philadelphia in the 1840s, he visited a predominantly black tavern called Almack's, where "corpulent fiddlers" played on stage and "demure young women led the dance."[3] Free black culture melded aspiration with rebellion and set the stage for a uniquely African American debutante ritual.

Enslaved people also held balls, particularly those who occupied more elevated positions in urban households. Some had direct experience with African high culture, and may have brought some of its aesthetics to these new world celebrations. Historian Katrina Hazzard-Gordon points out that "there were slaves familiar with the courts of African kings, tradition in which the court and its attendants would've had the best of everything. They could have composed a significant portion of the slaves who were personal servants to influential whites." These affairs were modeled on the balls held by their rich masters, and often were partially funded and attended by them. The parties could be extravagant. A Montgomery, Alabama, Christmas Ball held in the 1840s by a "slave club" petitioned the mayor to get the City Council to approve their plan to keep the city's gas lamps illuminated well into the night so that their guests could go home safely. Invitations to the ball were crafted from heavy paper stock and embossed in gold. The ball was attended by enslaved men and women, along with a "better class of whites."[4]

Most accounts describing balls of this period are from white travelers who were wealthy enough to have connections in whatever city they were visiting, and who often attended parties in a pseudo-anthropological role, recording what they saw for friends and family back home. A white visitor to a Charleston, South Carolina, ball organized by free blacks in 1853 recalled that the "the striking features of Negro evening dress consisted in astonishing turbans with marabou feathers, into which added accessories of squib shape and other forms were inserted." Anthropologist Annette Lynch asserts that African American debutante balls "must be interpreted as a part of a long history of African Americans using dress within public venues to display reconstructed versions of gender and identity." While free blacks and urban enslaved people were able to organize their balls, black women also used their clothing to separate themselves momentarily from their enslavement. "Having been robbed of their history, culture, and control over their own bodies," Lynch continues, "African Americans had limited safe arenas in which to define themselves. Celebrations were rare, but were opportunities to display both pride in their bodies, and the cultural values they fought to retain."[5] When enslaved women mended the clothing provided to them by their white owners, they used brightly colored fabric and weaving techniques from West Africa to create garments that reflected their heritage. Similarly, the culture of performance that grew up around balls, and later evolved into a debutante ritual, is a pastiche that became its own unique performance and expression.

Despite the "white tendency to lump African Americans into one homogenous mass of degraded people," as historian Willard Gatewood put it, there was a diverse black upper class in antebellum America. Groups of free blacks in northern and southern cities, as well as the Creole elite in Gulf Coast cities, had amassed wealth and property, so much so in some cases that less privileged black communities worried that "they'd become an oligarchy" and a separate caste to themselves.[6]

Indeed, this was the view of many in the Creole elite who preferred to use their whiteness to reap what privileges it had to offer them. Despite their wealth, it does not appear that Creole communities introduced debutantes, perhaps because it was customary for them to intermarry within their small community.

African Americans began to make more dramatic gains during Reconstruction, but those eroded quickly after a series of political and legal losses that helped white Americans strip blacks of their civil and voting rights. This began in earnest with the Tilden/Hayes Compromise of 1877, wherein the two presidential candidates resolved their contested election by cutting a deal wherein Rutherford B. Hayes would become president if he consented to Samuel Tilden's demand to withdraw federal troops from the former slave states so they could return to home rule. This compromise effectively ended Reconstruction. The decades of losses that followed culminated with the Supreme Court decision, *Plessy v. Ferguson* (1896), which cemented the constitutionality of resurgent segregation in its "separate but equal" clause. The Jim Crow laws that followed led to widespread white supremacist terrorism, as the white majority forced African Americans out of shared social space.[7]

Although the very small percentage of black Americans who were wealthy and lighter skinned were somewhat more insulated from the ills of the post-Reconstruction period, Jim Crow spurred a new urgency among black intellectuals and community leaders, who had few safe ways to address widespread racism and rapidly worsening social conditions. The towering black intellectuals of the day, and architects of what became known as the uplift movement, Booker T. Washington and W. E. B. Du Bois, approached black social and economic advancement in dramatically different ways. Washington urged blacks not to agitate too much for an improved lot, but instead to be patient, focus on self-employment and economic independence, and maintain a conciliatory manner, which he believed together would eventually win over white society. Du Bois, though initially an ally of Washington, parted ways with him after concluding that Washington's accommodation strategy would not be successful, and would only perpetuate white supremacy. He concentrated instead on obtaining political power and rights, co-founding the NAACP to press for greater access and power. He, too, however, was focused on cultivating an upper level of black intellectuals who would lift up those below them.

Overall, leaders of this period sought to dismantle pseudoscientific prejudices regarding black intellectual capacity and social behavior by supporting academic education as well as cultivating the manners of white society.[8] The pointed disagreements between black intellectuals over how to address social and economic conditions play out in the development of the debutante ritual, itself a by-product of the uplift movement. Theoretically, the uplift movement dovetailed well with the stated genteel moralism of white Victorians, but could not and did not dismantle the fundamental racism underpinning white upper-class society. Still, within the African American community the push toward gentility increased interest in social rites like the debutante ritual, and set the stage for ongoing debate about how to define respectability, and who was permitted to define it. Presenting debutantes was an effective way for wealthy black families to affirm their gentility, to provide them with more social options within an oppressive white culture, and to highlight the accomplishments of their daughters, and by extension, the entire family.

The wealthiest black families held debuts for their daughters starting in the 1870s, which closely resembled those held by white families. The events were quiet and private, with daughters often introduced when they were eighteen. Sometimes families opted to introduce their daughter on her birthday, but other parents timed the debut with the opening or closing of the social season for greater attention from black newspapers, which covered these events enthusiastically. In 1889, New York debutante Katherine Bowers Smith made her debut at a party her father William H. Smith held for her at his house in Bedford-Stuyvesant,

Brooklyn, where many wealthy blacks had settled after fleeing the Manhattan draft riots of 1863, creating a wealthy enclave with beautiful brownstones and a vibrant economy. William Smith was a prominent businessman with extensive social ties in New York and Newport, Rhode Island. The *New York Age*, the most popular black newspaper of the period, reported that Katherine's debutante ball was an elaborate social event and that upper-class families came to Brooklyn from Boston and Philadelphia to attend it. The debutante stood with her parents and her two best friends, the daughters of a Philadelphia doctor, and the three were introduced to guests as they arrived. Though the debut was for Katherine herself, having her friends by her side served a dual purpose. It allowed Katherine to shine and provided her support and camaraderie during this important event.[9] After the reception, there was dancing until well into the night.

While a private debut like Katherine's was an important ritual for the most elite black families, other young women made their debuts at group balls. After Reconstruction, social clubs took up the practice of presenting debutantes at Christmas time. There were group presentations in cities with large black populations; Cincinnati, Chicago, Providence, Philadelphia, Boston, and New York all had clubs that presented debutantes by the 1890s. The debutante balls raised money for local organizations by charging for admission, and an even larger amount still for the families of the debutantes. Some black newspapers inveighed against the practice of "giving society balls under the guise of charity dances" and viewed them as more costly than beneficial. A 1912 editorial in the *Washington Bee* criticized the organizations for using more "wood, coal, and provisions" for the balls than they provided for "the worthy colored poor of their town."[10] Society balls and parties were part of a larger discussion within the black intellectual community about how to uplift the race. Archibald Grimké, one of the preeminent intellectuals of this period, and a founder, with Du Bois, of the NAACP, lamented black aristocrats' "penchant for expending energy on matters of little significance" at the expense of business enterprise and education, and wished they were a more cohesive group, so they could approach social problems together.[11]

The debutante ritual, white and black, has always invited this sort of opprobrium, but wealthy whites did not feel they had to defend their philanthropy, or lack thereof, to others. Because so many African American charities were reliant on contributions from those in the black higher classes, the cost of a ball might mean a reduction in the size of their donations overall. Still, black debutante organizations funded hospitals, eldercare, and other charitable organizations, and in the 1950s, they began to offer scholarships to the young women who participated. Raising money for charity, and keeping that money within the community, remain central components of the African American debutante ritual.

While white debutante organizations require their debutantes to have some combination of family history, money, and aspiration, these debutantes have never been obligated to meet any educational or service requirements. This would undercut the priorities of a caste system. Black debutante organizations nearly always have these extra prerequisites, even when these organizations have a long history of presenting the daughters of elite families. The condition that these young women meet a certain educational and charitable standard reflects that what has allowed most African Americans to achieve sustained success, along with good business sense, has been a strong education, which, even if not an inoculation against racism, improves one's professional prospects. Historian Miya Carey, who researched African American debutante balls in her doctoral work, points out that "black girls overwhelmingly shoulder the responsibility of representing racial progress." This was particularly true at mid-century, Carey told me, when depictions of the black family as pathological were common in mainstream white media and among certain black thinkers, like E. Franklin Frazier, who blamed the decline of the conjugal family for the "disorganization" of black culture. In contrast to these cultural forces, black newspapers often offered an alternative view of black life.[12]

The black press depicted young black debutantes as respectable, well-mannered, and worthy of respect for their achievements. This empowering narrative ran counter to the racial stereotyping that had every black girl "instantly move, upon puberty, from child status to an image of either the promiscuous, enticing, and sexually threatening Jezebel or the unattractive, overweight, asexual Mammy."[13] Coverage of debutantes provided a strong contrast for these common racist tropes.

Social clubs, which would sponsor debutante balls, tended to open and shutter rapidly as affinities, the economy, and community status changed. Although the debutante ritual itself has been consistent, it's hard to find a single African American social organization that has held debutante presentations consistently for as long as the Original Illinois Club, a black social club in New Orleans that holds its debutante ball during Mardi Gras. Originally co-ed, the club was founded in 1895 by a New Orleans civic figure and dancing teacher named Wiley Knight, who envisioned the club as a place where black citizens of New Orleans could enjoy some of the city's high life. Many of its original members worked as Pullman porters, a respectable and well-paying job, on the railroad line that ran between New Orleans and Chicago, which gave the club its name. Knight felt it would benefit members to teach formal dancing and etiquette at the club. In the early years of it, balls began at 10 p.m. because some of their members were butlers and maids, and had to finish their workdays before attending. It was not until the 1920s that the club became more exclusive and transitioned to being a club for men.

Filmmaker Phoebe Ferguson's documentary about black upper-class society in New Orleans, *Member of the Club*, follows Marisa Ariane Mitchell as she goes through her Original Illinois Club debutante season in 2003–4. Ferguson, who is white and from New Orleans, tracks Marisa's attempt to become its queen. Like the other Mardi Gras men's clubs, the Veiled Prophet Society, and Dallas's Idlewild, the Original

Illinois's male members pick themes for each year's ball, make decisions on decor, and control invitations. Most importantly, they choose their queen through a complex and secret process—when the club's secretary is explaining the selection process to Ferguson, he shields the page of the club's ledger. The debutante committee of the Original Illinois conducts interviews with the girls who are nominated by members and chooses the debutante court based on the sponsoring member's seniority in the club. Daughters and granddaughters of longtime members receive precedence. If there are no close relatives of members, they cast the net more widely. The ball is popular, and the queen is almost always a member's relative.[14] Marisa's sponsor was her uncle, a longtime club member.

Marisa's family began planning formally for her debut by writing a letter to the men of the club in 1998, when Marisa was just eleven. Before the debutante committee arrive at her mother's house to interview her, Marisa explains, "My aunt was a deb, my mom was a maid [a queen's attendant]. If I was a queen, that would mean we moved up." Aspiration comes up repeatedly in the documentary, and aligns with what many African American debutante participants and organizers cite as the driving force behind presentations in their communities. William J. Washington, a member of the debutante committee, describes it this way: "Because the education system [in New Orleans] is not what it should be, we have most of the black population here living below the poverty line. To have black kids have a future, to look forward to something, to have aspiration, you've got to give them something." The ritual allows participants to keep their traditions going, honor their history, and build continuity, which is especially important, another member says, "when your history has been erased." At the end of the interview, the club members caution Marisa not to change her hair, which she's wearing in a neat and simple bob.

The debutantes begin preparing seven months prior to the ball, with rehearsals and etiquette classes. They take lessons in how to walk, speak, curtsy, and in how to dance the Chicago Glide, a waltz unique to the club, which members have been dancing since its founding.[15] The debutantes-to-be attend a dozen teas, where they refine their table manners, and a formal lunch where they are tested with a cream puff dusted in powdered sugar to ensure they can eat it without covering themselves with the sugar.

Marisa's aunt, Valerie Petit, explains how important Marisa's debut is to her mother, Marisa's grandmother, Lorraine Kelly Petit. "It was more important to my mother, she wanted this for us. Her family was not able to afford it. But she, a successful dance teacher, could." Marisa's family sees their participation in the debutante season as a way to enhance her prospects for a good life, and the social progress in the family seems to validate their feeling. Marisa, for her part, feels both the weight of her family's pressure and her own excitement not just for the ball, but also for her own party, which will be held shortly before it. The family has saved money to throw her a lavish presentation at a country club. She's chosen a Cinderella theme, complete with a castle ice sculpture and a glass slipper centerpiece on every table. Three hundred forty-two people are set to attend.

Marisa's mother has a prestigious job as Director of Clinical Trials at Xavier University, but picks up long shifts at a pharmacy, working twelve-hour days to afford the party. While the costs of the ball are paid for by the New Orleans businessmen who are Illinois club members (the only thing debutantes pay for are their dresses), it's Marisa's mother and grandmother who will pay for her party. The girls' elaborate and themed individual debutante parties, the likes of which are rarely seen any more in white communities, require a large investment by the family of each debutante. They are more like weddings or quinceañeras than the quick cocktail party or luncheon that a white family might throw for their daughter—emphasis on might.

The morning after Marisa's party, the family sits together discussing the night before. "You know I've got a few checks to write. What's done is done. It's over. It was worth every penny," says her grandmother. Her mother nods and responds, "I have a shoebox of receipts. I'll add them up one day." Reflecting on the evening, Marisa's grandmother states, "We could've gotten an expensive car or a small house. That's one thing about money. It's going to get away from you one way or another." She then says in a quiet voice, "This was the name brand. We got it." The name brand can be carried with you even when nothing else can.

The relationship between debutante balls and elitism has long been a subject of debate within the African American community. The sociologist E. Franklin Frazier included a critique of debutante balls of the 1950s and 60s in his seminal book *Black Bourgeoisie*, asserting that the balls were derivative of white society, and existed so upper-class blacks could get recognition. His key criticism, though, was that the balls were financially draining for participants. This is clearly true for Marisa's family, who manage the cost because of their years of meticulous preparation. The instability of African American socioeconomic life in the United States makes it easier to understand why a family would spend so much money to get "a name brand." Being a debutante has enduring cultural currency. *Member of the Club* was made just a year before Hurricane Katrina devastated the city—there is a note at the beginning of the film that informs the viewer that nearly all of the debutante memorabilia and club records shown in the documentary were destroyed by the storm. But Marisa and the other women who have debuted at the Original Illinois Club remain debutantes. After the storm, the *New York Times* interviewed two women who were to have come out at the Illinois club, but had their seasons destroyed by the storm when the club was forced to cancel the ball. Amanda Williams, who spoke to the *Times* from Texas, where she was sheltered with family, lamented the loss of her debut, telling the paper:

> There's nothing that compares to it. It's the way to say, 'I'm a woman now.' Everyone gets to hear your life story, your accomplishments, what you plan for the future. None of that happens at

a prom; there's no comparison. You're just hanging out with your friends. At the ball, you meet other girls and form a bond. It's a social thing that also connects you to everybody who's ever come out with the club.[16]

In his book about the black elite, *Our Kind of People*, attorney Lawrence Otis Graham explains the hierarchy of debutante cotillions within the uppermost levels of the black elite from an insider's perspective. Graham, who, by his own description, grew up on the fringes of this group, but now lives squarely within it, has developed the taste for minute difference that is most frequently found in people who slip back and forth between barriers of a ruling elite. Graham explains that upper-class, black children are expected to have impeccable résumés that reflect their parents' achievements. "Children's social and academic credentials are intended not only to prepare the child for life filled with competition and high standards but also to fill out a family's already stellar resume or shore up a less-than-perfect one."[17] From birth, children are funneled into the right groups, beginning with a Jack and Jill membership that will teach them what they need to know to move on to being debutantes and their escorts. Graham recounts that, while debutante cotillions are widespread, "the best families" would never present their daughters at the local church group or the YWCA, preferring instead a group of selective member-only organizations—The Links, The Girlfriends, The Smart Set, Jack and Jill—as well as two sororities, the AKAs (Alpha Kappa Alphas) and the Deltas.[18]

Most of the groups Graham mentions have presented debutantes for decades. Jack and Jill was founded in 1938 by Marion Stubbs Thomas and seven other mothers to forge friendships and a sense of community among children from like-minded, well-to-do African American families. Today, there are hundreds of chapters in cities and affluent suburbs, with a capped membership number that makes the organization more exclusive. The organization's annual yearbook, a kind of social register called *Up the Hill*, armed Graham with "a coast-to-coast directory of boys, girls, and parents who were just like me."[19] When describing debutante parties, Graham takes us through a long list of debutantes. He speaks to many women, and their answers about why they made their debuts are formulaic, the same answers white women give when asked about their debuts. Some daughters say they came out for their parents; some say they looked forward to it for years. Some parents say their daughters have looked forward to it; others say their daughters refuse to do it. However, Graham does not describe any party in great detail. While this might seem like an oversight, it's revealing. Elite black debuts have become as formulaic as their white counterparts. Rituals endure and are successful because of their sameness. Participants bow to the successes of the past, and agree to take them into the future. When the attendees are the only thing that changes from one party to the next, that means a ritual has settled in, become venerable, and reflects a community's success. Where you are most likely to see this happen is at the uppermost reaches of black society that Graham describes.

Sorority debuts are the most charity oriented of the parties that make up the African American debutante scene. The Alpha Kappa Alphas or AKAs are a historically black service-focused sorority founded in 1908 at Howard University. Chapters have provided a robust debutante experience to qualified young women since the 1950s. Though debutantes have to be sponsored by "a financially active member" of the sorority, they also need to meet the organization's academic requirements. AKA debutantes train in etiquette and perform community service before receiving recognition, in the form of scholarship money, at their ball. Although for many AKA chapters the debutante cotillion is part of a long tradition, some chapters that have not had a cotillion in the past are finding that the debutante ritual meshes well with the current social environment. The Minneapolis chapter inaugurated its debutante program last year, working toward hosting their first debutante ball in

February 2019, with the intention "to motivate and educate participants to grow academically, professionally and culturally." To achieve that, the young women participated in eight months of "Debutante Program and 'Charm' Workshops," which included the traditional mixers, mother-daughter teas, and cotillion rehearsals, as well as sessions on college preparedness, career planning, cultural activity, community service, and time management. This season's crop of debutantes also got a session called "Managing Your Personal Brand," to which presumably *debutante* can now be added.

Jack and Jill added "beautillions" in the 1970s, but they gained in popularity in the eighties, in response to widespread negative portrayals of young black men in the media. The phenomenon of the beautillion is unique to African American culture (rich heterosexual white men in the United States have never felt the need to come out; there's no need to ask for recognition when your social position guarantees it), and celebrates young black men as they come of age in a culture that does not welcome or support them. A recent study by researchers at Harvard, Stanford, and the US Census Bureau mapped the roots of social mobility among millions of children. The researchers learned that even when black and white boys grew up in families with "the same income, similar family structures, similar education levels and even similar levels of accumulated wealth," the black boys raised at the top, in wealthy families and wealthy neighborhoods, were still more likely to become poor than they were to remain wealthy as adults.[20]

Beautillion organizers may not have been armed with these statistics, but their community response to hostility toward black male teenagers, and their understanding that a wealthy background doesn't guarantee continued social mobility for black men, bears them out. Beautillions are open to boys who are high school seniors or college freshmen. The young men need to have an honor roll average, engage in many extracurricular activities, and perform community service to be eligible to make their debuts at a scholarship ball. Mentorship from successful black men in the community is a key component and attraction of the beautillion season, allowing the boys to make connections with and get advice from successful men who can model that success for them. For some African American communities, a ritual like the beautillion, which fortifies individual and community resilience, is a realistic, if rarefied, response to social conditions.

Within the black community, there is an ongoing expectation that debutantes of both genders will give back to their communities. African American debuts are much more likely to be hosted by organizations that offer lifelong memberships as well as ongoing networking and community service opportunities. Miya Carey explains that part of the reason why black families prioritized education and almost always offer scholarships at debutante balls was that many black women could not stay home with their families during the Jim Crow period, so there was an attendant push to educate daughters so that women could seek professional jobs. Educated women began to create a pipeline for their advancement that began with the debutante ritual. After the debut, women were funneled into the right schools, often historically black universities and colleges, where they joined the right sororities, and moved into the world with the same group of professional women. Once adults, these women kept their bond and keenly focused on giving back to their communities and keeping the pipeline open and flourishing.[21] Whereas white debutante balls do make a nod toward community service during the debutante season, and many balls do raise money for and publicize charities, there is no real infrastructure for ongoing volunteering within these organizations. A possible exception is the Junior League. However, most Junior League members join that organization later in adulthood, and it is the adult members who complete most of the community service work. Most of these women also were not debutantes. It's debatable how much any cotillion group raises for charity, and impossible to measure what value they bring to white debutantes.

Lawrence Otis Graham's work raises questions about what it means to be elite within the black community. Would the subjects of his book see most African American debutante presentations as decidedly middle class? African American debutante organizations have looked to provide an answer to challenges within their communities and have combined philanthropy with a social ritual that confers class advantages. While debutante balls within the African American community highlight achievement and service, they also raise questions about elitism and embracing such a traditional notion of femininity. But black women, as Carey points out, have traditionally been denied their femininity and, when they began holding debuts, claiming femininity was a subversive act. The black community has adapted the ritual to their own needs and desires, affirming the value of education and service for black women, and creating a community of women who can work together toward those ends.

CHAPTER 10

Nouveau Now

THE DEBUTANTE REIMAGINED

U ntil the mid-'90s, the newly rich attempted to assimilate by emulating the old families. They joined country clubs, sent their children to riding lessons and boarding schools, and set up foundations and family offices. But in the mid-1990s the nature of money began to change. The corporate raiders who clamored for inclusion were replaced by an infusion of tech millionaires who generally rejected traditions like the debutante ritual in favor of sweatpants and the latest robot. In combination and in contrast with a rising entertainment culture emphasizing gratuitous displays of wealth, the new ultra-rich ushered in a drastically different model for the "upper class," one that thoroughly changed the social order, making "old money" so insignificant that it was no longer even a target of satirists. Digby Baltzell, in his book *The Protestant Establishment*, showed fifty years ago how the WASP upper class was a caste that had lost its political and economic power because it was unwilling to accept worthy new members into its power structure. But WASP culture did not wake up to its own obsolescence until its *aesthetic* power was no longer valued by society at large. By the early 1990s, it seemed like most WASPs would retire quietly to the country, destined for a slow disintegration, taking their rituals with them.

But it is often at the moment when a tradition might slip into the aether that it is championed most vociferously, and debutante presentations have steadily increased in popularity since the late 1990s. Though the debutante ritual has always had nostalgia for better days built into its structure, the differences between old and new money presentations in New York was clear in the '80s and early '90s. That difference is minimal today. Some people from old money families have figured out that they can discuss their money and are doing so enthusiastically. Though the film itself lacked depth, Jamie Johnson's 2003 documentary, *Born Rich*, embodies the moment in the early 2000s at which a discreet older culture and a flashier new culture began to meld. The film ostensibly seeks to explore the taboo about talking about one's wealth, cleverly creating a venue in which to do so. Johnson features a publicity-seeking Ivanka Trump alongside some WASP mainstays, the latter of whom had apparently realized that now was the time to come out of hiding to embrace the new display culture, before all was lost, and they could no longer dine out on their social credentials. Today, a debutante is more likely to be a New Russian than a daughter of the American Revolution.

In New York, a few debutante presentations still survive as relics of the country club style or of nostalgia for debutante performance wherein girls nod to their parents that they will be taking on the mantle of upper-middle or upper-class power, and won't be rocking any boats. That was the sort of ball where I would have made my debut. At that time, you wouldn't have known the names of young women making debuts at the Mayflower Ball, or Junior Assemblies, or even the Infirmary, unless you were a committed reader of niche social magazines, or of colonial history. At the Mayflower Society, there might be only one or two debutantes at the annual dinner in New York. I remember hearing from a friend that in the '90s one of the debutantes showed up with a tattoo of a sinking Mayflower on her right shoulder, just visible above her white strapless dress. These establishment balls in New York are less significant each year. Attendance and interest are waning, and there are fewer photos in the press—media being the standard by which New York society measures and judges everything.

Because of waning interest in the old upper rung, both the press and the potential debutantes, who want to use a debut to attract attention, have turned enthusiastically to a series of glitzy international parties, which take place in New York, London, and Paris. They are for openly ambitious families and receive multiple features each year in major magazines like *Vogue*, *Town & Country*, and *Vanity Fair*. These balls cater to the children of celebrities, the new superrich, and to any authentic aristocrats or blue-blooded Americans they can get to attend. As businesses designed for profit, they secondarily raise money for charity. Their main aim is to generate press for their attendees. Performing a similar role to Julia Cutting, PR firms control and shape these parties, acting as vetting agents, and in some cases as procurers of the debutantes themselves.

The International Debutante Ball is unabashedly high profile. It was founded by the socialite Beatrice Joyce in 1954 and held in the week between Christmas and New Year every year until 2001, when it moved to a biennial schedule. Joyce had been a night owl, and was "a fan of the arty set/cafe society who hung around at the theatre," according to her niece, Margaret Hedberg, who now owns and runs the ball. "She was doing parties all the time by the time she was in her 30s, and was one of the first women in the career they used to call 'special events.' " Joyce was an unusual figure, according to her niece. At 5'2" and 350 lbs., she "had pointy fingernails and wore pink bows all over her clothes. Needless to say, in the New York of the 1950s, she stood out." Because Joyce was obese at a time and in a milieu when that was rare, she was able to do things like "run around New York at night" in ways that "the thin women were not able to do," according to Hedberg. After reading Consuelo Vanderbilt Balsan's autobiography, *The Glitter and the Gold*, in which Vanderbilt Balsan describes her international friendships, Joyce saw an opportunity to start a ball with a similar spirit of international networking.

Unlike a lot of deb parties, the International Ball was a business from the start. Beatrice Joyce got seed money from Evyan Perfumes (makers of the famous White Shoulders, perfectly branded for debutantes) and the ball took off. Joyce was conscious of how her ball differed from others and promoted it as a mini-UN. This was a good strategy, as it allowed her to cannily by-pass the strict social restrictions of the period. She said she wanted to introduce girls to people they *didn't* already know, which no ball in the country was doing.

In the eighties, in the midst of the revival of all things grandiose, the International aired every year on the lovably down-market local New York TV channel WPIX, a station known primarily for airing an image of a blazing Yule log all day on Christmas. In Whit Stillman's satirical film, *Metropolitan*, there is a scene during which his characters sit in a hotel room in evening dress, having returned from the more blue-blooded debutante parties, and watch the International on television. Later in the film, one of the main characters, Nick Smith, shows up with a smiling Texan deb and her military escort, her cheer flying in the face of the cadre of jaded upper-class New York debs, and Nick's look of resignation a commentary on the passing of the old guard and blasé WASP culture.

While the ball thrived in the eighties boom years, it barely scraped by in the early '90s. As Hedberg shrewdly said to me, "It costs the same for the orchestra if one person is dancing or a thousand are." When I asked Hedberg how she survived that low period, she said she did so due largely to the mothers who had debuted there, and who wanted to keep the tradition by presenting their daughters at the same ball. That, and the fact that the International has always been known as a more fun and relaxed ball, carried her through. Some high-profile debs, like Julie Nixon Eisenhower, had added an air of respectability to the International. Europeans, who have always made up a large contingent, were less disenchanted than American teenagers and had an easier time ignoring politics in a country that wasn't their own. Additionally, because it wasn't a ball associated with the social establishment, it didn't telegraph the kind of upper-class values that invited rebellion.

The debutantes who decide to come out at the International Ball do so to get press, or to get their family press, with the idea that they can use the event to insert themselves into a contemporary New York and international social scene, which is driven primarily by effective public relations. The modern debutante season, which is extending into more of the world's major cities, is a thriving business, managed by professionals. Hedberg understands that the purpose of the debutante ball is now different than it was initially. "I don't think anyone enters society through these balls. Maybe in Charleston or New Orleans." The goal now is "press," which can then be used to propel a career of any kind. That doesn't mean that girls or their families want people to know they're seeking publicity. Like the 1920s debutantes who wandered in front of cameras as if aimlessly, any yearning for the spotlight needs to remain invisible. On the delicate subject of publicity, Mrs. Hedberg is sanguine. "We do some press," she said. "We need to be known. Of course we don't want any horrible press, but we are not the St. Cecilia Society. They are one thing, but we need to be known. If I send you an invitation and you've never heard of us, it doesn't work. It helps us to be known a little bit as opposed to getting something weird in the mail from a person in New York." [1]

On the night of the fifty-eighth ball, I walked through the lobby of the Waldorf toward the Astor salon, passing many of that particular breed of hardy Midwestern tourist who can somehow wear shorts on a cold December day. People were flooding the lobby to see the guests arrive at the ball. Teenage boys stood with dropped jaws as young guests passed by in slinky evening dresses on their way to celebrate their friends' debuts. This was no ball of old where rope lines protected guests and the whole hotel was rented out. Today, you could find yourself on a tourist's Instagram page.

When I arrived at the Astor room, I was wrongly ushered by a publicist into the line for guests, a mistake on her part since I was technically press. I didn't correct her, thinking I would hear more interesting conversations. When I saw the length of the line she put me in, I took a glass of champagne and edged myself forward. One thing you learn at these balls is to never get into a receiving line without a drink. As we waited, I spoke with the people next to me, an elderly woman in a voluminous emerald green taffeta dress who attended each year the ball is held, despite no connection to the event. She was there to support the charity, she said, and to see the girls. "Why," I asked? "I always come," she simply said. Later, Hedberg told me that these people come every year "on their walkers. There are debutante groupies. Bless them all."[2]

The wait ended at a large, mirrored rectangular room, lined by the debutantes, who were arranged in front of the countries' flags. The sizable American contingent was also arranged by state. You are meant to merely say hello, not to ask questions. The girls were sweet and polite. They smiled broadly, and introduced themselves over and over again saying their names and where they were from. Well-coached in what to say to the press, they gave the sort of friendly, meaningless answers that actresses give on the red carpet. Do your shoes hurt? "Yes." Why are you a debutante? "Because it's tradition," "I thought it would be fun." But while actresses have lately waged a successful campaign to be asked about more than their clothing on the red carpet, the debutante's role is largely a silent one, or at least one with few preapproved scripts.

Hedberg had a few explanations for why people wanted their daughters to debut at her ball: "The ball is eclectic. It is a mix. It tends to [attract] people who want to keep tradition alive and aspire to some old values. They want to honor their daughter as she passes into adulthood." For some families, she said, it can be as simple as "getting the family out of jeans and into something glamorous. It's a ball." She says. "You want people there who like this sort of thing." It costs families $16,000 to have their daughter presented. All but $2,000 of this fee is tax deductible, and that $2,000 accounts for the cost of a table for ten, plus the ticket for the debutante and her escort. If the family takes a table alongside the dance floor, the cost goes up to $20,000, and the overage from the better table goes to the International Ball Foundation and, therefore, to the military charities (chief of which is the Soldiers', Sailors', Coast Guards', Marines' and Airmen's Club of Manhattan) that the foundation supports. "If people want to donate more, I'd take it, but that never seems to happen." Families also spend a lot of money on other expenses for the ball. A few of the dresses may cost as little as a few hundred dollars, but they can be priced into the tens of thousands of dollars, if ornate. Families also take on the expense of travel and hotel as well as the expenses of any guests. The military charities provide cover, and a tax write-off.

There are also several parties that lead up to the ball that are included in its overall cost. There's a "Bachelor's Brunch" where the girls meet and choose their escorts. It happens on the Saturday after Thanksgiving, when people are in New York, or can travel there. Girls are required to invite their escorts themselves, and are instructed, because of escort shortages, to find out right away if a boy at the brunch is already taking his sister. Committee members also help to provide escorts, who tend to be brothers of debutantes and former debutantes. The boys also have to apply and be informally vetted, and tend to be similar as the girls, between seventeen and twenty-three. There is also a mother-daughter luncheon before the ball, and a party the morning after, where the girls have an opportunity for a postmortem and to say goodbye to each other.

Looking at these awkward daughters standing in a line, I felt protective. I learned how to please as a teenage girl, too, and this behavior was not totally unfamiliar to me, even if I was more at home with Stillman's group of sarcastic teens. It had been a long time since I had been at a debutante ball and the age of the girls startled me, and made me think of how much this really is the first big party for many. Since the population still skews toward WASPs, most of these girls had not had a bat mitzvah. After the receiving line disbanded, the partygoers spread out for a cocktail hour with hors d'oeuvres. This serves not just to keep people from fainting, but also provides the press with a long period in which to take photos in a more natural setting. Generally speaking, the debu-

tantes don't eat. They are told beforehand that you don't want to be photographed with food in your mouth (true). The girls who want publicity
also give interviews under the watchful eyes of the event's public relations firm. While the people from *Fairfield County Look* magazine and
Patrick McMullan Photographers (though not McMullan, a longtime
event photographer) took endless photos, I spoke to the other reporters. Having been rushed ahead into the guest receiving line, I missed
the PR directives and was curious to hear what they were. I learned that
the press were told to "be nice to the girls." This reminded me of family
members telling me "don't say anything arch, now."

Earlier in the evening, I had spoken with the woman managing PR
for the night, Christine Mortimer Biddle, a blueblood herself, doing
something akin to what Julia Cutting did in the previous generation—
putting her venerable name to use to earn money. Ms. Biddle and her
business partner are known for producing successful charity events, due
in large part to the fact that they are friends with, or can get access to,
people who move within New York's circles of power. While the girls
still milled about being photographed, Ms. Biddle looked on nervously,
watching the crowd. Soon, I heard a swish of dresses and a collective
intake of breath. Bill Cunningham, the now-deceased legendary photographer from the *New York Times*, had arrived. I will never forget the
expressions of relief on the faces of the organizers when they saw him.
Some of his photos ran in the next day's paper. It wasn't important that
there was no story to accompany them; perhaps it was even better that
there was not.

I asked girl after girl how she felt about being part of such an enduring ritual, and if they knew how and why it originated. Most did not
know, but some were excited to learn they were part of something with
a long history. Others barely spoke at all. A few described themselves
as "philanthropists," but others were more down-to-earth. The Texans
were the most practiced. Most of them had already debuted many times
in cities where the press cares. I tried to talk to the one girl representing

China, the country in the process of its own coal-fueled Gilded Age, complete with all the tropes—robber barons, corrupt officials, and pollution hanging low in rising cities. I was told she didn't want any press, but I did manage to ask her why she was there. "To represent my country," she said in halting English. I learned her father was a "government official." With that, the door was closed.

After the lengthy photo-op was done, the debutantes were moved to an anteroom, where they awaited their official presentation. They sat on hotel chairs arranged schoolroom style, their voluminous dresses flowing over the chairs' sides. Each chair had a number, which made remembering the order of presentation easier. I slipped into the room, sat next to a girl and introduced myself. I was lucky, as she happened to be from North Carolina, where my father's family originates, and many relatives still live. I asked her if she knew any of my cousins—she only knew of us—but we began to talk. She knew quite a bit about the history of debutantes and had done a sociology paper on the topic "because nobody gets it right." "Nobody takes this seriously," she told me, "and they should." I agreed with her. "This is my third ball," she said. She had also debuted in Charlotte, and at the National Debutante Cotillion, though interestingly not at the Terpsichorean Ball in Raleigh, North Carolina's oldest ball, where some of my young cousins have come out. I asked her if her mother had been a deb, and she said no, that this was "new for my family." When I asked her how she got there, her story was perfect. She told me that when she was sixteen in 2008, she and her family happened to be visiting New York and staying at the Waldorf while the ball was happening. They sneaked in and watched the girls from the balcony. Greatly affected by the princess dresses below her, she said, "Mom, I want to do this." And so she did. For her being a debutante was a kind of achievement, conveying that she had attained the kind of beauty, poise, and status that she saw in the girls at the earlier ball.

Then it was time for guests to enter the ballroom. The iconic art deco room was hung with Christmas garlands, a mix of fir needles and

1950s style pink and red roses interspersed with thick gold ribbon. The Waldorf ballroom has the feel of an opera house because you can look down from boxes. When I entered the room, I felt the degree to which this would be a performance with the girls on stage. The lighting was theatrical, with spotlights directed at the stage. I was seated at one of three tables for press. The only way to describe the journalists at this party is jaded, as jaded as twenty-five-year-old reporters can be. But they know the story they're meant to produce, and they know they can't write too far out of the lines, or they won't be asked back. There is a formula to covering these events, and the publicists rely on the press to reproduce it: the girls look beautiful and have Real-Life Interests. One might play tennis, another might be studying to be an electrical engineer. They're all good students and none is at the ball to get married. Publicists feed journalists information and assume they will ask friendly questions. The debutante piece is an old chestnut—they are all exactly the same, and the reporters are there primarily as appendages to the photographers. It's the pictures that matter.

While reporters talked around me, I thought to myself that parents were still paying a fee for an exchange: girls for press. It bears an uncomfortable resemblance to the old exchange, since young women are still on one side of the barter and parents are still trying to buy a future for their daughters. In some cases, they are trying to buy a place in society for themselves. Jerry Jones, billionaire owner of the Dallas Cowboys, a man not known for his manners, was there with his debutante granddaughters. Even if there are too few dowagers with unimpeachable credentials and too few old families at this party to make it truly prestigious, most of the world doesn't know or care. This party will appear glamorous and exclusive in the press. Those who like to deride the rich will have plenty of ammunition for that as well.

We next heard an announcement: it's showtime. The announcer stated where the girl was from, her name, and then her parents' names. The girls were introduced one by one, first alphabetically by country, and then alphabetically by US state. The debs and their escorts entered from an anteroom and walk down the center of the ballroom. Each couple was followed by a cadet, who carried the girl's state or national flag. The debutante and her escort's youth juxtaposed with a cadet in uniform gave the ceremony a strong sense of hierarchy that felt odd in modern life. Then the debutante walked down to the dais to theme music from her home state. If this sounds hokey and rather undignified, that's because it is. Even the debutantes looked apologetic as they strolled to "New York, New York" or "Sweet Home, Alabama." Everyone was now waiting for the debutantes from Texas. They make up the biggest, most aggressive contingent, not because they are the most enthusiastic, but because, as we saw in the San Antonio ball, they do the Texas dip curtsy. I was standing next to another reporter, who said to me, "I hope they don't fall." I think she meant the opposite.

Once the Texans reached the center of the stage they stopped and waited. During this interminable period I wondered if the debutante was thinking, "Am I really going to do this?" The Texas dip is high kitsch—almost like a Vegas magic trick. You can't see the girl's feet so it appears like she's vanishing into a trap door, giving the entire thing an unintentionally comic element. What the girl has actually done, under her voluminous dress, is cross her legs, slowly bent her knees, and lowered herself onto her high heels. It is a feat. The whole move is designed to show no leg movement whatsoever, and involves complicated balance in order to absent all movement below the waist. Just before she reaches the lowermost point of her bow, which would bring her head directly into her own lap, she tilts her head slightly to the left to avoid smearing her white dress with her copious makeup. The Texas dip had been a major topic of conversation and a publicist selling point all night. We were told, in hushed tones, that the girls practice for months. But the move is so difficult that only one girl executed the curtsy with any real ease. The rest look relieved when it was over. One stumbled and fell, and was rescued by her escort, who became the hero of the night. The crowd cheered for her like the Americans we are. She blushed and left the stage as quickly as she could. I feel for her. It was painful to watch. Will Texas allow her to come home? At the same time, I couldn't get the absurd nod to submissive sexuality in this move out of my head. I wished I were with John Waters.

The girls were "out" after the last debutante's curtsy. The first dance was the ceremonial father-daughter dance. It was hard not to watch two tall sisters from the Netherlands who, not trusting the many official photographers to capture them well, had brought their own photographer. One danced with her father and the other with a designated stand-in, while the photographer circled them both making his own little quadrille.

After the father-daughter dance, the formality ended and the girls reverted to being the teenagers they were and started dancing in groups to Beyoncé, moving awkwardly in their bride-like dresses. When the party moved on to dancing Gangnam-style, I returned to a photographer I met earlier who had more lamentations for the demise of old money families than I'd ever heard from anyone actually in one. He wouldn't have a conversation with me on the record, but warmed to me when we talked about Lester Lanin, whose namesake band was playing, though Lester himself had died a while ago. I spoke in the codes he knows, joking with him about the Lester Lanin hat I still have somewhere. I can't remember at what party I got the hat—it wasn't at a debut—but they used to throw them into the crowds at the parties they played. Lanin played for a long time, so the hats could not really be exclusive, but they're still a WASP relic. We reminisced about the times we saw Lanin conduct. The seduction of old days has to be one of the greatest seductions we have. This line of conversation is a stand-by at debutante parties. For me, acting as a reporter, it was highly useful, a way of playing both good and bad cop at once. He opined that the debutante ritual is dying out. I assured him it's long dead but will never die and got an understanding high five in return.

I made my way through the crowd and talked to more girls. I received stock answers, but I wanted those, too, to check if they had changed. I was talking with a nationally ranked tennis player from New York who was telling me about civic duty and the responsibility of giving back. After a series of innocuous questions, I asked the young woman a final one—"What did you think about when you bowed down?" She looked confused. For the first time we were off-message. Her answer? "I just really thought about how important it is for me to be a debutante." She looked relieved. Her mother, who had been visibly nervous, relaxed. Her daughter had found her way out.

There had been drama enough earlier in the evening. The pomp and circumstance provided by the military escorts at the International Ball almost didn't come off that year. Military lawyers had decided to take seriously a long-ignored rule against wearing uniforms to certain types of events—like beauty pageants—which would degrade the uniform. The lawyers determined the debutante ball to be akin to a beauty pageant because the girls are escorted onto the stage, pageant style. With the ban on uniforms in place, only Citadel students were allowed to attend in uniform, because they are not directly affiliated with the military. West Point cadets didn't attend, and the Naval Academy escorts wore tuxes, forcing the organizers to recycle the same uniformed escorts to walk the girls to the stage. Party attendees, particularly the girls' parents, who were invested in their image, were horrified by the comparison to that festival of high vulgarity, the beauty pageant. This was a hot topic around the edges of the ballroom. People were embarrassed. But think about it from the perspective of an army lawyer: the girls are arranged by country or state, they wear formal gowns, regularly talk about their talents, and the role for the cadet is to escort them on and off of a stage. It's hard not to understand their point.

In order to separate this party from a beauty pageant, one mother, who had made her own debut at the International, was explaining to a group of reporters that the party was "about teaching them networking, etiquette and diplomacy. The girls make connections and friends with girls in other cultures." It's hard to argue that the girls really learn anything from this party that they don't already know from being socialized by aspirational parents and a private school system. Barring a proper curtsy, which these girls are unlikely to ever need, the ball is not really teaching etiquette. Networking might seem right, because the girls do meet others who have similar social aspirations. But it strikes me that diplomacy is the opposite of what this particular party teaches. Diplomacy is different from mannered denial. It's the recognition that there is a dark undercurrent to many commonplace interactions. That it is possible to soldier onward even when you know the ground beneath your feet is crumbling. Diplomacy is engagement—if diplomacy teaches us how to negotiate hard truths with decency and tact, and to know the right moment and in what tone to say something difficult, the current iteration of the debutante ritual teaches us that these are not women's roles. The debut teaches you to recognize your own kind, to revel in the status quo—and how to avoid what you plainly don't want to see.

I found another photographer leaning against a ribbon-wrapped column and asked how long he'd been attending these parties and how they've changed. He tells me that the ball had totally transformed. "It used to be more about the upper class, and people you had heard of, not this kind of new money," he said. He suggested that I go to the parties in Connecticut, to see how the old guard still does it. I tell him that the Connecticut Junior League ball folded last year. The girls who want to come out have been directed to go to the Infirmary Ball, which has enthusiastically welcomed them because it means more money for the hospital. And some, too, have been picked up by the Junior Assemblies, held at the Plaza. At the Infirmary, which is officially called the Debutante Cotillion and Christmas Ball, the girls still do a series of Christmas-themed cotillion figures. One of my older cousins remembers carrying, variously, a garland, a candle, and a marabou muff, and making different arrangements and shapes with the other girls while singing Christmas carols. The Infirmary Ball is endowed by NewYork-Presbyterian/Lower Manhattan Hospital, which organizes the ball and benefits from its proceeds. Their internal budget allows the ball to exist while remaining somewhat selective. It's doubtful they're raising much for the hospital, but the ball does a good deal to raise the hospital's pro-file, which brings in more donations. This helps them to keep their status as a blue-chip social charity, which matters in New York, and has rami-fications for how much a charity can raise.

In the mid-'90s, I went to my boarding school friends' debuts at Junior Assemblies. We drank a lot of vodka in the hotel room where we were staying, and went down to the party far from sober. The ball didn't feel like a ball because the girls weren't formally introduced on a stage and they didn't do any kind of proving ritual, like dancing a complex figure. At the end of a staid dinner, someone made an announcement and the girls stood in unison, were recognized with polite applause, and then sat down. There was music from a band in the background, and a simple father-daughter dance, but nothing that could invite cringing like curtseying. Most of the room knew each other. Even if you didn't, you knew their names. This was the world in which I grew up. The International, composed of what my dad would jokingly call "the real swells," using a supercilious accent straight out of old Hollywood, was unrecognizable to me.

At the International, there was a debutante I'd been watching. She had a great deal of style and looked different from the forty-six others. I learned that she's a Russian American from Pennsylvania. She had matte bleached blonde hair, and the sort of face you rarely seen on a young American girl; this girl is *jolie laide*. In America, we are only good at *jolie*. The other girls are smooth, preppie, clean, and shiny. She was the only girl who was not smiling from ear to ear for the entire party. This girl would be more beautiful later in her life, and had the sort of fierce, interesting face that doesn't wither with the meandering disappointments of country club life. While the others looked excited about the proceedings, this girl looked like she was in another place, and while in character, was counting the minutes until her presentation was finished. I got the distinct sense that she wanted to avoid the press. I tried, but was never able to talk to her.

The night waned. I left before the Lanin hats were passed out. Changing in the bathroom of the Waldorf, I suddenly remembered doing the same thing twenty years earlier, but in reverse. When I'd escape from boarding school, the Waldorf's first floor bathroom was where I would change into my clothing before heading to clubs downtown. They had good mirrors for the alarmingly adult makeup I put on before going out. Yet with its bright lights and proximity to the Upper East Side, the hotel was still safe and familiar. This time my escape was to my family, to go back home to my little son. The next morning, I woke up and googled the name of the Russian-American girl. In her nondebutante time, she is a Cosplayer and has photos of herself in various manga costumes and excellent wigs. I found myself hoping fervently that she would do debutante Cosplay, taking her strong, subversive face to Japan, where she would pantomime debutante presentations and send up the whole thing.

The International Ball provides a modern, openly corporate model for a social debut. Yet, this is not so disingenuous in the United States, where debuts have never been fixed to a real aristocratic system, and have always been a means of creating and sustaining family histories. In England, the season slowly declined after 1957, when Queen Elizabeth terminated court presentations because they didn't reflect her vision of a modern monarchy. Her husband, Prince Phillip, had famously called the debutante system "bloody daft." There is even a story about her sister, Princess Margaret, perhaps revealing the true reason for abandoning presentations when she remarked, "We had to put a stop to it, every tart in London was getting in." But after the demise of court presentations, a British property heiress, Lady Howard de Walden continued to sponsor and organize the season on a smaller scale. She was followed in her mission by Peter Townend, the social editor of *Tatler*, who compiled a "little black book" filled with the names and addresses of suitable potential debutantes and escorts. Every year, Townend, who was obsessed with lineage, wrote to parents—in flowery penmanship and turquoise ink—inviting their daughters to take part. If they did, he could guarantee them photos and favorable coverage in his magazine. He had a female analogue at *Harper's & Queen* and the two loathed each other from across opposite sides of central London (even after Queen Charlotte's Ball officially folded in 1997) until they both died in 2001. For many this meant the end of the season in London, and this was met, in most quarters, with relief.

In 2009, a friend of Townend's named Jennie Hallam-Peel, a former lawyer, decided the time was ripe to revive the season once again, telling the *Independent*, "I think people are sick and tired of New Labour's political correctness and this horrendous cult of the celebrity. People want to re-instate some of the proud institutions that defined Britain's identity and I believe debutantes are very much part of that."[3] With that unabashed nationalism at the heart of their mission, she and her partner Patricia Woodall have attempted to reanimate the London season, and have centered it around reviving Queen Charlotte's Ball. The organizers registered the domain name thelondonseason.org and garnered the patronage of minor Slavic princesses and British aristocrats, who are compensated for their time. The two have attempted to create the exclusivity of debutante ritual, using a lengthy application process to vet candidates. They choose 200 girls and their mothers to interview at the Grosvenor House hotel. At the end of the interviews, 180 of these families are told they're not suitable, and the remaining 20 go through a debutante season where they learn the manners they need and do unspecified charitable work. Each year, Hallam-Peel and Woodall choose a different designer to make the debutantes' dresses and a jeweler to loan them pieces, which allows the London Season organization to control the attire of young women who might not have the requisite taste, and to extend an excellent PR opportunity to whichever designers they pick. The season culminates at the ball itself, held at London's Royal Courts of Justice in early September. The debutantes perform the curtsy of old to the guests at the ball. Unlike the original Queen Charlotte's Ball, which supported only the West London hospital that still bears her name, the ball now supports a different charity each year. The ball receives eager press from tabloids like *The Daily Mail* and its share of open ridicule as well. The season's patrons get some publicity for their own ventures, and a new crop of debutantes get the imprimatur of legitimate, if not significant, royalty and a few peers. It is unclear if those associations last past the debutante season.

The possible motives for relaunching the social season and reviving debutantes became clearer when, after a few years of running the debutante ball in London, Hallam-Peel and Woodall launched a new venture called the London Season Academy. It runs business etiquette and global leadership courses in London, Dubai, and at Bradley House, the Wiltshire country house owned by the Duke of Somerset, a ball patron. The school offers these courses to individuals and corporations, with the stated mission, "Etiquette in a multicultural society is important in helping to navigate social occasions and to avoid unintentional offence when communicating with people from varying cultures." This is undeniably true, and a good business. The company has hired respected experts on protocol and leadership to mentor their attendees, as well as royal and aristocratic patrons, who also have expertise on manners.

The London Season Academy chose to launch their new business with a debutante ball in Dubai, where they had recently opened their foreign bureau. They held the party on a private island, where it would be easier to duck confusing Emirati alcohol laws that differ based on age, religion, location, and licensing, and provide a challenge for organizers, who need to balance the need for a festive atmosphere with respect for the Muslim debutantes and their families. Some of the debutantes who come out in Dubai are British, and first came out at the ball in London. They travel to Dubai as part of their season because, according to the organizers, the Emiratis "want British tradition." The debutantes in Dubai are considerably younger than their counterparts in the rest of the world. Their ages range from sixteen to twenty, while other debutantes are almost always in college. The Duchess of Somerset and Princess Katarina of Yugoslavia teach them how to serve afternoon tea, shake hands, and properly cut a scone. Then the girls go through a one-day training in business and corporate etiquette. The absurdity of combining scone-cutting instruction with a day of rapid-fire corporate etiquette training to women who aren't in a life phase where either is relevant makes it clear that the debutantes aren't the ones who are meant to benefit from their seasons; they're a product that enhances the school's corporate offerings. And it has worked. The school is a success. However, whether the Academy will manage a full resurrection of the debutante season remains to be seen.

The most exclusive debutante ball today is barely a debutante ball, and takes place in France, which has never had a strong tradition of coming out. *Le Bal des Débutantes*, once known as the Crillon Ball and now just called *Le Bal*, began in 1992, when Ophélie Renouard, who was then the director of events at Paris's famed Crillon Hotel, organized a charity couture show where the clothes were modeled by young French socialites. Renouard came up with the show to garner publicity for the hotel, the couture industry, and the women who participated, and it was such a success that, in 1994, she transformed her event into a ball, which was held at the hotel between Christmas and New Year, and found "cavaliers" to escort the girls she invited. *Le Bal* remains the only debutante ball to which you can't apply—unlike most balls, tickets aren't available to interested outsiders—you must be invited. Renouard relies on her network of contacts, many made through the parents of former debutantes and the women themselves, to construct a list of daughters of aristocrats, celebrities, politicians, and high-profile businesspeople. The only additional requirement is that prospective debutantes be able to fit into a couture sample.

If any contemporary debutante ball can be said to have real prestige beyond a small circle or in-group, it is this one, and that's because Renouard is savvy. There is no nod to virginity or tradition by insisting on white dresses. The children of European aristocrats, maharajahs, and pretenders to defunct thrones comingle with the children of Reese Witherspoon, Forrest Whitaker, Larry David, and Bruce Willis and Demi Moore, among many others. The daughters and granddaughters of high-profile politicians also come out at *Le Bal*. Lauren Bush, Kick and Kyra Kennedy, Barbara Berlusconi, Xenia and Anastasia Gorbachev all debuted at the ball. There are a few debutantes from Silicon Valley, and, increasingly, the daughters of Chinese, Russian, and Indian billionaires. Isha Ambani, daughter of industrialist Mukesh Ambani, the richest man in Asia, made her debut at *Le Bal*. Even if you don't know an individual debutante's name, her presence can be explained by revealing her parents are Annette Bening and Warren Beatty, or her grandfather, the Duke of Devonshire.

Displaying an understanding of the cultural moment that other ball organizers don't seem to have, Renouard outlines how she sees the ball directly on its website: "At the time of Facebook, the Debs need not to make their social débuts, *Le Bal* is rather the unforgettable moment of their couture and media premières." What results is something like the *Vanity Fair* Oscar party, a tightly edited mix of people that tells a story about who is currently most relevant within a specific milieu. While there are articles about debutantes from a few of the other balls, especially the International, this one is widely covered every year in prestige publications, the dresses are authentically interesting and beautiful, with long photo spreads appearing in magazines like *Vanity Fair* and *Teen Vogue* (it helps that the daughters of Graydon Carter and Anna Wintour came out at the ball). By being a good editor, Renouard has gained the trust and imprimatur of today's loosely connected elite, combining them intelligently, limiting the size of the party, and keeping the luridly ambitious away, creating the most modern debutante ritual we have today. *Le Bal des Débutantes* is traditional only in its unabashed emphasis on family status and a refreshingly honest lack of interest in the debutantes' accomplishments.

The contemporary debutante scene reached a kind of stasis in the 2010s, with a variety of debutante balls still popular in US cities, and a few more high-profile balls happening in Paris, London, and New York. They provide some sort of entree to the social life in one's community and are settling into a routine. But they don't feel dynamic, or like they were indicators of cultural change. In the 2010s, things started to become more interesting. After years of industrialization and development, there were large groups of unimaginably wealthy people in Russia and China. Unlike in other countries with an active debutante ritual, these formerly Communist countries had authoritarian governments that had long eschewed a Western cultural model, but, once again, the new class of industrialist and oligarchs were beginning to embrace the debutante ritual.

The Russian ultra-rich resemble the American robber barons of the nineteenth century. They have had no exposure to any kind of time-honored definition of good taste, but are eager to be seen as cultivated, so tend to do just what nouveau riche Americans did during the Gilded Age—buy entire collections of historical objects with the aid of outside advisers. When *Tatler*, the British society magazine, launched a Russian edition in 2008 to cover the decadent and rapidly expanding social scene in Moscow, it was a natural fit to start a debutante ball as well. Though Russia never had a strong debutante tradition, they did have an imperial past with a long tradition of formal balls. When the magazine organized this ball, Russian fathers were eager to display their wealth through their daughters.

The *Tatler Russia* debutante ball is part concierge service, part nationalistic effort. While other international billionaires send their daughters to debut in Europe and America each year, the Russians generally haven't. The Russian presence in London is politically and economically controversial. Russians who live there are not usually integrated into the London society scene that is covered by the UK edition of *Tatler*. Some oligarchs, particularly in the past few years, are under sanction, and can't travel to the United States, and, even if they could, are unlikely to want their daughters blessed by what their government considers a political adversary. Finally, the Russian leader, Vladimir Putin, has an imperialist vision of Russia, and is committed to restoring the country to its former glory. While that has generally meant reasserting Russian control over, or influence in, former Soviet Republics, or meddling in Western elections, a glamorous debutante ball in Moscow also fits the bill.

The ball takes place at the eighteenth-century House of the Unions, in a ballroom built for the Russian nobility during the reign of Catherine the Great. State support of the ball is tacit. While Putin does not attend, his presence is evident throughout. The daughters of Putin's energy minister and close confidante Alexander Novak, as well as Kremlin spokesman Dmitry Peskov came out at the 2018 ball, further signaling Kremlin approval. At the ball, the Russian National Philharmonic played Tchaikovsky's *Eugene Onegin* as the debutantes danced with their partners—male dancers from the Bolshoi Ballet. It would be similar to Yo-Yo Ma headlining the International Ball, or Misty Copeland providing dance training to a crop of young debutantes. Basically, unimaginable. The ball evokes an imperial past, while also making the statement that the present-day Russian oligarchs are fit heirs to that legacy. This is further heightened by the appearance of some Russians who have aristocratic pasts. The *Tatler* ball communicates that Russians don't need to debut in London, Paris, or New York; it is far more glamorous to come out at home.

The debutante ritual is not only appealing to Europeans looking to revive the tradition, or to repurpose it for their modern ambitions, but it's also going beyond that continent. The first signs that the debut was becoming truly international came in 2012, when a Chinese socialite and entrepreneur named Vivian Chow Wong founded the Shanghai International Debutante Ball—modeled on the ball in New York—with girls from around the world attending. The ball, held at Shanghai's Waldorf-Astoria (like the International Ball in New York), was the first debutante ball in China.

When asked why she launched the ball, Chow Wong told CNN: "The time was right," adding that there is "high demand for such events in China, where the girls are striving to have a certain quality of life other than brand names and materialistic things." Despite this, she wasn't able to get any debutantes from Mainland China to attend during the ball's first year because she concluded they did not meet her standard. The debutantes came almost entirely from England, with two young women coming from Taiwan. More recent balls have been mostly made up of Chinese debutantes, who began to participate once the ball proved itself elegant enough. When I asked Margaret Hedberg about the similarly named ball back in 2013, she told me that Chow Wong had proposed a debutante ball modeled on hers to the Waldorf when they were opening a new hotel in Shanghai. Hedberg's ball is trademarked and she was considering her legal options. Any problem seems to have vanished, as they now coexist without an issue.[4]

As China's wealth has grown, and the power of its industrialists along with it, Chinese debutantes, called "Red Princesses" by the Chinese press, have sought out debuts at balls in Europe and the United States. I spoke with Noël Duan, a Chinese American woman who made her debut at Queen Charlotte's Ball in 2013, to gain a better understanding of how the debutante ritual is expanding in Asian and Asian American communities.[5] Duan, who grew up in Silicon Valley and came out at the same time she was getting her master's degree in women's studies at Oxford, told me that she met the organizers of Queen Charlotte's through contacts at a magazine where she had been interning. She thought they were going to hire her to do social media for them, but instead they invited her to make her debut. Though she's from an affluent background and was invited to come out in San Francisco, she was surprised they asked her to be a part of the ball only a few weeks before it happened, especially because British debutantes tend to be white. Now she says she's seen such a major transformation in the composition of the ball that she can understand what they were trying to do. Hallam-Peel and Woodall, who Duan said are genuinely committed to British traditions, clearly saw where the future of the debutante ritual is, and it's not in Britain. Two years after Duan debuted, a quarter of the debutantes were Chinese.

The Chinese have been increasingly interested in British aristocracy, playing polo and seeking out British etiquette training. Duan attributes this to the loss of history that occurred during the Cultural Revolution, when the Communist government destroyed antiquities and records. Duan can't trace her family back farther than her grandparents' generation. As a result, the children of the Chinese superrich, called the *fuerdai*, meaning "rich second generation," have become entranced with the trappings of aristocracy, particularly British aristocracy. The debutante ritual, enhanced by its portability, holds real currency in China.

While nearly all of the British debutantes who came out with Duan were still in their teens, Chinese debutantes, both in China, and those who debut abroad, tend to be older. Reflecting on why a Chinese friend of hers who had graduated from a prestigious university, and would be moving on to an MBA, wanted to use the debutante ritual as a way to become a socialite in China, Duan told me: "It's not enough these days to achieve what you want to achieve, you need to get that press recognition. I don't know how to explain it. It's about having your own personal brand." She continues, "being a debutante, I think, gave her that prestige, at least in China."

Their participation also helps their families to forge business and social connections. The young women, often educated in Britain or the United States, are ambassadors for their families. It is rare for the daughter of a Russian oligarch to work in his company. It's almost always the case that a Chinese daughter does something that is at least tangentially related to her family's business. Wendy Yu, the daughter of billionaire Jingyuan Yu, founder of the Mengtian Group, Asia's largest manufacturer of wooden doors, attended boarding school and university in England, after which she became vice chairman of her family's businesses. A few years later, when she was looking to set up her own fashion and tech-focused venture capital fund, she decided to come out at both Queen Charlotte's Ball and the International Ball in New York. At twenty-six, she was much older than the average debutante, and as a billionaire, much richer, but she used the balls to promote her businesses, and was widely written about in the press.

In 2017, UK television station Channel Four aired a documentary about ultra-rich Chinese immigrants to Britain and featured Yu going through her London season (culminating in Queen Charlotte's Ball). We see her learning to shoot clay pigeons with the Duke of Somerset—and misunderstanding when she's meant to fire. We see Jennie Hallam-Peel singling her out during the pre-ball rehearsals as the one debutante who can't get the walk right, berating her in front of her father, "Wendy, you really need to walk with dignity and slowly," and then, slowly surveying the room, says: "This really applies to everyone. Although I have to say that everyone else has walked . . . um . . . walked in a very nice way." Despite this treatment, Yu is unfailingly polite, and her clearly sincere desire to impress her father is at times wrenching to watch. When she is not awarded "debutante of the year," her family leave the ball early. She manages to take it in stride, and writes it off as cultural difference. Her honesty about wanting to show she has achieved a certain level of grace and to impress her father is endearing and makes anyone who would want to degrade her come off as jaded and condescending. Yu has since become successful in her own right, having chosen to take a stake in a taxi-hail app that promised to be the Uber of China (and ended up taking over Uber in China). She is a major donor to a number of fashion-related charities, including the Costume Institute at the Metropolitan Museum of Art. She serves on the committee for their high-profile annual gala, chaired by Anna Wintour, which has raised her visibility as a player in the fashion business.

Annabel Yao, daughter of the reclusive telecom billionaire Ren Zhengfei, founder of the telecom giant Huawei, is a computer science student at Harvard who came out at *Le Bal*. Annabel, who does not have her father's name and had rarely been seen by the Chinese public before her debut was suddenly in the spotlight at *Le Bal*. For Ren Zhengfei, the timing of Annabel's debut was crucial. He has been beset by accusations of cyberespionage and embroiled by investigations in several countries, possibly hampering a huge merger. He and his wife appeared together at Annabel's debut, and the reclusive family posed for a big photo spread in *Paris Match*.

Sabrina Ho, daughter of gambling tycoon Stanley Ho, known as the King of Macau, also came out at Queen Charlotte's Ball. It is not uncommon for a Chinese debutante to come out at more than one ball, suggesting a desire to make as many connections as possible, as there isn't much social overlap between the different balls. Duan emphasizes that the women she knows view the ritual as a stepping stone—not the vital component of "their personal brands," but something that can demonstrably help, particularly in China.

Almost immediately after I began thinking about writing this book, I started thinking about the future of the debutante ritual. I didn't wonder if it would continue, but I did wonder where it would be most relevant. The debut has proven, perhaps unsurprisingly, to be a natural fit for this new generation of ultra-rich in authoritarian states, whose leaders rely heavily on ceremony to maintain power for themselves and their circle. For the leaders of those countries, it's important that wealthy industrialists are well fed and quiescent. Allowing their daughters to become debutantes and then socialites is one important concession. Whether the debut becomes popular enough to expand the upper class in these countries in any significant way remains to be seen. But with the explosion of debutante balls in China, and their growth in Russia, it is trending in that direction.

AFTERWORD

At one time, the debutante ritual was the ultimate expression of rarefied knowledge. It was esoteric, exclusive, and often incomprehensible to outsiders, if they could even glean some of it its details. Presentation at court and the ensuing London season were the culmination of years of training that began in childhood and were designed to render manners so natural as to seem innate. Today, a debutante goes through a few rehearsals, moving awkwardly through curtsies and dance figures, a hint of her college sweatshirt hanging in the air around her. The more formal etiquette is replaced by modern corporate etiquette, and the hierarchies the debutante ritual once created recede from young women's daily lives, the more disjointed it feels to watch debutantes don their white dresses, dance a waltz with their fathers, and perform what is surely the only curtsy of their lives.

Historically, preparing for the season meant learning how to hide any appearance of effort. Once the ritual expanded beyond the uppermost reaches of society, young women from newly rich families studied how to behave like aristocrats and tried to mirror their effortlessness. In doing so, they hoped to conceal their bourgeois origins well enough to marry into the aristocracy without causing real embarrassment to themselves or their new husbands. This specialized ritual limited to the upper classes—or those working on their behalf—transmitted accepted taste and social power to the next generation, so as to keep out parvenus.

By facilitating marriages between the aristocracy and wealthier members of the gentry and the bourgeoisie, the debutante ritual gradually increased the size and scope of the upper class, changing both its values and its socioeconomic composition to be more inclusive. This made it a stabilizing force for England and its colonies for several hundred years. However, its very success at expanding the ruling class through intermarriage eventually led to the more democratic socioeconomic conditions that rendered its original purpose obsolete.

Americans have always longed for an amorphous, older, and more exclusive glamour, to be comforted by beauty, without thinking of its complex production. Our ongoing attachment to the debutante ritual is wrapped up in our unremitting Anglophilia. America, with its rickety social system, is conformist but unstable—tradition is all we have, if we even have that. Any small slip can deprive us of our status. Unlike the titled Brits confidently loaning out their country houses, a kind of shabby pride covering over their resignation, when our wealth vanishes our names do, too.

Exploring how we think of the debutante ritual exposes the awkward relationship between wealth and social class in America. While 70 percent of Americans identify as middle class, only 50 percent qualify when using objective economic measures. Since most of that extra 20 percent are people striving upward, even the rich may insist they are middle class. When I was growing up, I knew many ultra-rich people from old families who tried to squeeze themselves into the upper middle class, even though family history, education, and net worth placed them squarely on the upper rung. Their urge to hide in a vast middle is more common and more possible in the US, where people are both anti-elite and obsessed with the trappings of wealth, both old and new.

For Americans who have had money for quite some time, what class is and who possesses it is even more slippery. This is likely why among the old WASP upper class, minute distinctions are of paramount importance, and subtle insider signaling creates an elite among the elite. One is taught from an early age to discern difference, however meaningless it might seem outside of this group. Growing up, I often heard people confer "class" in an entirely idealistic—and non-financial—way, never using the word of course—the gardeners had it, so did the garbage man, but the neighbors who cut down too many trees had none at all. I never heard anyone question why they had the authority to demarcate who had class and who didn't, nor what happens when you start removing social class from its economic underpinnings. Kindness holds inestimable valuable, but it can only put food on the table in a utopia. Unmooring denies the reality of our society, and keeps things as they are.

Today, the purpose of the debutante is more fluid. Still, I would not say it's a ritual that has been modernized, despite the best efforts of its proponents to sell it as such. No modern iteration of the presentation fits naturally into young women's lives, which have become casual across all social classes and ethnic groups. The debutante's prize was once a husband, which modern organizers and debutantes now dismiss with embarrassment. Instead, organizers, who earn money from hosting balls or organizing seasons have alighted on the agreeable and convenient idea that being a debutante is good for any potential business you might create, for creating a persona that can sell you, and for all the ideas and products related to you: the personal brand. A catchall term with limitless use but little real meaning, the personal brand is malleable and can be retrofitted for every person. It is made and remade just as the debutante ritual has been.

Many of the debutante's attendant luxuries have bled outward into women's culture at large, scattering aspiration among larger and larger groups of girls. Products first commissioned or purchased by members of the European aristocracy and then by the larger groups of upper class women are now available to everyone who can pay for them. Luxury clothing and accessories are accessible online at a moment's notice, but fashion houses work to maintain a veneer of exclusivity, including holding shows attended by a select group of people. Fashion shows still follow the same timetable created to serve women during their social seasons. The exclusivity is smoke and mirrors, as most of the runway shows are immediately streamed online. Everything is accessible if you have enough money, but as people's lives are more public than ever, the hunt for privacy and exclusivity has become more urgent. Dressmakers like Worth paved the way for generations of couturiers who now dress the world's superrich, but whose work we see more often on actresses during awards season. Women's magazines, which grew out of the conduct literature and dress catalogues so crucial to debutantes, fill that advisory role today, counseling women on style, health, beauty, and relationships. Some teen magazines still cover debuts, especially on their websites, where you can click through images without being overburdened by much text. It's not difficult to see how the debutante ritual would appeal to teenage readers who are navigating through one of life's most challenging transitions. The photos are glamorous, escapist, and make life look easier than it is.

When working on this book, I tried to keep in mind how young debutantes truly are, what teenage girls want, and to what degree what they want reflects the social expectations of their families. Many mothers, especially those from rich, conservative backgrounds where there are financial perks for remaining compliant and attractive, direct daughters toward what worked best for them, emphasizing their looks and manners, because those things were what made their own lives possible. At the beginning of this project, I aligned myself with the debutante ritual's critics. After all, I had not wanted to do it, and I had not understood why anyone would. While I still have negative feelings about the ritual's elitism, and its key role in enriching men at the expense of young women's self-determination and without care for their desires, my research has complicated some of my views. I can't completely write off something that some women actually enjoyed and considered a bonding experience. It was harder still to dismiss the importance of the debut to African American communities. When black organizations began to present debutantes, they were effectively asserting that their daughters were elegant, smart, hardworking, and worthy of the admiration they had been denied by a racist society that hyper-sexualized them at a very young age. To reclaim this ritual on their own terms, using it to provide scholarships and fund community service, has had transformative power, even as it simultaneously raises questions about classism within the black community.

The history of debutantes is the history of change within families, and of the most elegant sort of control over daughters. Humans have a native terror of instability and the debutante ritual has been, above all, an attempt at social control, a response to fears about losing one's footing. That young women have historically been the means by which families have been saved has not escaped me. I have watched young women being observed. There is no other secular ritual that marks or defines the blurry space between teenage and adulthood, celebrating the end of one and the beginning of another in a way that takes into account the sum total of experiences that young women might have had, and imparts wisdom about what might come. The debutante ritual provides an opportunity to mark this right of passage, and to receive admiration, but we always need to ask: Admiration for what? Quiescence? Beauty? The vision of women that the debutante ritual celebrates is narrow, and it sets women up to compete for concessions meted out by powerful men. Still, when people ask me if I think the ritual will continue, I assure them that it will. They almost always give me a dubious look, but I know what the rewards of elitism are, and they are very hard to give up.

ACKNOWLEDGMENTS

When writing feminist history, you learn that the past is a painful mess, punctuated by moments of creativity, bravery, and relief. The women whose letters and diaries I read were self-aware and often funny, and I'm grateful to them for recording their thoughts and experiences even though the world did not yet value them.

I'd like to thank my agents, Andrew Wylie and Jackie Ko, for providing loyal support during every stage of the writing process. It's hard to describe the miracle that is working with a great editor after a long time working alone. My editor at Norton, Amy Cherry, was lovelier than I could have imagined, and deftly eliminated all my worst tendencies. I'm grateful to everyone at Norton who worked on the book, especially Zarina Patwa, Erin Sinesky Lovett, and Michelle Waters.

So many of my friends held me together through this process. My brother Stuart Richardson, aunts Mary and Nora Fay, and friends Alex Stone and Amie Myers have fielded so much of my panic that I am grateful that they'll still talk to me. Randy Hartwell, Chris Milenkevich, Karin Schaefer, Rebecca Schoon, Amber Hruska, Catherine Ikner, Jill Stephenson, Susanne Cunningham, Jen Rawlings, Emily Simmons, and Hilda Saffari have all seen me at my most gruesome and have kept me sane and laughing throughout. Thank you all.

I'd like to thank my ex-husband, Sinclair Smith, for being a sounding board and support throughout our marriage and a wonderful co-parent after we ended it. I also want to thank two young women who took care of my son while I was writing. Without the time and love that Deborah Hartranft and Jda Gayle gave to Henry, this would have been a far more difficult process.

I'm grateful to my mother and father for raising us partly abroad, and then in the country. Thank you for laughing at my requests for a phone and television in my bedroom, because reading is the best cure for boredom. Alas, by letting me read all the time and putting no limits on the subject matter, you unintentionally created a writer.

Finally, I'd like to express my particular gratitude to my father, who took the leading role in helping me through the major detour of unexpected illness. He was there for every hospital visit, he ferried my son around when I was not able to drive, and was, ultimately, the single most important factor in my being able to finish this book.

NOTES

INTRODUCTION: TOO MANY DAUGHTERS

1. Kate Van Winkle Keller, *Dance and its Music in America, 1528-1789* (Hillsdale, NY: Pendragon Press, 2007), 238.

CHAPTER I: THE GIRL STANDARD

1. *The History of Herodotus*, vol. 1, bk. 1, trans. and ed. George Rawlinson (New York: D. Appleton and Company, 1885), 178–200.
2. Olwen Hufton, *The Prospect Before Her: Women's History in Western Europe 1500–1800* (New York: Knopf, 1996), 146.
3. Antonia Fraser, *The Weaker Vessel: Women's Lot in Seventeenth Century England* (London: Wiedenfield and Nicholson, 1984), 12.
4. Cited in Roy Porter, *English Society in the Eighteenth Century*, Revised Edition (London: Penguin Books, 1990), 26.
5. Richard Steele, "207: 5th August, 1710," in *The Tatler*, vol. 3, ed. Donald F. Bond (Oxford: Clarendon, 1987), 99–100.
6. James Boswell, *Life of Samuel Johnson Vol 2: March 19, 1776–Dec. 13, 1784* (London: Pitman & Sons, 1907), 770.
7. Margaret Jacob, *The Radical Enlightenment: Pantheists, Freemasons and Republicans* (London: George Allen and Unwin, 1981).
8. Quoted in Ian Watt, *The Rise of the Novel: Studies in Defoe, Richardson and Fielding* (Berkeley: University of California Press, 2001), 143.
9. Watt, *The Rise of the Novel*, 160.
10. Roy Porter, *English Society in the Eighteenth Century*, 27.
11. Watt, *The Rise of the Novel*, 145.

12. David Lemmings, "Marriage and the Law in the Eighteenth Century: Hardwicke's Marriage Act of 1753," *The Historical Journal* 39, no. 2 (June 1996): 348.

13. Lemmings, "Marriage and the Law in the Eighteenth Century," 355.

14. Lemmings, "Marriage and the Law in the Eighteenth Century," 357–8.

15. Amanda Foreman, *Georgiana, Duchess of Devonshire* (New York: Modern Library, 2001), 11–12.

16. Quoted in Venetia Murray, *An Elegant Madness: High Society in Regency England* (New York: Viking, 1999), 132.

17. Fanny Burney, cited in Nigel Arch and Joanna Marschner, *Splendour at Court: Dressing for Royal Occasions Since 1700* (New York: Harper Collins, 1987), 41.

18. Quoted in Murray, *An Elegant Madness*, 132.

19. Cited in Stephen Turner, "Almack's and Society," *History Today* 26, no. 4 (April 1976): 241–9, 242.

20. Horace Walpole, cited in Beresford E. Chancellor, *Memorials of St James's Street together with the Annals of Almack's* (London: G. Richards Ltd.), 1922.

21. Jane Rendell, *The Pursuit of Pleasure: Gender, Space and Architecture in Regency London* (New Brunswick, NJ: Rutgers University Press, 2002), 88.

22. Rendell, *The Pursuit of Pleasure*, 89.

23. Cheryl Wilson, *Literature and Dance in Nineteenth-Century Britain* (New York: Cambridge University Press, 2009), 48.

24. Reese Howell Gronow, *Reminiscences of Captain Gronow* (London: Smith and Elder, 1862), 44.

25. Maria Edgeworth, Letter from Maria Edgeworth to Fanny Beaufort Edgeworth, March, 1822, in *The Life and Letters of Maria Edgeworth*, vol. 2, ed. Augustus Hare (London: Edward Arnold, 1894), 353.

CHAPTER 2: REVOLUTION AND REPUBLIC

1. "Teaching Visitors about the Consumer Revolution," *Colonial Williamsburg Teacher Gazette* 9, no. 10 (June 1, 2011).

2. "Teaching Visitors about the Consumer Revolution."

3. Cited in Alice Morse Earle, *Two Centuries of Costume in America* (New York: MacMillan, 1903), 299.

4. Richard Bushman, *The Refinement of America: Persons, Houses, Cities* (New York: Knopf, 1992), xiv.

5. *Pennsylvania Magazine of History and Biography* 39 (1915): 115.

6. Judith Cobau, "The precarious Life of Thomas Pike, A Colonial Dancing

Master in Charleston and Philadelphia," *Dance Chronicle* 17, no. 3 (1994): 229–62, 231.

7. Nancy Shippen, *Her Journal Book*, ed. Ethel Armes (Philadelphia: Lippincott, 1935), 244.

8. David Shields, *Civil Tongues and Polite Letters* (Chapel Hill: University of North Carolina Press, 1997), 144.

9. Thomas Willing Balch, *The Philadelphia Assemblies* (Philadelphia: Allen, Lane and Scott, 1916), 62.

10. General Nathanial Greene to Colonel Jeremiah Wadsworth, Middle Brook, New Jersey, Mar. 19, 1799.

11. James Tilton to Gunning Bedford Jr., Annapolis, Maryland, Dec. 25, 1783.

12. Francis T. Brooke, Journal, 1784. Brooke Family papers, Special Collections, University of Maryland Libraries.

13. Miss Charlotte Chambers to her mother, Mrs. James Chambers, Wednesday, Feb. 25, 1795, *Memoir of Charlotte Chambers By her grandson, Lewis H. Garrard* (Philadelphia: 1856) 15.

14. Shields, *Civil Tongues and Polite Letters*, 153.

15. Eric Homberger, *Mrs. Astor's New York: Money and Social Power in a Gilded Age* (New Haven: Yale University Press, 2002).

16. Shields, *Civil Tongues and Polite Letters*, 149.

17. Shields, *Civil Tongues and Polite Letters*, 150.

18. Quoted in Richard Bushman, *The Refinement of America: Persons, Houses, Cities* (New York: Knopf, 1992), 56–57.

19. Lucinda Lee Orr, *Journal of a Young Lady of Virginia in 1782* (Baltimore: John Murphy & Co., 1871), 37.

20. Philip Vickers Fithian, *Journal and Letters of Philip Vickers Fithian, 1773–1774: A Plantation Tutor of the Old Dominion*, ed. Hunter Dickinson Farish (Charlottesville: Virginia University Press), Jan. 8, 1774.

21. Bushman, *The Refinement of America*, 57.

22. Dixon Wecter, *The Saga of American Society: A Record of Social Aspiration 1607–1937* (New York: Charles Scribner's Sons, 1937), 91–92.

23. Quoted in Anya Jabour, *Scarlett's Sisters: Young Women in the Old South* (Chapel Hill: University of North Carolina Press, 2009), 118.

24. *A Season in New York 1801: The Letters of Harriet and Maria Trumbull*, ed. Helen M. Morgan (Pittsburgh, PA: Pittsburgh University Press, 1969).

25. Harriet Trumble to Maria Trumbull, Apr. 7, 1801, in *A Season in New York 1801*.

26. Philip Hone, quoted in Edward Pessen, *Riches, Class and Power before the Civil War* (New York: D.C. Heath, 1973), 17.

27. A contemporary wrote: "Nobody's affairs were too sacred, too august, or too disreputable for his prying investigations. He had society at the end of his fingers and could have told you with amazing glibness thousands of genealogical facts concerning it." Fawcett's *A Demoralized Marriage* (Philadelphia: JB Lippincott, 1889), 69–70.

28. Mrs. Burton Harrison, *Recollections Grave and Gay* (New York, 1911, London: Smith, Elder, 1912), 315–16.

CHAPTER 3: FROZEN IN TIME

1. Amy Stallings, "Dance during the Colonial Period," *Encyclopedia Virginia*, Jan. 31, 2012, http://www.EncyclopediaVirginia.org/Dance_During_the_Colonial_Period.

2. *A Huguenot Exile in Virginia*, trans. and ed. Gilbert Chinard (New York: Press of the Pioneers, 1934), 142.

3. Carter was colonial representative to the British aristocrats who owned Virginia's "Northern Neck." He was so successful that Lord Fairfax himself decided no better money could be made than in the colonies, and sent his son and then came to the colonies himself.

4. Robert Carter wrote to the county clerk again and again: *This is to Desire You to make out a Marriage Lycense for the Nuptials of Man Page Esqr with my daughter Judith Carter to wch I give my full Consent & I Suppose You want not more to Enable You to Perform Yor Duty with Safetie, & then You are to deliver it to Mr. Thomas Carter [on my behalf]*, April 1719.

5. The marriages of his daughters and sons illustrate in striking fashion the custom of the gentry families intermarrying to help keep their influence and power within a tightly woven circle. "King" Carter's daughter, Judith, married Mann Page of Rosewell; daughter Anne married Benjamin Harrison of Berkeley; and daughter Elizabeth married Nathaniel Burwell. King Carter's eldest son married Elizabeth Hill, whose father built Shirley plantation for her use. Charles Carter married William Byrd II's daughter, Anne, while Landon Carter married Byrd II's other daughter, Maria. The power of the Carter family would last for several generations from such marriage practices.

6. Robert Carter, Diary, April 12, 1726.

7. Gail Collins, *America's Women: 400 Years of Dolls, Drudges, Helpmates, and Heroines* (New York: Harper Collins, 2006), 64.

8. Lawrence Butler to Mrs. Anna F. Craddock, Oct. 15, 1784, *Virginia Magazine of History and Biography*, 266–67, cited in Daniel Blake Smith, *Inside the Great*

House: Planter Family Life in Eighteenth-Century Chesapeake Society (Ithaca, NY: Cornell University Press, 1986), 130.

9. Thornwell, ed. *Diary of Nicolas Cresswell*, 53, cited in Daniel Blake Smith, *Inside the Great House*, 131.

10. The top 1,000 planter families brought in $50,000,000 per annum. The remaining 666,000 families who constituted the "gentry" brought in $60,000,000 per annum.

11. Dancing schools for all social classes were opening all over the South.

12. Philip Vickers Fithian, *Journal and Letters of Philip Vickers Fithian, 1773–1774: A Plantation Tutor of the Old Dominion*, ed. Hunter Dickinson Farish (Charlottesville: Virginia University Press), Dec. 17, 1773.

13. He did this, much to the dismay of his maternal relatives, the powerful, landowning Randolphs of Virginia. Jefferson, himself, acquired a fortune through marriage to a wealthy young widow.

14. Stephanie E. Jones-Rogers, *They Were Her Property: White Women as Slave Owners in the American South* (New Haven: Yale University Press, 2019).

15. Anya Jabour, *Scarlett's Sisters: Young Women in the Old South* (Chapel Hill: University of North Carolina Press, 2009), 18.

16. Jabour, *Scarlett's Sisters*, 34.

17. Lloyd Noland to Ella Noland, Mar. 3, 1845, and Elizabeth Noland to Ella Noland, Nov. 14, 1849, Ella Noland Mackenzie Papers, Southern Historical Collection, University of North Carolina, Chapel Hill.

18. F. William Wirt to Elizabeth Wirt, Sept. 9, 1810, quoted in Anja Jabour, " 'Grown Girls, Highly Cultivated': Female Education in an Antebellum Southern Family," *Journal of Southern History* 64 (Feb. 1998): 30.

19. Elizabeth Noland to Sally Gibson, cited in Jabour, *Scarlett's Sisters*, 113.

20. Ella Noland to Elizabeth Noland, cited in Jabour, *Scarlett's Sisters*, 114.

21. Jabour, *Scarlett's Sisters*, 113.

22. Charles Lockhart Pettigrew to William Shepard Pettigrew, Oct. 9, 1837, Sarah McCulloh Lemmon, Pettigrew Papers, 2:354; Penelope Skinnner to Tristrim Lowther Skinner Oct. 21, 1838; Mary Maillard, ed., *On the Carpet: The Coming of Age Letters of Penelope Skinner 1832–1840* (self-pub., Amazon Digital Services, 2014), loc. 2516–2518, Kindle.

23. Penelope Skinner to Tristrim Lowther Skinner, Jan. 29, 1839.

24. Joseph Blount Skinner to Tristrim Lowther Skinner, December 4, 1838.

25. Frederick Nash to his daughter Maria, Oct. 15, 1839, Frederick Nash Papers, Private Collections, State Archives, Office of Archives and History, Raleigh, N.C; Mary Maillard, *On the Carpet: The Coming of Age Letters of Penelope Skinner 1832–1840* (Mary Maillard, 2014), Kindle.

26. Cited in *An Evening When Alone: Four Journals of Single Women in the South 1827-67*, Michael O'Brien, ed. (Published for the Southern Texts Society in Charlottesville: University of Virginia Press, 1993), 24.

27. O'Brien, *An Evening When Alone*, 25.

28. O'Brien, *An Evening When Alone*, 165.

29. O'Brien, *An Evening When Alone*, 166.

30. O'Brien, *An Evening When Alone*, 205.

31. Jabour, *Scarlett's Sisters*, 131.

32. Jabour, *Scarlett's Sisters*, 131.

33. Willis, whose name is now mostly forgotten, was an American writer and editor and the highest paid writer of his day. With his writings on leisure and stable of magazines, including *Home Journal* (later *Town and Country*), Willis was the first American writer to make a living off of writing about the rich.

34. Cited in Thomas A. Chambers, *Taking the Waters: Creating An American Leisure Class at Nineteenth-Century Mineral Springs* (Smithsonian Institute Press: 2002), 149.

35. Netta, "First Impressions of Saratoga," no. 6, *National Era*, Sept. 15, 1859: 163, cited in Thomas Chambers, *Taking the Waters*, 149.

36. Cited in Thomas Chambers, *Taking the Waters*, 152.

CHAPTER 4: THE FOUR HUNDRED AND BEYOND

1. Eric Homberger, *Mrs. Astor's New York: Money and Social Power in a Gilded Age* (New Haven, NY: Yale University Press, 2002), 126.

2. Eric Homberger, *Mrs. Astor's New York*, 124–25.

3. Dixon Wecter, *The Saga of American Society: A Record of Social Aspiration 1607–1937* (New York: Charles Scribner's Sons, 1937), 244.

4. Wecter, *The Saga of American Society*, 246.

5. Mrs. John King Van Rensselaer and Mr. Frederic Franklin Van de Water, *The Social Ladder* (New York: Henry Holt and Company, 1924), 80.

6. King Van Rensselaer and Franklin Van de Water, *The Social Ladder*, 38.

7. Ward McAllister, *Society as I Have Found It* (New York: Cassell Publishing Company, 1890), 125.

8. Huybertie Pruyn Hamlin, *An Albany Girlhood* (Albany: Washington Park Press Limited, 1990), cited in Maureen E. Montgomery, *Displaying Women: Spectacles of Leisure in Edith Wharton's New York*, (New York: Routledge, 1998), 49.

9. Montgomery, *Displaying Women*, 46–7.

10. Montgomery, *Displaying Women*, 50.

11. Wecter, *The Saga of American Society*, 226.

12. Montgomery, *Displaying Women*, 49.

CHAPTER 5: TRANSATLANTIC CROSSINGS

1. Anne Sebba, *American Jennie: The Remarkable Life of Lady Randolph Churchill* (W. W. Norton, 2010), 28.

2. Elizabeth Davis Bancroft to her sons [unnamed], May 30, 1847, cited in Elizabeth Davis Bancroft, *Letters from England 1846-1849* (London: Smith, Elder & Co. 1904).

3. Leonore Davidoff, *The Best Circles: Women and Society in Victorian England* (Totowa, New Jersey: Rowman and Littlefield, 1973), 50.

4. Davidoff, *The Best Circles*, 63.

5. David Cannadine, *The Decline and Fall of the British Aristocracy* (New Haven, CT: Yale University Press, 1990), 342.

6. Ralph G. Martin, *Jennie: The Life of Lady Randolph Churchill* (New York: Prentice Hall, 1969), 167.

7. Amanda Stuart MacKenzie, *Consuelo and Alva: Love, Power and Suffrage in the Gilded Age* (London: HarperCollins, 2005), 84.

8. Consuelo Vanderbilt Balsan, *The Glitter and the Gold: The American Duchess—in Her Own Words* (London: Hodder, 2012), 29.

9. Stuart MacKenzie, *Consuelo and Alva*, 102.

10. Balsan, *The Glitter and the Gold*, 34.

11. Balsan, *The Glitter and the Gold*, 35.

12. MacKenzie, *Consuelo and Alva*, 120.

13. E. Digby Baltzell, *Philadelphia Gentlemen: The Making of a National Upper Class* (New Brunswick, NJ: Transaction Publishers, 2004), 232.

14. Cannadine, *The Decline and Fall of the British Aristocracy*, 91.

15. Van Rensselaer, cited in Wecter, *The Saga of American Society*, 1937.

16. Elizabeth Drexel Lehr (Lady Decies), *King Lehr and the Gilded Age: With Extracts from the Locked Diary of Harry Lehr* (Carlisle, Mass.: Applewood Books, 2005), 81.

17. "Some Happenings in Good Society," *New York Times*, Dec 2, 1900, 18.

18. Robinson Family Papers, New-York Historical Society.

19. Wecter, *The Saga of American Society*, 345.

CHAPTER 6: THE BRIGHT YOUNG PEOPLE

1. Mabell Airlie, *Thatched with Gold: The Memoirs of Mabell, Countess of Airlie* (London: Hutchison, 1962), 143.

2. Lady Muriel Beckwith, *When I Remember 1936*, cited in Leonore Davidoff, *The Best Circles* (Cresset Library: London, 1986), 68.

3. D.J. Taylor, *Bright Young People: The Lost Generation of London's Jazz Age* (New York: Farrar, Straus and Giroux, 2007), 115.

4. Cynthia Asquith, *Remember and Be Glad, 1952*, cited in Davidoff, *The Best Circles*, 66.

5. Mary Packenham, *Brought Up and Brought Out* (London: Cobden-Sanderson, 1938).

6. Gioia Diliberto, *Debutante: The Story of Brenda Frazier* (New York: Knopf, 1987), 92.

CHAPTER 7: CAFÉ SOCIETY, CELEBRITY, AND CONFORMITY

1. Gioia Diliberto, *Debutante: The Story of Brenda Frazier* (New York: Knopf, 1987), 106.

2. Diliberto, *Debutante*, 69.

3. Sherrie A. Inness, ed., *Delinquents and Debutantes: Twentieth-Century American Girls' Cultures* (New York: New York University Press, 1998), loc. 2726–2730, Kindle.

4. Cleveland Amory, *Who Killed Society?* (New York: Harper & Brothers, 1960).

5. "Party: The $250,000 debut of Charlotte Ford: Automaker gives his daughter the most lavish coming-out party in 25 years," *Life Magazine* (January 11, 1960): 101.

6. Bob Ickes, "The Debutante from Animal House," *New York Magazine* (Jan. 14, 1991): 33.

CHAPTER 8: PROPHETS, KREWES, AND FIESTA QUEENS

1. Jan Jarboe Russell, "Fit for a Queen," *Texas Monthly*, April 1994, https://www.texasmonthly.com/articles/fit-for-a-queen/.

2. Russell, *Texas Monthly*.

3. Thomas Spencer, *The Saint Louis Veiled Prophet Celebration: Power on Parade 1878–1995* (Columbia: University of Missouri Press, 2000), 7.

4. Spencer, *The Saint Louis Veiled Prophet Celebration*, 56.

5. Lucy Ferriss, *Unveiling the Prophet: The Misadventures of a Reluctant Debutante* (Columbia: University of Missouri Press, 2005), 6–7.

6. William Powell, "Behind the Scenes with the Veiled Prophet Maids," *St Louis Magazine*, Jan. 14, 2016.

CHAPTER 9: CREATING A BLACK ELITE

1. Graham Russell Gao Hodges, *Root and Branch: African Americans in New York and East Jersey, 1613–1863* (Chapel Hill: University of North Carolina Press), 151.

2. Annette Lynch, Dress, *Gender and Cultural Change: Asian American and African American Rites of Passage* (Oxford: Berg, 1999), 84.

3. Hodges, *Root and Branch*, 203–4.

4. Katrina Hazzard-Gordon, *Jookin': The Rise of Social Dance Formations in African-American Culture* (Philadelphia: Temple University Press, 1992).

5. Lynch, *Dress, Gender and Cultural Change*, 83.

6. This was a common concern for blacks in New Orleans when they considered the Creole elite in their city.

7. "Racial Uplift," American History Through Literature 1870–1920, Encyclopedia.com.

8. "Racial Uplift," American History Through Literature 1870–1920, Encyclopedia.com.

9. Willard B. Gatewood, *Aristocrats of Color: The Black Elite 1880–1920* (Fayetteville: University of Arkansas Press, 2000), 209.

10. Gatewood, *Aristocrats of Color*, 235.

11. Gatewood, *Aristocrats of Color*, 237.

12. Miya Carey, "A well-talked-about affair: Black Debutantes and the Cotillion in the *Washington Afro-American*," Society for the History of Children and Youth Biennial Conference 2015 (University of British Columbia, Vancouver, BC, June 24–26, 2015), 2–3.

13. Miya Carey, "A well-talked-about affair."

14. Lolita V. Cherrie, "History of the Original Illinois Club (1895)," *CreoleGen*, Feb. 7, 2015, www.creolegen.org/2015/02/06/history-of-the-original-illinois-club-1895/.

15. Cherrie, "History of the Original Illinois Club (1895)."

16. Susan Saulny, "No Cinderella Story, No Ball, No Black Debutante," *New York Times*, March 2, 2006.

17. Lawrence Otis Graham, *Our Kind of People: Inside America's Black Upper Class* (New York: HarperCollins, 1999), 45.

18. Graham, *Our Kind of People*, 46.

19. Graham, *Our Kind of People*, 14.

20. Emily Badger, Clair Cain Miller, Adam Pearce, and Kevin Quealy, "Extensive Data Shows Punishing Reach of Racism for Black Boys," *New York Times*, Mar. 19, 2018, https://www.nytimes.com/interactive/2018/03/19/upshot/race-class-white-and -black-men.html.

21. Author Interview with Miya Carey, January 15, 2019.

CHAPTER 10: NOUVEAU NOW

1. Author interview with Margaret Hedberg, January 25, 2013.

2. Author interview with Margaret Hedberg, January 25, 2013.

3. "The Return of the Debutante," *Independent*, Aug. 10, 2009, https://www .independent.co.uk/news/uk/this-britain/the-return-of-the-debutante -1769953.html.

4. Author interview with Margaret Hedberg, January 25, 2013.

5. Author interview with Noël Duan, January 9, 2019.

INDEX

THE SEASON

Kristen Richardson

THE SEASON

Kristen Richardson

DISCUSSION QUESTIONS

1. In what ways do daughters serve as currency in the debutante ritual?

2. How did curtseying before Queen Elizabeth I in the sixteenth century solidify the matchmaking power of a debut?

3. What does Richardson mean when she states that having a daughter debut is a way for families to "purchase their social legitimacy" (p. 6)?

4. How did Almack's change the debutante ritual in London? What about it set the standard for other assembly rooms in both London and America?

5. What insight about the ritual can be gleaned from the Duke of Wellington being refused entry into Almack's for "wearing the wrong trousers" (p. 40) after a victory in the Napoleonic Wars? What precedence did that set?

6. Though debutante balls were primarily for matchmaking, how were they used to communicate societal rank? What role did married men play in this?

7. How did the debutante rituals in the Antebellum North and the Antebellum South differ? Why were regional implications of marriage so crucial?

8. Why was Caroline Astor successful at taking charge of New York society? What role did Ward McAllister play in this success?

9. In what ways did American cities mold the debutante ritual to fit the culture of a specific city? Did the individuality of some cities' rituals make it more difficult to join?

10. How did World War I issue in the modern era of the debut? How

did the evolving roles of women post–World War I contribute to the changes that began to take hold?

11. The debutante ritual has historically been for the white elite and has taken on an attitude of exclusivity. How did the African American debutante ritual foster inclusivity?

12. How has the debutante ritual evolved for the twenty-first century? Would it be recognizable to the original patronesses of Almack's or Caroline Astor? Is it out-of-date in modern society?

SELECTED NORTON BOOKS WITH
READING GROUP GUIDES AVAILABLE

For a complete list of Norton's works with reading group guides,
please go to wwnorton.com/reading-guides.